Getting into

Oxford & Cambridge

2023 Entry

Matthew Carmody

25th edition

Getting into guides

Getting into Art & Design Courses, 12th edition
Getting into Business & Economics Courses, 14th edition
Getting into Dental School, 12th edition
Getting into Engineering Courses, 6th edition
Getting into Law, 14th edition
Getting into Medical School 2023 Entry, 27th edition
Getting into Pharmacy and Pharmacology Courses, 2nd edition
Getting into Physiotherapy Courses, 10th edition
Getting into Psychology Courses, 14th edition
Getting into Veterinary School, 12th edition
How to Complete Your UCAS Application 2023 Entry, *34th edition*

Getting into Oxford & Cambridge: 2023 Entry

This 25th edition published in 2022 by Trotman Education, an imprint of Trotman Indigo Publishing Ltd, 21d Charles Street, Bath BA1 1HX

© Trotman Indigo Publishing Ltd 2022

Author: Matthew Carmody

21st–24th edns: Matthew Carmody
20th edn: Lucy Bates
17th–19th edns: Seán P. Buckley
15th–16th edns: Jenny Blaiklock
13th–14th edns: Katy Blatt
7th–10th & 12th edns: Sarah Alakija
11th edn: Natalie Lancer

British Library Cataloguing in Publication Data
A catalogue record for this book is available from the British Library

ISBN: 978 1 912943 64 7

Printed and bound in Gloucester, UK by Severn.

Contents

About the author

Matthew Carmody read Philosophy at Queens' College, Cambridge. He continued his studies at King's College London, obtaining an MPhil and then a PhD in Philosophy. He has taught in a number of schools and universities and is currently a Head of Faculty and tutor at MPW London, where he oversees the Oxbridge programme.

Acknowledgements

I am very grateful to the Oxbridge students who kindly agreed to share their personal statements and to take the time to write the case studies. I am also grateful to the many members of staff at MPW London who suggested interview questions and recommended reading. I would also like to thank the following Oxbridge coordinators and advisers for their views on the application and preparation processes: Harriet Brook, Zoe Makepeace-Welsh, Richard Pember, Michelle Russell and Lesley Sharples. Final thanks are due to my wife Jessica for proofreading, helpful suggestions and cups of tea.

Foreword

I suspect that the first thought that occurred to me on arriving in Cambridge for my interview has occurred to many others for whom disembarking from the train in mid-December is their first experience of the place. That thought would be: why is it so perishingly cold? I fished the paper map Queens' College had sent me out of my coat (this was some years before smartphones with maps existed) and started to walk to the centre, something that prompted a second thought (which, again, must have been thought by many before me making a similar trip), namely, why was it that the railway station was such a distance from the centre? It was some time before the shops gave way to colleges, the market square and King's Parade. After a few wrong turns – map-reading was not a skill I possessed – I arrived at the Porters' Lodge to be given a key to my room and a second map to get me there that I also failed to read correctly. Thankful that none of this was part of an initial assessment, I eventually found it and spent the next hour pressed up against a small radiator.

I had been invited to attend an interview for Computer Science and I had very little idea what to expect. I can remember sitting on a wooden bench outside the interview room in a very nervous state of mind. Of what happened when I went in, I remember very little. We talked about some software I'd written and then it was all over. I know I felt that it had gone too quickly and that this was not a good sign. I returned home to Bristol and tried to forget all about it. A couple of weeks later, around Christmas, a letter arrived with an offer. Eight months later, I had the results that I needed and a year or so after that, with my gap year over, I arrived back in Cambridge with a car full of material possessions, almost all of which I instantly regretted bringing when I realised that my room was at the end of a long corridor on the third floor of a building without any lifts.

I had applied to read Computer Science but, during my gap year, I decided to change to read Philosophy. Requests to change one's course were quite understandably frowned upon and I was very lucky to be accommodated. (I should take this opportunity to say that in these days of even greater competition, I would expect such requests to be firmly rejected. If you change your mind about what you want to study, be prepared to re-apply.) I would like to say that I proved my doubting Director of Studies wrong with an exemplary first term, but it was quite the opposite. I was not as prepared as I should have been for the intense academic environment that I had been accepted into. I was given long reading lists and short deadlines. Whereas at school I had had relatively little trouble absorbing what was thrown at me, I now had to read dense academic material on a wide range of topics of which I had little prior understanding. It was a difficult first year and I did not perform well in the exams at the end of the year. Oxbridge students are used to getting high grades in school and my very-far-from-high grades came as quite a shock.

It was not until the second year, after a busy summer among the books, that I felt I was able to keep up and deserving of the opportunity I'd been given. I was now able to read and digest information at a rate I could not have envisaged a year earlier. I was able to benefit properly from the supervisions and lectures I attended. The subject finally came fully alive for me. A further year and I was filling out forms to apply for post-graduate study.

My academic experience at Cambridge was therefore not the simple one of continuing school-level success for a further three years. I know I was not alone. Very many students who are used to doing well, and indeed doing well with relative ease, have the shock of finding that they are no longer top of the class and not able to carry on as they were before. This may well apply to you, in which case I would say to you that it is not cause for despair. If you have got in, you have been judged capable of handling the academic pressures characteristic of Oxbridge. It may just take a while for you to realise your potential.

One feature of my time that did start well and continued to grow was the friends that I made. You will meet a very wide variety of people and it is impossible not to be able to find people with shared interests. I had the good fortune to make friends with people who stretched me intel-lectually, supported me in difficult times, and generated very happy memories. They continue to do these things a full 30 years after we all first met.

Oxford and Cambridge present you with brilliant minds and beautiful places to create a very special environment in which to live and study. Whether it be in the form of lectures, clubs, orchestras, sporting events or second-hand bookshops, there is more there to keep you occupied than you could want. You will learn a lot about your subject but also about yourself and others. You will do things that will surprise you and make you smile many years later. But don't delay! The terms are short and three years really will fly by. If you find yourself on the threshold of freshers' week in 2023, make sure you allow yourself to enjoy it and take it all in.

Matthew Carmody

Introduction

The title of this book says it all. Its purpose is to tell you everything you need to know to help you get into Oxford or Cambridge. It will also try to give you a flavour of what it's like to live and study in these historic cities. My hope is that this book will help to demystify the whole application process and encourage you to apply if you feel you've got what it takes to get in.

You may already know quite a lot about the Oxbridge system and think you simply need a checklist of things you should do to ensure your application is as strong as possible. However, this book aims to be comprehensive and will cover all stages of the admissions procedure in detail. Or, you may know nothing at all about how to get in.

In many ways, an application to Oxford and Cambridge is similar to an application to study at other UK universities. You will need to submit a personal statement, a reference and your educational history. These factors, along with your predicted grades, will be relevant to whether you are made an offer. What *is* different in an application to Oxford or Cambridge is the quality of these factors. Your personal statement will need to reflect a profound intellectual interest in and engagement with the subject or subjects you hope to read. So make sure you get started on a programme of reading and research as early as possible so that your academic potential is evident. Also different to a standard application are the additional steps you have to make. There will be an interview and very possibly an entrance examination. And from conversations with tutors involved in helping students prepare for Oxbridge, these elements carry ever more weight.

Many potential applicants can be put off applying on the basis that Oxford or Cambridge somehow isn't right for them, or that the odds of getting in are weighted towards a certain type of student – one with 'connections'. This simply isn't true today. Oxford and Cambridge are interested in academic excellence alone, and have over the last decade or so boosted their outreach activities to encourage students from 'non-traditional' schools to apply. Ironically, this in turn has led to another myth: that students from the independent sector are being discriminated against unfairly. Again, to judge from those I have spoken to, this is also not true. We'll break down these myths more in Chapters 2 and 3, but having spoken to many admissions tutors in researching this book, I can guarantee that your application will be judged, more than ever before, on your potential to succeed and your willingness to work hard.

You also shouldn't be dissuaded because you're worried that you're not a geeky Oxbridge type or that you somehow won't hold your own there.

If you're passionate about your subject and have the ability to excel at university, you're almost certainly a strong candidate for admission and to happily succeed in either institution.

How this book works

This book will take you through the application process step by step: from making sure you're studying the right A levels, or equivalent qualifications, to giving you tips to help you sail through your interview.

Chapter 1, Why study at Oxford or Cambridge?, explores why Oxford and Cambridge are so special and how they differ from other universities, giving the reader some idea of what it's like to study there. It also aims to demystify the selection process by outlining Oxbridge's equal opportunities policy.

Chapter 2, Choosing your university and college, considers the best way to choose a university and college. It mentions the differences between Oxford and Cambridge, highlighting the importance of choosing the university that offers the subject that most suits you, and explains the option of the 'open application'.

Chapter 3, Entry requirements, discusses things to consider well before the UCAS application. It includes a section on choosing your A level subjects or the alternatives to UK A levels that are accepted by Oxford and Cambridge (including the International Baccalaureate and Scottish Highers). It also discusses the importance of high grades, and considers the issue of applying from a state school versus from an independent school.

Chapter 4, Money matters, explains the financial aspects of studying at Oxbridge. There is a common misconception that studying at Oxbridge is more expensive than at other universities. This chapter gives a breakdown of costs incurred over a year, and introduces the bursary schemes and music scholarships at the universities.

Chapter 5, The early stages of preparation, discusses the importance of choosing the right subject for you. Your choice of subject is more important than any other decision you will have to make during this process. This chapter encourages would-be applicants to read widely and in depth, and includes reading lists that will give you a few ideas.

Chapter 6, Experience to support your application, discusses the importance of 'super-curricular' experience in the application process – activities students have engaged in outside of their school curriculum that are directly relevant to their chosen course and which will strengthen their personal statements. The pros and cons of a 'gap year' are considered. The chapter also looks at the importance of work experience, particularly if you wish to study a vocational subject, and the importance of being aware of events in your area, current affairs and news stories that are relevant to your chosen subject.

Chapter 7, The UCAS application and the personal statement, gives advice on how to make your application shine, and provides example personal statements with analysis. After you have completed your personal statement, Cambridge (but not Oxford) automatically sends a Supplementary Application Questionnaire (SAQ), and there is advice on how to complete this form. Many subjects require you to send in examples of written work; the chapter explains why written work is required and how best to satisfy the universities' requirements.

Chapter 8, Non-standard applications, discusses the application procedure for mature students and international students and gives information on specific issues relating to these categories. It also provides information about the Lady Margaret Hall Foundation Year.

Chapter 9, Succeeding in written tests, discusses the exams that are taken in addition to A levels (or equivalent) for most subjects. These are taken either in advance of interviews or during the interview week. This chapter also provides example questions, dates for testing and useful website links so that you can find out more for yourself.

Chapter 10, Surviving the interview, explains the interview process. General information about interview practice is given, as well as a breakdown of what interviewers are looking for. In addition, there is information about different interview styles and how to deal with them; a comprehensive list of interview questions for a range of subjects; and interview stories from previous applicants. Finally, there is a word of advice about presentation skills and an explanation of the pooling system.

Chapter 11, Getting the letter, looks at the final stages of the process: receiving an offer or coping with rejection; and how you can make this experience a success, whether or not you obtain a place at Oxbridge.

College profiles provides bite-size information on each college at Oxford and Cambridge, covering courses offered, accommodation and catering provision, facilities, financial aid and interesting facts specific to each college. Here you will also find the Norrington and Tompkins tables, tables showing which subjects are offered by each of the colleges, and maps of Oxford and Cambridge showing the locations of the individual colleges.

In the **appendices** you will find a useful timeline of the application process and a **glossary** of important terms.

PART I

First Considerations

1 | Why study at Oxford or Cambridge?

What makes these two universities such special places to study? And why are places there so fiercely fought over?

When people think about those who have passed through Oxford and Cambridge, they tend to think of politicians – especially Prime Ministers – and prize-winning academics, such as Professor Stephen Hawking and Dame Mary Beard. However, Oxford and Cambridge provide environments in which talents of all kinds can flourish. Both universities have a good history of producing comedians. Cambridge gave us most of the Monty Python team, Fry and Laurie, Mitchell and Webb, Richard Ayoade and Sue Perkins. Oxford has provided Rowan Atkinson, Armando Ianucci, Al Murray and Sally Phillips. The many opportunities to play sport have resulted in world-class rowers, rugby players and cricketers, to give three obvious examples. A notable recent alumna was Lily Cole, who received a double first from Cambridge while continuing to work as a model and actor. And the tranquil but intensely academic setting has been the breeding ground for many a great eccentric, my favourite being the Reverend William Buckland, a 19th-century theologian, early palaeontologist and geologist at Oxford. He conducted his fieldwork in his academic gown, lectured on horseback, and saw it as his mission to sample as great a variety of the animal kingdom as possible for dinner. Dinner guests might have found themselves served a rhino pie, crispy battered mice, slices of porpoise head or elephant trunk.

What is important is that Oxford and Cambridge are at the forefront of academic excellence and produce rates of graduate employment that are among the highest in the UK.

Top of the league tables

According to the latest *Guardian* survey that ranks UK universities by teaching excellence (www.theguardian.com/education/ng-interactive/2021/sep/11/the-best-uk-universities-2022-rankings), Oxford topped the league table, with Cambridge in second place. The tables rank universities according to the following measures:

- how satisfied their final-year students are with the course, teaching and feedback they received
- how many students complete the first year of their course and continue into the second year
- how much they spend per student
- the student–staff ratio
- the career prospects of their graduates
- the average entry Tariff
- a value-added score, which compares students' degree results with entry qualifications to determine how effective the teaching is.

The tutorial system

Unlike at most universities, teaching at Oxford and Cambridge is built around the tutorial system. Tutorials (or supervisions as they are called at Cambridge) involve a meeting with your tutor, alone or with one or two other students, and generally last about an hour. Often, one of you will read your essay or written work aloud and this will act as a catalyst for discussion of the work that has been done independently during the week.

What makes an Oxbridge education so special is that you'll have personal access to some of the world's experts in your chosen subject. Your tutor may be the person who literally 'wrote the book' on the subject you're studying, so being able to discuss topics with them in depth every week is an invaluable experience.

Case study: Harry, Cambridge

'As I approach the end of my first term at Cambridge, I am struck by how quickly it has gone, how much I've learnt and how many great experiences I've had. As a mature student I was offered a place at Wolfson College. Initially I was anxious about how mature undergraduates, postgraduates and doctoral students would interact and about being a bit further out of the city centre than other colleges. I feel fortunate now that my college heavily promotes equality. We have no high table, and everyone sits and mingles together, which creates an open and friendly atmosphere. Luckily, Wolfson is a four-minute cycle ride to where my language lessons and lectures are held and a seven-minute ride into town. For me, it is a haven away from the crowds of tourists the city attracts.

'Before applying I was told that you would only have time for two disciplines: academics and one other interest. However, I quickly realised that you can do sport, music and have a social life as long as you are organised. For me, knowing that if I work hard during the day, I can do something I enjoy at the end, keeps me going.

'There are some incredibly smart and hardworking people here, but I've learnt it is important not to compare yourself to them. Working hard and putting the effort in is definitely something my supervisors recognise. Although the workload can feel quite heavy sometimes and the pace can feel intense, it's important not to get put off. Something that has really helped me is the study workshops my college provides. Sitting in a lecture room and making notes with a hundred or so people around you was something I had never experienced before and the workshops have given me ideas and techniques to combat this, as well as other skills such as speed-reading and planning my time effectively.

'I have been incredibly lucky with my supervisors and supervision partners. I know that if I'm stuck on my work or need something explaining I can always email my supervisor and they will point me in the right direction. Alternatively, if I want to discuss a French passage or a Russian article with my supervision partner, they are happy to meet for a coffee and some cake. For languages I have roughly ten contact hours a week in the form of lectures, supervisions, language and translation classes. I have been blown away at the knowledge and enthusiasm my teachers and lecturers have for their subjects, and the time they take over my work to make sure I am getting the most out of it. Recently I had a lecture by one of the leading experts on the foundation of Russia and it was something special to listen to the person who wrote two of the books I cited in an essay.

'My college has been amazing at organising events for us. We have had pub quizzes, BOPs (Big Open Parties), Mario Kart tournaments and wine tastings. There's also a dance night with a different dance style on almost every night which attracts students from other colleges and is a great way to meet new people.

'If you are looking to party all the time then Cambridge isn't for you; but if you're willing to work hard, enjoy your subject and get involved with what's on offer, then I couldn't recommend Cambridge enough. I honestly wouldn't want to be anywhere else!'

Case study: Tayo, Oxford

'Without trying to sound too teacher-like, a definite realisation that hits you from as early as "freshers' week" is that Oxford truly is very different to other universities. This was obvious from my second day when faculty inductions had already kicked off: people were set work due for the upcoming first full week and there was a clear message emphasised by all our tutors that work was of paramount importance over the course of our degree. A definite mistake I made, common throughout the regrets of freshers countrywide, was to sign up for anything and everything at the freshers' fair, which meant I spent an hour the following evening unsubscribing from various activities which in retrospect I really wasn't that interested in. Given the demands of academic life that I am now encountering, this was just as well.

'On the social and academic side of my experience so far, I definitely had some qualms over the standard of work and the sorts of people I would meet at Oxford and I'm pleased to report that all the tutors are incredibly supportive and understanding of your academic background and will only push you as far as your own ambitions allow. Obviously, there are elements of competition, in terms of weekly language morphology tests and the like, but there is definitely a lot more of a chilled consensus among the student body which isn't necessarily reflected to those outside of the university. I still haven't quite yet figured out the most efficient way of handling the writing of one 2,500-word essay each week as well as delivering language homework and attending tutorials and lectures. Nevertheless, I would stress that as long as you don't intend to secure a "blue" for being in the first rowing team or to get a first all while aiming to maintain a high social presence, there is more than enough time during the week to meet your academic requirements while fulfilling your own goals for your time here at Oxford.

'An observation I've made that might be of importance to applicants is that the college you are in does have an impact on your workload and the support you get. For example, at one college, English students get three essays every two weeks, whereas at another college they only get one a fortnight. (I've been told by friends that they gained this inside knowledge by talking to people already at Oxford doing their subject at different colleges and by looking at online discussion sites.) For Classics at my college we have one essay each week and from the third term we will be required to submit three essays every two weeks.

'Overall, Oxford is definitely a hard-working environment but there is plenty of time to take advantage of the many extra-curricular opportunities on offer. Good luck with your applications!'

Case study: Shiyoun, Cambridge

'Life in Cambridge can be wonderful and confusing simultaneously, and that is fine if you accept the idea that getting into this university is only the beginning. The workload in Cambridge is manageable, yet it requires conscious management of one's priorities and the will to put study before all the enchanting social occasions, opportunities and entertainments the university offers. Beyond the special tutorial system, the famed club activities and the brilliant people you will meet at Oxbridge, I would like to share some of the episodes and observations I have had here, hoping that it may offer a realistic glimpse into this place.

'An observation I made during my first term is that one has to be really dedicated to the subject one has chosen. This sounds like an obvious statement, yet by the end of week one, more than two freshers from my faculty discussed the option of changing their course. In one extreme case from another faculty, a student decided to take a year off altogether. The reasons for these situations vary; it may be because they found the course too demanding or stressful, or because they chose the wrong course for the wrong reason, thinking that some courses are "easier to get onto" than others. One should choose a course that one is truly passionate about, a subject on which one can devote a considerable amount of time every day as independent study hours. I know it's an overused cliché, but, do what you love and love what you do. Otherwise the time here will not be as rewarding and illuminating as it can be.

'Enough caveats. On a more positive note, Cambridge is an undeniably thrilling environment. On Tuesdays I have this surreal experience of having Professor Mary Beard, the author of legendary titles such as *SPQR* and whose BBC documentaries I used to watch as an A level student, as my lecturer.

'Beside the lectures, weekly supervisions can be stressful, during which we are questioned, pushed and challenged on the 2,000-word essay we have written after studying the target texts and over ten suggested readings in a week. But personally, I find those hours of sitting and discussing with my supervisors, while surrounded by the casts of Greek and Roman sculptures in the Museum of Classical Archaeology, electrifying. Alongside well-known academic brilliance, you may also meet some extraordinary people of your age. Overall, if you can work hard and (optionally) play hard, I recommend applying. I wish the best of luck to future candidates!'

The collegiate system

The Oxford and Cambridge collegiate system is an integral part and a key strength of both universities. The colleges are independent, self-governing communities of academics, students and staff. Students and academics have the benefits of belonging both to a large, internationally renowned institution and to a smaller, interdisciplinary, academic college community. Colleges and halls enable leading academics and students across subjects and year groups, and from different cultures and countries, to come together and share ideas.

The relatively small number of students at each college also means that you receive plenty of personal academic and pastoral support. Your college can provide you with the perfect forum to discuss your work in seminars, over meals in the dining hall or in your room late into the evening. It will help you to make friends quickly, and give you the opportunity to try a wide range of social and sporting activities.

All colleges invest heavily in facilities for library and IT provision, accommodation and pastoral care, and offer sports and social events. Undergraduate students benefit from the junior common room or junior combination room (JCR) in their college – both a physical space and an organisation, it provides social events, advice and a link to the undergraduate community.

The standard of accommodation and food offered by some colleges is generally superior to that offered by most UK universities. Certain colleges even have Michelin-starred chefs overseeing their kitchens, and wine cellars that equal those of some of the best clubs in the world. Unlike most universities, many colleges can accommodate you for the whole of your time at university, saving you the trouble and expense of finding your own accommodation.

The best libraries and research facilities

Oxford and Cambridge are consistently placed among the highest-ranked universities for their research performance and have been shown to outperform UK competitors in the scale and quality of their research across a wide range of subject areas. The two universities also far outstrip other universities in terms of income from endowments and other private sources because of their age and their ability to attract funds from alumni and other donors.

Case study: Keith, Cambridge

'The facilities at Cambridge are amazing. There are facilities in your own college, but you can also join university-wide societies. I enjoy doing drama productions and being involved in the university paper. Over the past couple of years I have gained particularly fond memories of the social community of my college – I know I have made friends for life. In terms of teaching, there is an incredibly high standard. My lecturers are extremely dedicated and the other students are very engaging to debate ideas with. Mixing with people in college who study other subjects at an equally high level means that without realising it you are constantly exposed to interdisciplinary thinking.

'I am a keen musician and am part of CUMS (Cambridge University Musical Society). CUMS gives you real opportunities to nurture your choral or orchestral talents to the highest level and take part in concerts not only in Cambridge and around the UK but even internationally. Similarly, given the small size of the city, it is amazing how many top international musicians play in Cambridge venues. I have found that my musical education has broadened a great deal too with exposure to so many talented individuals with so many different musical tastes and backgrounds.'

Oxford students have access to the Bodleian Library and Cambridge students to the Cambridge University Library; both are copyright libraries and therefore hold a copy of every book, pamphlet, journal and magazine ever published in the UK. They are also non-lending, so students can always access the texts they need quickly, no matter how obscure. There are lots of other libraries in Oxford and Cambridge, including at least one for each faculty and college.

The people you'll meet

Contrary to popular belief, people who study at Oxford and Cambridge come from very diverse backgrounds and have many different interests and personalities. There really is no such thing as an 'Oxbridge type'. If you enjoy art, music, sport, acting, drinking, clubbing or just about any sort of activity imaginable, there will be many like-minded souls waiting to share your interests. Students come from private schools, state schools and from overseas. It's up to you to decide whether you want to spend your time punting along the river, attending May balls, writing for the university magazines, speaking at the Students' Union, drinking in the JCR or doing none of these things. Your Oxbridge experience is one only you can create, so forget the clichés.

It is true, however, that Oxford and Cambridge attract the highest-performing undergraduate students, so you will be keeping company with some of the brightest people in the country and from abroad. Indeed, you may find yourself moving from the top of the academic tree to the bottom and this can require a period of adjustment. Not everyone you meet will become your friend or be your type, but you are sure to find their company stimulating and intellectually satisfying.

Case study: Jessica, Oxford

'I'll be honest and admit that I wasn't the hardest worker at school and had a very casual attitude to academic study, but I was smart enough to promise myself that if I got the A level grades I needed to get into Oxford, to read Classics, I would apply myself fully to the course and its rich and varied curriculum. Looking back, I am happy to say that I did.

'I viewed Oxford as a place full of possibilities and it never failed to deliver. I found the pace and depth of studying hugely stretching as I had daily language classes in Ancient Greek at 9am, as well as language classes in Latin, lectures, and an essay to write per week – and this was just in the first year. Halfway through freshers' week I realised I needed to stop focusing just on fun. I went on to make my life at Oxford both rich in study and in the fantastic friendships I made through my subject, college, music and journalism interests.

'I learned a huge amount about self-discipline and about what I could achieve if I really pushed myself. The academic training and critical thinking I learned through my studies of literature, original languages, ancient history and philosophy have taught me to keep questioning and seeking answers, and keep seeking truths and new discoveries in whatever I do, whether that be teaching or a career in the city, both of which I have done since graduating.

'I was fortunate enough to have been able to explore different cultures, countries, periods in history and the rich diversity of life during my time in Oxford. I have continued to make this exploration a part of my life, and in today's truly global society I have found myself better equipped to be a high performer in my career and a global citizen through the education and principles I learned in my university experience.'

The location

Both Oxford and Cambridge are undeniably lovely places to live, and each has its own very special character. Cambridge is much smaller than Oxford and has a market-town feel about it. The university buildings are set much closer together, with a few exceptions such as Girton. Oxford feels more like a university set inside a city; colleges and faculty buildings are spaced out over a wider area and you will probably need a bike to get around easily. The universities themselves have many beautiful buildings – each with its own architectural integrity. The colleges are stunning, whether you're into ancient architecture or modern chrome and glass.

Employers are impressed by an Oxbridge degree

While having a First Class degree will improve your employment prospects more than anything else, employers are always impressed by an Oxbridge degree. The tutorial system will have taught you many useful skills: how to formulate and articulate a logical point of view, how to work independently, how to assimilate large amounts of information and how to prepare for tight deadlines. Oxbridge graduates have the confidence, intellect and skills that employers are looking for.

It can also be easier to get an internship while you're studying at Oxbridge because the university terms are shorter so you are available for work experience for longer periods.

Are there any disadvantages?

The eight-week terms do make your study time very intensive, and you will have to work hard outside term time too. Some students find the atmosphere highly pressured; you will constantly be called upon to meet deadlines and assimilate large amounts of information in a very short time. You will also have to balance your extra-curricular activities alongside your demanding academic schedule.

Both universities do not consider it appropriate for students to take on paid work while they are studying as the terms are so short and the workload so intense. See page 30 for more information.

Some people will tell you that Oxford and Cambridge are not good places to go if you want to play lots of sport or be in a band or basically do anything other than study. It is certainly difficult to strike the right balance but many fine sportspeople, musicians, actors, artists and novelists have managed to do just that. Nonetheless, it's worth noting that the atmosphere is shifting at both universities, and it is now harder to devote lots of time to extra-curricular activities than it once was.

Will it be suitable for me?

Just because Cambridge and Oxford are two of the leading universities in the world doesn't mean you should be daunted by their reputations. Their sole criterion for accepting new undergraduates is academic excellence. This is assessed through academic qualifications, during interviews and through special written tests prior to or during the interview stage. If you have good academic qualifications and are passionate about learning, you are eligible and they will welcome your application.

Equally, being eligible does not necessarily make Cambridge and Oxford a good choice for you – you have to be prepared to consistently put your studies first and you'll find yourself working harder than your friends who are studying elsewhere. If this is not for you, then consider other options.

Case study: Tom, Oxford

'I had always done well at school, but didn't really have the confidence to consider applying to Oxbridge, partly because I didn't know anyone who had gone there before. In fact, I didn't know many people who had been to university at all. However, when I got my AS grades, my head teacher suggested it might be worth trying, especially as I also had a strong track record at GCSE.

'I had already undertaken some work experience in a legal firm and had been visiting law courts on a regular basis. Once I had made the decision to apply to read Law at Oxford, I began to read more widely around the subject, keeping up to date with legal developments through articles in newspapers, magazines and journals, as well as watching items related to law on the television news. I also made my visits to law courts more systematic and kept notes of what I had observed and learned.

'I was conscious not to over-prepare for the interview, but I was also proactive in getting some interview practice from family or friends. Although they did not have direct experience of law at university, it was really useful for them to ask me questions about what I had learned in my research and why I wanted to study Law. My school also put on a couple of practice interview sessions. All of this made me more confident about the real interview. I knew I would feel prepared, but would still be natural.'

Your school

Does the school you attend have any bearing on your Oxbridge application? (NB: This is a much-discussed issue for students attending UK schools, but if you are applying from a school outside the UK, then you can pass over this section.)

Schools in the UK can be divided into independent schools, often called 'public schools' (although the categories do not quite overlap) and state or maintained schools. The view that Oxford and Cambridge are largely populated by students from the independent sector and that the universities have a preference for such students is outdated. Admittedly, at one time it was true that such students formed the majority of undergraduates (partially due to the fact that some schools had ties to sister colleges), but this hasn't been the case for some years.

Until recently, it was also commonly accepted that it is easier to get into Oxbridge for students in the independent sector, but there have been many stories in the media recently that suggest that the opposite is now true and that preference is given to state school students. Let's examine the facts to see if we can shed some light on this debate.

- Less than 7% of students in the UK are educated in independent schools, but they make up around 30% of the student body at both Oxford and Cambridge.
- In 2000, 40% of Oxford undergraduates came from state schools whereas in 2021, it was about 70%.
- An independent school student is four times more likely to gain a place than a state school student.
- In 2020, four of the top ten schools to receive the most offers from Oxbridge colleges were state sixth forms.
- See also Tables 1 and 2 on pages 18–19 for more comprehensive data on state school and independent school admissions and acceptances to Oxford and Cambridge colleges.

So although the percentage of students at Oxbridge from the independent sector has largely been getting smaller over the last few years, it is undeniable that students from the independent sector still have a statistical advantage. It is important to understand that this advantage is not because being in an independent school confers a special status upon you. Fees and entrance exams mean that such schools can have smaller classes and extra tuition. They also have better resources and the ability to expose students to a wide range of super-curricular activities and interests, such as clubs and societies, external speakers and educational trips. Finally, many public schools resemble, from the architecture to the house system, the Oxbridge world of quads, chapels and colleges, and so their students are unlikely to experience a 'culture shock' on going up.

This said, not all independent schools are equal. According to a recent guide to independent schools, Westminster School managed to secure places for 42% of their upper-sixth students, with St Paul's and St Paul's School for Girls securing 33% and 31%, while Eton secured places for 26% of their cohort. Another ten schools secured about 20%, and the school in 25th place – Dulwich College – secured 13%. Of course, compared to the state sector these are still big numbers; a study by the Sutton Trust revealed that, over 2015–2017, the top eight independent schools filled 1,310 places compared to 1,220 from nearly 3,000 other schools, the overwhelming majority of which were state schools.

Similarly, not all state schools are equal. A significant number of the state school students entering Oxbridge will come from highly selective sixth form and grammar schools; schools that commit to preparing their students for the Oxbridge application process in much the same way as the private sector does. Undeniably, however, state schools are producing more high-achieving students; in turn, more applications are made and the competition to get a place gets ever tougher. For example, since 1981 the number of annual applications to Cambridge has risen from just under 5,000 to 20,246 in 2020.

Oxford and Cambridge are committed to improving representation, and are most concerned with reaching students in schools that historically have not sent many, or even any, students to them. Nevertheless, independent school students shouldn't feel concerned that their status puts them at a disadvantage (just as it confers no special benefit), and all students should use the resources at their school to make themselves as academically competitive as possible.

Ultimately, Oxford and Cambridge are looking for students who are not only academically gifted, but passionate about their subject choice. Finally, remember that, as with all university applications, there is always an element of luck. It's not the end of the world if you don't get a place at Oxford or Cambridge, as there are many more great universities out there.

State schools and outreach programmes

Oxford and Cambridge have worked very hard over the last decade or so to bring the sort of students into their orbit who would traditionally have not considered making an application, even if there is still a lot to do (as they themselves readily admit). If you are an academically top-rank student, don't let the disparity between admission rates from the state sector and independent sector put you off. And don't allow yourself to be discouraged by others – the Sutton Trust has observed that a significant factor in applications to Oxbridge is the teachers; many state school teachers continue to hold an incorrect picture of Oxbridge as somewhere that would look down on their students and therefore discourage their students from applying. Do your own research! A good place to start is with Oxford's Increasing Access project and Cambridge's Widening Participation project.

- Oxford: www.ox.ac.uk/admissions/undergraduate/increasing-access
- Cambridge: www.undergraduate.study.cam.ac.uk/find-out-more/widening-participation

These similar enterprises provide students and schools with helpful advice and resources, and the range of provision is impressive. There are links to a wide range of online material, from actual lectures to explorations of 'big questions' (take a look at Oxford's Oxplore: www.ox.ac.uk/admissions/undergraduate/increasing-access/oxplore). There is also a lot of information on events, from open days through academic support programmes to residential summer schools. For example, Oxford's UNIQ programme helps students explore subjects that might interest them by inviting them to a residential week in which they work with students and academics. Cambridge's HE+ programme offers year-long academic support to students to enhance their prospects of a successful application.

Table 1 UK applications to Oxford, students admitted by school type and gender and college, three-year total 2018–2020

Oxford college	State school	Independent school	State proportion of total UK students admitted	Female	Male	Female proportion of total UK students admitted
Balliol	162	89	64.5%	126	131	49%
Brasenose	196	76	72.1%	148	130	53.2%
Christ Church	163	139	54%	148	161	47.9%
Corpus Christi	103	67	60.6%	88	91	49.2%
Exeter	140	95	59.6%	145	105	58%
Hertford	225	76	74.8%	173	136	56%
Jesus	151	104	59.2%	126	143	46.8%
Keble	210	121	63.4%	160	183	46.6%
Lady Margaret Hall	206	90	69.6%	184	119	60.7%
Lincoln	123	95	56.4%	116	103	53%
Magdalen	156	102	60.5%	137	127	51.9%
Mansfield	186	11	94.4%	112	87	56.3%
Merton	132	70	65.3%	115	93	55.3%
New College	180	139	56.4%	168	158	51.5%
Oriel	123	79	60.9%	100	112	47.2%
Pembroke	148	107	58%	129	133	49.2%
Queen's	132	97	57.6%	146	91	61.6%
Somerville	200	106	65.4%	176	139	55.9%
St Anne's	214	86	71.3%	181	131	58%
St Catherine's	221	122	64.4%	162	185	46.7%
St Edmund Hall	146	99	59.6%	127	127	50%
St Hilda's	163	103	61.3%	169	109	60.8%
St Hugh's	162	122	57%	156	132	54.2%
St John's	161	96	62.6%	142	127	52.8
St Peter's	127	103	55.2%	117	119	49.6%
Trinity	128	89	59%	106	115	48%
University	185	83	69%	153	120	56%
Wadham	227	94	70.7%	194	135	59%
Worcester	240	83	74.3%	195	136	58.9%

*Source: www.ox.ac.uk/sites/files/oxford/
AnnualAdmissionsStatisticalReport2021.pdf.*

Table 2 UK applications to Cambridge, student acceptances by school (2020) and gender (2018) and college

Cambridge college	State school	Independent school*	State proportion of total UK students accepted (2020)	Female	Male	Female proportion of total UK students admitted (2018)**
Christ's	85	30	74.1%	50	73	40.6%
Churchill	114	37	75.4%	51	86	37.2%
Clare	125	53	70.4%	71	70	50.7%
Corpus Christi	89	26	77.5%	39	47	45.3%
Downing	111	62	64%	62	66	48.4%
Emmanuel	122	55	68.9%	70	66	51.5%
Fitzwilliam	121	32	79.3%	58	73	44.3%
Girton	127	39	76.4%	68	73	48.2%
Gonville and Caius	154	116	57.1%	69	88	43.9%
Homerton	154	56	73.4%	92	86	51.2%
Jesus	136	34	80.1%	68	77	46.7%
King's	110	31	78.2%	61	63	49.2%
Magdalene	90	45	66.7%	46	60	43.4%
Murray Edwards	111	36	75.7%	104	-	100%
Newnham	106	44	70.8%	119	-	100%
Pembroke	128	39	76.6%	66	63	51.2%
Peterhouse	61	30	67.2%	37	47	44.0%
Queens'	145	53	73.1%	74	77	49.0%
Robinson	101	107	48.5%	47	78	37.6%
St Catharine's	115	44	72.2%	64	70	47.8%
St John's	158	84	65.2%	72	96	41.4%
Selwyn	111	31	78.4%	63	56	52.9%
Sidney Sussex	97	50	66%	43	65	39.8%
Trinity	157	97	61.8%	69	142	32.7%
Trinity Hall	104	40	72.1%	53	47	53%

*Source: www.undergraduate.study.cam.ac.uk/sites/www.undergraduate.study.cam.ac.uk/
files/publications/ug_admissions_statistics_2020_cycle.pdf
and the University of Cambridge Registrary's Office.*

* Approximate figures calculated from information provided in columns 2 and 4.
** Approximate figures calculated from information provided in columns 5 and 6.

Both universities also offer shorter-term shadowing schemes where you can spend anything from a day to a few days learning about what life at these universities is like under the wing of current undergraduates. For more details, see:

- Oxford: www.oxfordsu.org/activities/target-schools/shadowing-days
- Cambridge: www.applytocambridge.com/shadowing/apply

Oxford and Cambridge also have teams of school liaison officers whose job it is to help schools that do not have a history of Oxbridge applications learn about how best to prepare their students. Both universities divide the UK up into a number of regions, each of which is associated with a number of colleges and their liaison officers. If your school has not established a connection, then ask a relevant staff member to set up a relationship. To find out which colleges you should contact, use the following links:

- Oxford: www.ox.ac.uk/oxfordforUK
- Cambridge: www.undergraduate.study.cam.ac.uk/area-links

Another excellent resource is InsideUni (www.insideuni.org) which is a non-profit organisation run by ex-Oxbridge students who want to share their experiences. They have advice on mentoring, how to extend your reading on a budget and hundreds of testimonials. Finally, the Access Programme (https://oxbridgeapplications.com/the-access-programme) has been providing advice and support for students from non-fee-paying schools for over 20 years.

Useful websites

- Oxfizz: https://oxfizz.org/accessprogramme – has over 200 graduate volunteers providing students from disadvantaged backgrounds with tuition (via summer schools) and advice to help them apply.
- Target Oxbridge: https://targetoxbridge.co.uk/index.html – a year-long programme for black students in Year 12 which provides advice on courses, mentoring, seminars, personal statement advice and interview practice.
- UniRise: www.unirise.co.uk – a free online course on how to write a winning personal statement.
- Zero Gravity: www.zerogravity.co.uk – provides mentors to students to help them increase their chances.

Students with disabilities and special educational needs (SEN)

Students with disabilities and SEN students are welcome at both universities and are in no way disadvantaged in their application. Disabilities must be declared on the UCAS form in order for the university and college to pool their resources and you must contact the admissions office at university and college level to discuss your individual needs.

For students with physical disabilities and impaired movement, living in older colleges can be tricky. Because Oxford and Cambridge are so old, much of the architecture is 'listed', which can make it illegal to make changes to the buildings. This means that it is sometimes impossible to install lifts. The same is true of some faculties, for example, the Architecture faculty at Cambridge. There are, however, many faculties with new buildings that do not pose such problems, and several colleges in both universities have recently been renovated. You will need to consult your chosen college to advise you on whether it is able to accommodate your needs.

Students with Specific Learning Difficulties (SpLDs), such as dyslexia and dyspraxia, are given the opportunity to write using a computer and extra time during exams; they should feel in no way anxious about applying. Those with visual or hearing impairments are also welcome to apply.

Each college should have a member of staff responsible for disabled students. You should ring the admissions tutor at your chosen college, who will put you in touch with the disability staff member to discuss its resources and your needs. Students can also apply for the Disabled Students' Allowance (DSA). Cambridge offers advice on this at www.disability.admin.cam.ac.uk/students/financial-support/disabled-students-allowance, while information about the DSA at Oxford can be found at www.ox.ac.uk/students/welfare/disability/needs. For more information in general, look at the Cambridge Disability Resource Centre at www.disability.admin.cam.ac.uk, or the University of Oxford Disability Advisory Service at www.ox.ac.uk/students/welfare/disability.

Students with children

Both Oxford and Cambridge welcome applications from prospective students who have children. Several colleges provide accommodation for couples and families and some colleges have their own nurseries. They each also have a university-wide nursery. You should ring the admissions office at your chosen college for more information.

Although the Access to Learning Fund has been scrapped, there is a Parents' Learning Allowance; more information about this can be found at the following link: www.gov.uk/parents-learning-allowance.

UK students at both universities can ask to be considered for a university and college hardship fund (www.gov.uk/extra-money-pay-university/university-and-college-hardship-funds). Students should contact the student services department at their university to see if they are eligible. Students with children, especially single parents, could qualify, as students with children are one of the priority groups for support. More information is available at the following websites:

- Cambridge: www.childcare.admin.cam.ac.uk
- Oxford: https://childcare.admin.ox.ac.uk/finance.

The 'Cambridge Guide for Student Parents' is written yearly by the Cambridge University Students' Union (CUSU) and is available online at www.studentadvice.cam.ac.uk/welfare/childcare. Some colleges are also members of the Central Childcare Bursary Scheme, which currently offers means-tested grants to overseas and EU students to help with the costs of childcare (www.childcare.admin.cam.ac.uk/supportwithchildcarecosts/central-childcare-bursary-scheme-eu-and-overseas-students). This is not a loan and does not need to be repaid. Application forms are available from college offices, the childcare information adviser and CUSU. Applications can be made at any time during the academic year, though the university advises applicants that most funding will have been allocated by the Easter Term.

The University of Oxford provides similar support, heavily subsidising the cost of local nursery care, as well as funding holiday play schemes. See https://childcare.admin.ox.ac.uk/home for further details. Oxford University Students' Union (OUSU) provides useful information on childcare, funding and other necessities for students who are also parents (www.oxfordsu.org/support/advice).

Students from ethnic minorities

The issue of BAME (Black and Minority Ethnic) students has been in the news for a number of years now with claims that relatively few such students are admitted, showing that the universities are not doing enough to broaden access. This is not the place to enter into a detailed discussion of the causes of the low numbers. It should be said that both universities have significantly improved, and continue to improve, their outreach programmes over recent years; it should also be said that some of the problem lies with some schools whose students traditionally did not go to Oxbridge still feeling – erroneously – that their students are 'not of the right kind'.

Oxford now has a page dedicated to ethnicity statistics (www.ox.ac.uk/about/facts-and-figures/admissions-statistics/undergraduate-students/current/ethnicity). It shows that, of the 2020 intake, 76.4% of students identify as white and 23.6% as BAME. This is to be compared to 19.4% of the population between the ages of 18 and 24 declaring themselves BAME, as opposed to 80.6% white, and to 26.9% of the 2018 intake for *all* UK universities achieving AAA or better declaring themselves BAME as opposed to 73.1% white.

The BBC reported an all-time high of 29.3% undergraduates declaring themselves as BAME in Cambridge's 2020 intake (www.bbc.co.uk/news/uk-england-cambridgeshire-57156553), with detailed information available in section 8 of the University of Cambridge's 2020 undergraduate admissions statistics document (www.undergraduate.study.cam.ac.uk/sites/www.undergraduate.study.cam.ac.uk/files/publications/ug_admissions_statistics_2020_cycle_0.pdf).

While these statistics necessarily simplify a complex picture, they do show that the universities are becoming ever more representative.

Students from disadvantaged backgrounds

Both Oxford and Cambridge are firmly committed to increasing the representation of students from disadvantaged backgrounds at their institutions. Oxford claims that about 15% of their students at the moment come from such backgrounds and they intend to increase that percentage to 25% by 2023. Cambridge claims that it has hit the target of one in four students already and has pledged to increase the proportion to one in three by 2035.

Oxford has a number of ways of increasing access (www.ox.ac.uk/admissions/undergraduate/increasing-access), notable among which are two initiatives to help students from disadvantaged backgrounds. Foundation Oxford (www.ox.ac.uk/admissions/undergraduate/increasing-access/foundation-oxford) is a foundation-year course offered to state school students from less advantaged areas and to students who have suffered some sort of serious disadvantage or disruption to their education. Opportunity Oxford (www.ox.ac.uk/admissions/undergraduate/increasing-access/opportunity-oxford) is a bridge programme for offer-holders to help students to develop the academic skills necessary to get the most out of their time at Oxford.

Cambridge also has a number of programmes for increasing access (www.undergraduate.study.cam.ac.uk/find-out-more/widening-participation), and now participates in the UCAS Adjustment programme which allows students who have met the conditions of their conditional firm offers and exceeded at least one to make an application to another university without risking their places. Cambridge restricts Adjustment to students from disadvantaged backgrounds, and claims it will make about 100 places available (www.undergraduate.study.cam.ac.uk/adjustment).

Lesbian, gay, bisexual, transgender and queer (LGBTQ+) students

Oxford and Cambridge are inclusive universities. Not only is there a central LGBT society at each university but each college also has its own LGBT representative. There are plenty of events to help you feel comfortable. For further information have a look at these websites:

- Cambridge: LGBT+ information from CUSU: www.lgbt.cusu.cam.ac.uk
- Oxford: LGBTQ+ Society at OUSU (OULGBTQ): www.oulgbtq.org.

Educationally disadvantaged students or students who have had a disrupted education

Oxford and Cambridge are committed to helping applicants who have in some way been disadvantaged by significant disruption to their educational career, which may have resulted in candidates getting lower grades at A level than they might otherwise have achieved.

The Extenuating Circumstances Form (ECF) (www.undergraduate. study.cam.ac.uk/applying/decisions/extenuating-circumstances-form) enables teachers to provide detailed background information about Cambridge applicants so they can be assessed fairly. The admissions tutors will also have access to publicly available data on school perfor- mance that can help them place a student's educational achievement in context. Cambridge no longer lists factors that identify someone as being in extenuating circumstances, saying instead that the form is for those who believe they have suffered 'particular personal or education disadvantage' and wish this to be considered. In previous years, they've identified the following and I suspect they still provide a good guide:

- having a medical condition that has significantly affected their educational progress, particularly since the age of 14
- having major caring responsibilities, suffering a recent bereavement or having a close family member with a serious illness
- being estranged from and living independently of their family
- having experienced significant disruption to their education provision at school or college or significant disruption due to family circumstances
- being a victim of a serious crime.

ECFs can be obtained from any college admissions office, from the uni- versity's admissions office or from the university website (shown above). If in doubt as to whether your circumstances merit consideration, you should ask the college to which you are applying directly. The form must be returned by 22 October (a week after the UCAS deadline).

Oxford does not have a separate form. It asks that the UCAS reference contain details of any special circumstances similar to those listed above.

Both Cambridge and Oxford make use of publicly available information for applicants who may have been subject to educational or socio- economic difficulties. They advise that if an applicant shows evidence of the academic prowess required, it is likely that they will be given consid- eration for interview alongside those shortlisted in the normal way. Aspects of contextual data that will be considered include:

- the socio-economic characteristics of an applicant's local area, and rates of progression to higher education in an applicant's local area
- how the applicant's school or college performs at GCSE, A level or equivalent
- students who have spent longer than three months in care.

For more information, visit www.ox.ac.uk/admissions/undergraduate/ applying-to-oxford/decisions/contextual-data and www.undergraduate. study.cam.ac.uk/applying/contextual-data.

2 | Choosing your university and college

As an undergraduate, you may only apply to either Oxford **or** Cambridge. You should try to make an educated choice between the two; ideally, do your research and visit both, have a look around the various colleges and university buildings and absorb the atmosphere. Talk to friends who are currently at Oxbridge and teachers who have been there. You also need to understand the courses each university offers; for example, Cambridge offers Natural Sciences in place of Physics, Chemistry or Biology; Philosophy, Politics and Economics (PPE) is on offer at Oxford, while Human, Social and Political Sciences (HSPS) is on offer at Cambridge. A very good guide on some of the similarities and differences between Cambridge and Oxford universities can be found on the Oxford website here: www.ox.ac.uk/admissions/undergraduate/applying-to-oxford/teachers/oxford-and-cambridge-similarities-and-differences.

Which university?

There are several reasons to choose one university over the other but Oxford and Cambridge agree that the most important decision a prospective applicant has to make is the degree they wish to study, not which university they want to apply to. Both universities are committed to recruiting the most talented students regardless of their background and both are world-class in teaching and research in both arts and science subjects.

First, choose your course

It is essential to check that the university you prefer teaches the subject you wish to study. There are various subjects that Oxford offers that Cambridge does not and vice versa. On the following page is a table of the undergraduate courses offered in 2021 for both universities, with shared or highly similar courses in bold.

Table 3 Courses offered at Oxford and Cambridge

Oxford Courses	Cambridge Courses
Archaeology and Anthropology	Anglo-Saxon, Norse, and Celtic
Biochemistry (Molecular and Cellular)	Archaeology
Biology	Architecture
Biomedical Sciences	Asian and Middle Eastern Studies
Chemistry	Chemical Engineering
Classical Archaeology and Ancient History	**Classics**
Classics	**Computer Science**
Classics and English	Economics
Classics and Modern Languages	Education
Classics and Oriental Studies	**Engineering**
Computer Science	**English**
Computer Science and Philosophy	**Geography**
Earth Sciences (Geology)	**History**
Economics and Management	**History and Modern Languages**
Engineering Science	**History and Politics**
English Language and Literature	**History of Art**
English and Modern Languages	Human, Social, and Political Sciences
European and Middle Eastern Languages	Land Economy
Fine Art	**Law**
Geography	Linguistics
History	Management Studies (Part II course)
History (Ancient and Modern)	Manufacturing Engineering (Part II course)
History and Economics	**Mathematics**
History and English	**Medicine**
History and Modern Languages	**Medicine (Graduate Course)**
History and Politics	**Modern and Medieval Languages**
History of Art	**Music**
Human Sciences	Natural Sciences
Law (Jurisprudence)	Philosophy
Materials Science	**Psychological and Behavioural Sciences**
Mathematics	**Theology, Religion, and Philosophy of Religion**
Mathematics and Computer Science	Veterinary Medicine
Mathematics and Philosophy	
Mathematics and Statistics	
Medicine	
Medicine (graduate entry)	
Modern Languages	
Modern Languages and Linguistics	
Music	
Oriental Studies	
Philosophy and Modern Languages	
Philosophy, Politics and Economics (PPE)	
Philosophy and Theology	
Physics	
Physics and Philosophy	
Psychology (Experimental)	
Psychology, Philosophy and Linguistics (PPL)	
Religion and Oriental Studies	
Theology and Religion	

For more information go to the websites listed below:

- Cambridge: www.undergraduate.study.cam.ac.uk/courses
- Oxford: www.ox.ac.uk/admissions/undergraduate/courses.

Course flexibility

At Oxford, most subjects include compulsory courses for the first year, and then give students the opportunity to choose options in subsequent years. At Cambridge, courses cover the subject very broadly in the initial years and then become more specialised within a wide range of options in the later years.

Comparing the Tripos system at Cambridge with the two-part system at Oxford can be another way to help you decide which university is better suited to you. One of the great attractions of Cambridge is the flexibility of its Tripos system (the name Tripos is said to have been derived from the three-legged stool that undergraduates in the Middle Ages sat on at graduation ceremonies). The Tripos system at Cambridge gives you the opportunity to gain a broad overview of the subject and to discover areas of interest before specialising later on in the course.

Each course, or Tripos, is usually divided into two parts: Part I and Part II. After each part there is an exam that counts towards your final undergraduate mark. Part I can take one year (in Economics, for example) or two years (in English). A two-year Part I is divided into Part IA and Part IB. Once you have completed Part I (A and B), you have the option of continuing to specialise in the same subject, or swapping to a related but different subject for Part II. There is also an optional Part III offered in some subjects, such as the Mathematical Tripos.

The exact details vary from subject to subject but, in theory, this gives students quite a bit of flexibility; there have been students who have studied three different but related subjects during the course of their three years at Cambridge and have come out with a First Class degree. In reality, however, you should *not* go to your interview thinking that you will be able to change courses easily as admissions tutors, particularly those interviewing for humanities, arts and social sciences, will see this as a sign that you're not committed to your subject, and may give the place to someone who is. If students want to change subject when they get to Cambridge they have to work very hard at convincing their current director of studies (DoS) that they want to change for the right reasons, and then convince the DoS in their new subject to take them on.

On the other hand, there are subjects where elongated undergraduate degrees are encouraged. Natural Sciences and Mathematics students have the option of adding a Part III, while Engineering students take Parts IA, IB, IIA and IIB over four years, leading ultimately to the award of MEng.

The system works slightly differently at Oxford. As at Cambridge, students have to pass exams in two parts. However, students don't have to take examinations at the end of each year, as is the case in many Cambridge courses. The Preliminary Examinations (or 'Prelims') are taken at the end of the first year (apart from a few exceptions) and the Final Examinations ('Finals') are taken at the end of the third year. In some courses, such as Classics, the first set of examinations are called Honour Moderations (or 'Mods') but the structure for subsequent study remains the same. Most arts and social science undergraduates at the University of Oxford do not take exams in their second year; mathematics and science students take exams at the end of each year.

In general there are more courses at Oxford that are designed to take four years. Classics takes four years. The Joint Honours courses of Mathematics and Philosophy and Physics and Philosophy, Mathematics itself, Physics and Earth Sciences can take either three or four years (your choice), but in the case of Molecular and Cellular Biochemistry, Chemistry, Engineering Science, Materials Science and Physics, students are normally expected to progress to the fourth, research-based year leading to the award of a master's degree.

You should research the similarities and differences that apply to your particular subject choice carefully, and be prepared to discuss your discoveries at interview.

Other factors to consider

The location

Oxford is located about 100km (62 miles) north-west of London, with excellent links to the capital and the rest of the country by car, coach and train. It is a lively, medium-sized city with a total student population of over 30,000 (including students at both Oxford and Oxford Brookes). Most university and college buildings are located in the centre and are easily reached on foot or by bike.

Cambridge lies 88.5km (55 miles) north of London, off the M11 motorway, and is a 45-minute journey by train from the capital. There are also excellent rail links to Scotland and the north of England (via Peterborough), with direct regional services from Birmingham, the Midlands, East Anglia and the north-west of England. The city is also very well served by bus services to and from other cities. Stansted Airport is 48km (30 miles) away. The city has also become the centre of the hi-tech 'Silicon Fen' industries. It is smaller than Oxford and this can make Cambridge feel claustrophobic for some, but there are plenty of open green spaces in this undeniably beautiful place.

The student mix

In the 2020 intake for Oxford, 54.2% of students were female and 45.8% male; 79.8% of students were UK (Home) students, 7.2% were

EU students and 13% were overseas students. Maintained (state) school students accounted for 68.6% of Home undergraduates.

In the 2020 intake for Cambridge, 48% of students were female and 52% male; 74% were UK (Home) students, 10% were EU students and 16% were overseas students. Maintained (state) school students accounted for 70.6% of Home undergraduates.

Both Oxford and Cambridge have seen a dramatic rise in the percentage of students from the state sector over the last decade, and record numbers of state school pupils were offered places in 2020. There has been a jump of around 18% (from 51% to 69%) for Oxford and 16% (from 54% to 70%) in the case of Cambridge. Given that over 90% of UK pupils are educated in the state system, it is arguable that there is a long way to go, but these figures are nevertheless a testament to the huge amount of 'outreach' work that both universities have undertaken in recent times. (See pages 15–20 for more detail.)

Teaching

Teaching methods are very similar at both universities, as students will attend lectures, classes and laboratory work, as appropriate for their course. Unlike at many other universities, students at Oxford and Cambridge also benefit from one-to-one teaching from world experts in their field; the only difference is in the name: Oxford refers to these sessions as 'tutorials' while Cambridge calls them 'supervisions'.

Assessment

Students at Oxford and Cambridge are assessed informally throughout their course by producing work for their tutors/supervisors for weekly tutorials/supervisions. Formal assessment is almost entirely based on examinations, although in the final year of many courses one examination paper can be replaced with a dissertation. For certain subjects, such as Music, additional coursework papers and performance options can replace examination papers.

At Oxford, the final degree classification result is usually based on the examinations taken at the end of the final year, though for some science subjects, such as Biology, the final classification is based on results achieved in second- and third-year examinations. Cambridge students are assessed through examinations in more than one year of their courses.

Research standards

Oxford has more world-leading academics than any other UK university and was ranked number one in the 2014 national Research Excellence Framework; 48% of Oxford's research was rated 4* ('world-leading') in 2014, while 39% was rated 3* ('internationally excellent'). It has consistently boasted the highest research income from external sponsors of any UK university (in 2018–19, £624.7 million – of income came from this source).

Cambridge is equally blessed financially, and performance league tables consistently place Cambridge among the world's top-ranking institutions. Academics associated with Cambridge have been awarded more Nobel prizes in recognition of their research than any other university, nationally and internationally. In the Research Excellence Framework in 2014, 47% of the research submissions from Cambridge were judged to be 4*, while 40% were rated as 3*.

International reputation

In the 2021 Academic Ranking of World Universities published by the Shanghai Jiao Tong University, Cambridge was placed third globally for academic and research performance and Oxford was positioned in seventh place, placing both institutions at the forefront of the most prestigious universities in the world.

Availability of part-time work

Oxford offers opportunities for a limited amount of paid work within college, for which you may need your tutor's permission, and colleges sometimes offer employment during the vacations. It does not allow students to have a part-time job outside of the university except in exceptional circumstances and only with the agreement of the college. The University Careers Service facilitates summer internship and work opportunities through the University of Oxford International Internship Programme and on-campus employer events and fairs.

Cambridge states that since the university terms are short and highly demanding on students' time and intellectual capabilities, it does not allow students to take on part-time work. This said, they note that some colleges will allow for small exceptions in the form of work in the college bar or library, or as a student helper on open days. Furthermore, as a Cambridge undergraduate, you will find it relatively easy to procure internships and holiday work if you are prepared to put enough effort into researching and applying.

Which college?

Your next decision is which college to choose. Many students are thrown into a complete quandary about this and at first sight it seems hard to know how to decide. Your college will be the centre of your academic and social life so it is worth putting a bit of thought into why you might prefer one over another. On the other hand, at both universities there is the very real possibility of being moved to another college before, during or after (in the case of Cambridge) the interview process. So while you should put some thought into which college to apply to, you shouldn't agonise over it too much. Rest assured that whichever college you end up in, by the end of your first term you will think it's the best one!

Detailed information on the colleges at both universities is provided in the College profiles section from page 177 onward.

Oxford and Cambridge are comprised of 45 (39 colleges and six permanent private halls) and 31 colleges respectively although not all of them will offer undergraduate courses (currently there are 37 undergraduate colleges at Oxford and 29 at Cambridge). See page 10 for more information on the collegiate system.

Your college will have a senior tutor whose role includes general oversight of all undergraduate members of the college, although your academic studies will be directed by your department or faculty. The relatively small number of students at each college allows for close and supportive personal attention to be given to the induction, academic development and welfare of individual students. At some Oxford colleges each student has a college adviser, who is a member of the college's academic staff and will be able to offer support and advice. This person is almost always the student's personal academic tutor. At Cambridge, a director of studies has oversight of academic welfare, while a tutor can help with issues to do with finance or other personal matters. Colleges at Oxford and Cambridge may also have college counsellors.

How do I choose a college that is right for me?

You might consider the following factors when making your decision.

Does it offer the right course?

Not every college will offer every course offered by the universities. To find out which colleges offer your course, visit www.ox.ac.uk/admissions/undergraduate/colleges/a-z-of-colleges for Oxford and www.undergraduate.study.cam.ac.uk/colleges for Cambridge.

Do you want to be with a certain type of student?

A minority of colleges admit only certain groups of students, so if you want to be in a women-only college or with more mature students your options are limited.

Women only: Murray Edwards and Newnham at Cambridge.

Mature students (over 21) only: Hughes Hall, St Edmund's and Wolfson at Cambridge; Harris Manchester and Wycliffe Hall at Oxford.

Does it have the right character?

There's no question that each college has its distinct character, whether it is highly academic, sporty or literary. Certainly, there's an element of 'horses for courses', if you'll pardon the pun. Being with like-minded students may make you work harder, but if you aspire to captain a sports team or run a student society, then you may want to pick somewhere that will be sympathetic to your aspirations.

Every year, Oxford publishes the Norrington table and Cambridge the Tompkins table (see pages 208 and 241), which rank the colleges in order of the number of First Class degrees achieved by their students in their final exams. This may give you some indication of the colleges' academic prowess. But beware of placing too much importance on this; colleges go up and down the tables at an alarming rate, and those at the top of the tables one year may find themselves halfway down the next.

What are the admissions criteria?

The colleges all have different admissions criteria for the subjects they offer. In addition to the information provided by your UCAS application, some colleges will request some sample work and some will require candidates to sit a test at interview. If you're applying to Oxford, you should check your course webpage to see what's required for your course. At Cambridge, most applicants will be asked to sit a written admissions test, either pre-interview or at interview (there are exceptions, for example for Mathematics and Music, although Mathematics applicants interviewing overseas are required to take a written mathematics assessment). Colleges may also set their own additional requirements: some may ask you to submit a few examples of school essays, which may form part of the discussion at interview; check the college to which you are applying for individual requirements. For further details, see Chapters 7–9. You need to read the admissions criteria for your course very carefully and this may help you decide. You might find that there are admissions criteria you aren't comfortable with or colleges whose criteria particularly appeal to you.

Is the location convenient?

It's definitely worth locating your faculty buildings and lecture halls and seeing which colleges are nearby. This may sound faintly ridiculous when most of the colleges are located quite centrally, but it's great to be able to fall out of bed and be at your lecture within 10 minutes of waking up after a hard night of working or playing. Bear in mind that a lot of people cycle around Oxford and Cambridge, so you may wish to consider cycling distance and walking distance.

Equally important is the college's location generally: consider what facilities are nearby, and whether you'd rather be right in the middle of it all or somewhere with more space to yourself.

Does it have the right facilities for me?

At this stage it might be useful to consult the alternative prospectus provided by students at each university (these can be found on almost every college website) – students already at Oxbridge are experts at discussing their own college's good and bad points – to eliminate colleges that don't have a particular facility (such as provision for sports or music) you really want. If you're unsure, contact the college directly for clarification. You may think now that all you will do at university is study, but you will be grateful that your college has a decent JCR bar with ping-pong tables or playing fields nearby or a fantastic music venue. You may not necessarily want to row for the university but you might have fun rowing for your college, for example. It's worth doing a bit of research into what colleges offer before you make a decision.

Should I visit the college and check it out?

If you can, you should. On open days you can ask questions of current students and professors. If you are unable to attend an open day, it's still possible to get a feel for a college by visiting at another time, although the areas you can explore may be restricted. Just a wander around the grounds and a look at the current students will probably give you a feeling that a college is or isn't right for you, and you are bound to prefer some over others. Each college has its owns prospectus, which will provide more detailed information than its entry in the university prospectus.

Should I think about the accommodation?

You'll be spending three or four years at university and the standard and range of college accommodation varies quite dramatically from college to college. If the size and standard of room matters to you, a bit of research will pay dividends. What's more, some colleges offer accommodation for the whole of your course, whereas at others you may find yourself competing against everyone else in the private rental sector (and 'living out' can prove more costly as you will have to rent a flat or house for the whole of the academic year, not just during term time).

Open application

If you still can't decide which college to apply to, it's possible to make an open application – this is where you are assigned a college by the admissions board. Allocation is often to 'less popular' colleges; this does not make them bad colleges, simply colleges that have fewer applicants than others in the current cycle of applications. Both universities stress that making an open application in no way disadvantages you.

You may decide to make an open application if you really don't mind what your college life will be like. However, college life is such a great and unique aspect of Oxbridge that it's worth putting at least some thought into it. But, as making an open application doesn't disadvantage you, don't be afraid to take this route if you really feel it's best for you.

If you decide not to make an open application, the next step is to narrow down the list of colleges at Cambridge and colleges/permanent private halls at Oxford to make your personal shortlist from which you will make your final choice.

Should I make a tactical decision?

So you're nearly there. You're close to deciding on your choice of university and your course. Lots of people now try to make a tactical choice based on which colleges are less popular, less centrally located, less well endowed; the theory being that somehow they'll be easier to get into. But don't be fooled.

A question that many students ask is whether certain colleges lean towards independent school students over state school pupils or vice versa. Both universities publish annually detailed statistics on the student intake at www.ox.ac.uk/about/facts-and-figures/admissions-statistics/undergraduate-students/current/college and www.undergraduate.study.cam.ac.uk/apply/statistics. Consulting the data will allow you to see the acceptance rates in a given year and trends over recent years. In the case of Cambridge, the figures for the last three years show that, for example, Gonville and Caius, Magdalene and St John's are consistently at the lower end of the range of offers made to state school students (around 63%) and Murray Edwards and King's at the higher end (around 85%). As for Oxford, Christ Church, St Peter's and New College are at the low end of this range (around 57%) with Hertford and Worcester at the top end (around 78%) and Mansfield is very much isolated at the top with around 95% of its offers made to state school students. These statistics are certainly interesting, but it's important to understand that they don't determine a state pathway and an independent pathway. Take a look at the data if you're curious, but don't rely on it for decision-making.

Another commonly asked question is whether some colleges are easier to get into for a given subject than others. Both universities are very clear on their websites that this is not the case! Again, all the relevant statistics are publicly available, and close inspection shows that the percentage of applicants made offers for a given course at a given college varies considerably from one year to the next, meaning that there are no 'easy' colleges. Do bear in mind that colleges don't have to fill up their places from those who have applied to them. If it happens that a college has relatively few applicants for a given course they may well reject those applicants and see whether other colleges have students that are more worthy of consideration. (This happens during the interview process with Oxford and later, in the winter pool, with Cambridge). They may even simply reduce the offers they make.

It should be clear also that if a certain college and course does accept a relatively high percentage of applicants over a given period of time, and becomes considered an easier pathway, more students might apply and the percentage of successful applicants will be driven down. Where such changes happen, it is impossible to know that this is the cause, but it should not be excluded; and such changes are visible. For example, over 2015–2017, St Hilda's (Oxford) was top of the list for acceptances to reading Classics with 50% of those who chose it for Classics being offered a place; but over 2018–2020 it was near the bottom of the list with just 25% of applicants being accepted. Inspection of other courses and colleges shows similar fluctuations.

In sum, there's no clever way around the system, so don't waste any time worrying about it in the belief that there is a right college for the type of student you are and the course you want to follow. Simply consider the other factors discussed in this chapter to guide your decision, and choose a college based on where you think you might be happy, rather than on where you think you have the 'best' chance; or opt for an open application.

Case study: Ray, Cambridge

'My experience of applying to Cambridge was similar to a roller-coaster ride. Having completed secondary school in Hong Kong (but with grades much lower than those I was capable of), I came to the UK to complete one-year intensive A levels at MPW Cambridge in English Literature, Sociology, Chinese and History. During that year I applied to Magdalene to read Law. After an intense but enjoyable interview, I waited for the result. Finally, on 3 January, a response: I had been pooled. In some ways this was more frustrating than a rejection as it meant yet more of an agonising wait, but on the other hand it meant I still had a chance. I had been deemed a suitable candidate. I remained hopeful. Then, sadly, on 8 January I was rejected. I was crushed.

'I busied myself with my other university offers. I secured a place at KCL, winning the Dickson Poon undergraduate law scholarship, as well as an offer from a prestigious Hong Kong University. On results day I was thrilled to secure A*A*AA but this was tinged with sadness as I knew I would have been able to meet a Cambridge offer had I managed to secure one. After much soul-searching, I decided to take a huge risk. I rejected my university offers and took a gap year during which I reapplied to Cambridge. Thankfully, my gamble paid off and I received an unconditional offer.

'I am now in my second year at Wolfson College reading Law. I am so glad I persevered. I love my college and my course, although it is very hard work (I am currently writing my fourth essay this fortnight!). I had heard lots of rumours about how little chance I had of securing a place: firstly because I had retaken my final school exams and secondly because I had been rejected the previous year. However, I am proof that these rumours are unfounded. If you are good enough, Oxbridge will take your application seriously. However, I do recognise that luck does play a part. I certainly took a big gamble and I would only encourage others to follow the same path if, like me, they could cope with a second rejection.'

3 | Entry requirements

Everyone knows that it's not easy to get into Oxford or Cambridge. In this chapter, we'll look at what examination results you can expect to be asked for, but it's important to bear in mind that it's not all about formal qualifications. And given that almost everyone applying will have or have been predicted excellent grades, to enable Oxford and Cambridge to make a more informed decision on who to offer places to they conduct interviews and/or admissions tests.

Oxford and Cambridge will almost always interview students as part of the application process. Cambridge says that it will interview all students with a realistic chance of a place, which amounts to a little over 75% of applicants. Oxford interviews a little under 50% of applicants and typically interviews three candidates for every place. So, here are some important factors to consider before you apply.

Your A level (or equivalent) subjects

The A level subject choices you make in Year 11 (or equivalent) can have a significant impact on the course options available to you at university.

The Russell Group, which represents the 24 leading UK universities (including Oxford and Cambridge), runs the website www.informed choices.ac.uk which provides students with tailored advice on what A level options will best place them to pursue the courses they want to study. The guide states that even where these choices are not specified as required subjects, universities may still have a preference for them.

Many Oxford and Cambridge courses require prior knowledge of certain subjects. Oxford has an extremely useful 'traffic-light' table that indicates, for each course, which subjects are essential, which are recommended and which are helpful: www.ox.ac.uk/admissions/ undergraduate/courses/admission-requirements/admission-requirements-table. Information on what subjects are mandatory and which are recommended at Cambridge can be found for each course on the respective course page (the list of courses can be found here: www. undergraduate.study.cam.ac.uk/courses). Cambridge also publishes a booklet on post-16 choices in a PDF format (www.undergraduate.study. cam.ac.uk/files/publications/the_subject_matters.pdf).

By way of general guidance, the following points may be helpful.

- No course requires a particular choice of three specific A levels.
- Many courses require one specific A level.
- A small number of courses require you to study two specific A levels. These are almost always science courses or courses with a science component. For example, Medicine requires chemistry with one of maths, biology and physics; Engineering requires maths and physics, as does Philosophy and Physics (Oxford). English and Modern Languages (Oxford) and History and Modern Languages (Cambridge: some colleges only) are examples of non-science courses requiring two specific A levels: English/history and a modern language.

Arts and social science courses

If you're undecided about which arts or social sciences course you would like to study at university, then A levels in English literature, history and languages provide a good foundation. If you are good at maths, this is always a good A level to have as well. Alongside these subjects there are many A levels that will put you in a good position, such as philosophy, history of art, and government and politics on the humanities side, and economics, psychology and the sciences on the science side.

Science courses

If you're interested in studying a science course at university but are not sure which one, you are advised to take at least two, and ideally three, of biology, chemistry, mathematics and physics. Some pairings of these subjects are more natural than others. The most natural pairs are biology and chemistry, chemistry and physics, and mathematics and physics.

In practice, the vast majority of applicants for science courses at Oxbridge take at least three of these subjects. Another useful combination is mathematics, further mathematics and physics. Many students take four of biology, chemistry, mathematics, further mathematics and physics.

If you're planning to study biological or medical sciences you should take chemistry; for physical sciences or engineering you should take mathematics and physics and, ideally, further mathematics.

Other possible subject choices, for instance computer science, design and technology, electronics or psychology, may be useful preparation for some science courses but as always it is advisable to check for any more information about the course at the time of applying.

Medicine

All candidates to Oxford or Cambridge have to take the BioMedical Admissions Test (BMAT) as part of their application (see Chapter 9).

To read Medicine at Oxford, you will need to achieve A*AA in three A levels (which does not include critical thinking or general studies) taken in one sitting. The minimum requirements are a grade A in both chemistry and at least one of biology, physics or mathematics.

Scottish students must have AA (taken in the same year and to include chemistry) in their Advanced Highers plus AAAAAA in their Highers, which must include biology or mathematics or physics (taken in the same year). IB students need a minimum total score of 39 including core points depending on the course with 766 to higher level. Candidates must take chemistry and one of biology, physics or maths to higher level (www.ox.ac.uk/admissions/undergraduate/courses-listing/medicine). If you have any concerns about what subjects are suitable, you can email Oxford at admissions@medschool.ox.ac.uk.

If biology, physics or mathematics haven't been taken to A level (or equivalent), applicants must show that they have received a basic education in those subjects (achieving at least a grade C/4 at GCSE, Standard Grade (Credit) or Intermediate 2, or equivalent). The GCSE Dual Award Combined Sciences is also acceptable (www.ox.ac.uk/ admissions/undergraduate/courses-listing/medicine).

To read Medicine at Cambridge requires A levels in chemistry and in one of biology, physics or mathematics, with the typical offer being A*A*A. Most applicants for Medicine at Cambridge have at least three science or mathematics A levels, and some colleges require this or ask for particular A level subject(s). You can find the details of each college's requirements at www.undergraduate.study.cam.ac.uk/files/ publications/medicine_subject_requirements.pdf. If you apply with only two science or mathematics subjects at A level, your likelihood of success will be reduced: in the past three admissions rounds, 95% of applicants had three science/maths A levels and 25% of them success-fully gained a place against only 5% of the 4% who had only two science/maths A levels.

As with Oxford, those sitting Scottish Highers and those sitting the IB must take chemistry as an Advanced Higher (Scottish) or higher-level subject (IB) along with one of biology, physics and maths at the same level. Applicants should expect to receive AAA (Scottish) or 776 with an overall score of at least 40 (IB). You can find full details at www. undergraduate/study.cam.ac.uk/courses/medicine.

Other A level subjects

There are other subjects not mentioned above, such as general studies and critical thinking, but Oxford and Cambridge will usually only con-sider these as a fourth A level subject.

Case study: Alex, Cambridge

'The thing with Medicine at Cambridge is that when you apply you aren't just applying to Cambridge but you are applying to a specific college, with its own rules and expectations. Although this can be said about all subjects at Cambridge and Oxford, it is especially true for Medicine. For example, different colleges often have different BMAT score requirements, with different colleges placing different emphasis on different sections of the test. It is useful to make sure you are aware of these different expectations before you decide which college to apply for.

'It is also important to keep in mind when writing your personal statement that the course offered at Oxbridge is quite different to that offered at other medical schools. It is helpful to mention your more scientific interests, given the strength of the scientific section of the course at Oxford and Cambridge. However, there is no need to go overboard as the admissions tutors do understand that Oxbridge is just one option for which you are applying.

'When preparing for your interview don't worry about the little things, like what to wear, as these should all be covered in your interview invitation (if not, then a suit for medical interviews is always a good bet, although I did not follow this very sound advice and still got in). The formats of the interviews themselves are another aspect of the application that varies between colleges. My college gave me two interviews, one which was a standard medical interview containing some unusual data analysis questions and the other followed the format that a biological NatSci (Natural Sciences) applicant may expect from his/her interview. This goes to highlight the importance placed by Oxbridge on the scientific side of studying Medicine, something that applicants need to make sure they are happy with before applying. It is worth mentioning that I wasn't asked any questions specific to extracurricular reading I had done, but some of the topics covered in such reading helped me in my approach to answering questions at interview.

'Although I found my interview challenging and the process as a whole demanding, I thoroughly enjoyed the experience. At the end of the day, like any other university, both Cambridge and Oxford are looking for applicants who do have a similar passion and interest in medicine.'

Your grades

There are no set 'grade requirements' for applying to Oxbridge, but that doesn't mean that you don't have to be an excellent student to gain a place. Oxford and Cambridge are considered Britain's 'elite' universities; in the words of one Cambridge admissions tutor: 'We are the best university in the world and we want the best undergraduates in the world.'

There is an interactive graph generator into which prospective students can enter the name of the college and the course to which they wish to apply in order to see specific statistics on applications and acceptance rates on the Cambridge website: www.undergraduate.study.cam.ac.uk/apply/statistics. The figures for Oxford can be found at www.ox.ac.uk/about/facts-and-figures/admissions-statistics/undergraduate-students.

On average, six applications were made for each undergraduate place at Oxford in 2020 (23,414 applications, 3,932 offers and 3,695 admissions) and over five per place at Cambridge (20,426 applications, 4,710 offers and 3,997 admissions). All of these applicants will have been intelligent and talented students. The average successful applicant has around eight GCSEs at grade 8 or 9/A*. For the 2020 cycle, at A level, 99% of successful applicants to Cambridge obtained A*AA or above, and 69% obtained A*A*A*; and over 90% of successful applicants to Oxford in the same cycle obtained A*AA or above and nearly 60% obtained A*A*A*. It is a very competitive business acquiring a place at Oxford or Cambridge.

Oxford grade requirements

The University of Oxford makes conditional offers where the precise entry requirement depends on the course. For A level students, offers range between A*A*A and AAA. For students on the International Baccalaureate (IB) programme, offers range from 38 to 40 points (including core points), with 6s and 7s in the higher-level subjects. For students taking Scottish Highers, offers are AAAAB or AAAAA (supplemented by at least two Advanced Highers).

For humanities subjects, the offers are generally AAA; for most sciences A*AA; and for Mathematics, Mathematics and Philosophy, Mathematics and Statistics, Chemistry and Engineering Science A*A*A (with A* in mathematics and further mathematics if taken). Specific A level (or equivalent) subjects may be required to apply for some subjects, especially in the sciences, and some subjects require applicants to sit a written test or submit written work. See www.ox.ac.uk/admissions/undergraduate/courses/admission-requirements/admission-requirements-table for comprehensive details.

Cambridge grade requirements

For A level students applying to Cambridge, normal offers will be A*AA or A*A*A in three A level subjects (or equivalent), although they have the discretion to make non-standard offers where appropriate as part of their holistic assessment of candidates. The typical conditional A level offer for humanities subjects (except Economics), as well as for Psychological and Behavioural Sciences and Veterinary Medicine, for 2022 entry was A*AA; the typical offer for the other sciences and Economics was A*A*A.

Offers for certain applicants may be dependent on them achieving A* in a specific subject or subjects. For IB applicants, offers range from 40 to 42 points with 776 in the higher-level subjects. For students taking Scottish Highers, the usual offer is AAA at Advanced Higher Grade. Applicants may also be asked to submit written work, depending on the subject, and most applicants are required to take a written admission assessment, either pre-interview or at interview (see www.undergraduate.study.cam.ac.uk/applying/admission-assessments and Chapter 9 for more details).

Do AS levels matter?

With the decoupling of the AS from the A level, most students now study three subjects at A level and do not sit AS exams midway through their sixth-form. While some schools will encourage students to study a fourth subject, be it to AS level or A level, Oxford and Cambridge are aware that most will not.

You won't get a conditional offer that includes AS grades. However, if you do sit a reformed AS examination, you must declare the result in your application, and Oxford and Cambridge reserve the right to use it in helping them make a decision. So, while a top-grade AS may help, a low-grade AS may be a hindrance. This is one reason why many schools opt not to enter potential Oxbridge students for AS levels.

Cambridge requirements in detail

Although the website mainly talks in terms of GCSEs and A levels, other school and national examinations at an equivalent level are equally acceptable. Whatever system you're being educated in, Cambridge requires top grades in the highest-level qualifications available for school students. Most of the information below has been taken from the Cambridge admissions website (www.undergraduate.study.cam.ac.uk/applying/entrance-requirements). It is always advisable to check the website in case there have been any changes since the publication of this book.

If you are taking any other examination system (including the Advanced International Certificate of Education offered by Cambridge Assessment), it is a good idea to make early contact with the Cambridge admissions office to check that it provides an appropriate preparation for the course you hope to study.

A levels

The usual conditional A level offer for arts subjects and for Psychological and Behavioural Sciences for 2022 entry was A*AA, while the usual conditional offer for the other sciences was A*A*A. The subject in which the A* is to be achieved is unlikely to be specified in most cases.

As noted above, most students study three A levels. The advice from Cambridge is that a fourth A level will not typically be an advantage. They note that for STEM subjects, Further Maths is looked favourably on as a fourth subject but stress that it is not mandatory.

Colleges may alter offers depending on an individual's case. For instance, mitigating circumstances may be taken into account if an Extenuating Circumstances Form has been completed; conversely, higher offers may be made if there is some doubt about a student's potential.

Access to HE Diploma

The Access to HE (Higher Education) Diploma is considered acceptable preparation (with Distinctions in all relevant units) for a wide variety of courses: most arts subjects and Psychological and Behavioural Sciences. It is not sufficient for science subjects or Economics. Applicants may also have to meet certain subject-specific requirements; for example, an extra A level in maths or evidence of proficiency in languages may be required. A list of extra requirements for each subject can be found on the subject pages for the courses: www.undergraduate.study.cam.ac.uk/courses.

Advanced Diplomas

The Advanced Diploma in Environmental and Land-based Studies is accepted for Geography and Natural Sciences (Biological) so long as two appropriate A levels have been taken within the Additional Specialist Learning component. For Natural Sciences (Biological), these should be A Level Chemistry and either A Level Biology, Maths or Physics. The requirements for Geography are more flexible.

The Principal Learning components of the Advanced Diploma in Engineering suffice for Engineering, on condition that A Level Physics and Maths are taken (the Level 3 Certificate in Maths for Engineering is an acceptable alternative to A Level Maths).

Advanced Welsh Baccalaureate

Students taking the Advanced Welsh Baccalaureate should normally be taking three subjects at A level as part of their qualification. Conditional offers will be made on the basis of how well they are likely to do in the individual A levels rather than on the overall award. The Skills Challenge will not normally form part of an offer but it may be taken into consideration. The details of any modular legacy A levels being studied as part of the Baccalaureate should be stated as part of the SAQ.

American qualifications

Applicants are expected to have five or more Advanced Placement (AP) scores at grade 5 along with (a) high passing marks on their school qualification (such as a US High School Diploma) and (b) a high score on the SAT (I) Reasoning Test or American College Testing Tests (ACT). Applicants are advised that the SAT II (Subject) Tests are not normally accepted as equivalent to APs. For the SAT (I), a high pass equates with scores of 750 in each component to give a combined score of 1,500 for most science courses and economics; and 730 in Evidence-Based Reading and Writing and 730 in Mathematics, to give a combined score of at least 1,460 for all other courses. If you took the American College Testing (ACT), a score of at least 32 (for Arts and Humanities) or 33 (for Sciences) out of 36 may be acceptable in place of the SAT.

Cambridge Pre-U

Cambridge Pre-U students and students who are studying a combination of Pre-U and A levels may apply to Cambridge. Conditional offers are made on a case-by-case basis; however, these are usually dependent on students achieving Distinctions (D2 or D3) in their Principal Subjects.

Extended Project Qualification (EPQ)

The Extended Project Qualification (EPQ) is taken by some students in addition to their A levels, which focuses on planning, research and evaluative skills – skills that are valued by higher education bodies, such as Cambridge, as well as by future employers. The EPQ is worth half the UCAS Tariff points of a whole A level. Although neither Oxford nor Cambridge will use the EPQ in its offers, Cambridge has stated that the EPQ may be used for discussion at interview and it may even form the basis of written work, in some circumstances. Cambridge further states that it welcomes the EPQ as it helps to develop independent study and the research skills valued in higher education.

International Baccalaureate (IB)

Conditional offers are frequently made on the IB, with scores between 40 and 42 points out of 45, with 776 in the higher level subjects being required. For certain subjects, students may need to achieve 7. Students should look on the Cambridge website for precise requirements and the best IB subject combinations.

The maths component of the IB has recently been revised. Students beginning the IB in 2019 (for first exams in 2021) will be able to choose between (i) Analysis and Approaches and (ii) Applications and Interpretations. Both options will be available at both standard and higher level. Cambridge asks that students take the Analysis and Approaches option. If your school does not offer it, you are advised to contact the college to which you want to apply for further guidance.

Irish Leaving Certificate

Republic of Ireland applicants who are taking the Irish Leaving Certificate would typically receive offers as follows.

- For courses with an A level entrance requirement of A*AA: H1,H1,H1,H2,H2,H2 at Higher level.
- For courses with an A level entrance requirement of A*A*A: H1,H1,H1,H1,H2,H2 at Higher level.

Scottish Highers and Advanced Highers

Courses that normally ask for A*AA at A level generally require A1, A2, A2; and for courses that normally ask for A*A*A at A level will typically ask for A1, A1, A2. In some cases, two Advanced Highers and an additional Higher may be acceptable, particularly if you have been prevented from studying more than two Advanced Highers. If so, you are advised to contact the college to which you are applying for more advice. Similarly, if your school/college only offers a limited range of Advanced Higher qualifications, please seek more advice from the colleges you are interested in.

T levels, VCE and Applied A levels, GNVQs and BTECs

Cambridge do not consider T levels appropriate by themselves and suggest that students who are taking T levels as part of a mix of qualifications contact the college to which they are considering applying to find out more.

Vocational qualifications are not considered an appropriate route to Cambridge, because of the vocational rather than academic focus. That said, if preferred subjects at A level have been covered, applicants may take an applied A level in lieu of a third A level or as a fourth subject to demonstrate breadth of learning. It is always worth checking with the college admissions tutor about what is acceptable, as indeed it is if you are taking any of the non-standard qualifications discussed in this section.

Oxford requirements in detail

- Many students who apply to Oxford are taking A levels but any candidate who has already taken, or who is currently studying, any other equivalent qualifications is also most welcome to apply.
- Oxford will assess a student's application on their ability, regardless of their age.
- The information below outlines the general entrance requirements. The Oxford website should also be consulted: www.ox.ac.uk/ admissions/undergraduate/courses/admission-requirements/uk-qualifications.

A levels

Conditional offers of between A*A*A and AAA, depending upon the subject and course being applied to, are made to Oxford applicants. General studies is ruled out as an approved A level, as is Critical Thinking for Biomedical Sciences and Medicine, but Oxford admissions officers say that almost any other subject may be considered, on the proviso that you meet the requirements laid out by the colleges. Colleges make their offers based on your predicted final A level grades.

Advanced Welsh Baccalaureate

Students taking the Advanced Welsh Baccalaureate should normally be taking three subjects at A level as part of their qualification. Conditional offers are likely to range between A*A*A and AAA at A level, depending on the course. Each course page gives details of the specific requirements. It should be noted that the Welsh Baccalaureate Advanced level Core Certificate will not form the basis of any offers.

American qualifications

Oxford requires all US students to have Advanced Placement (AP) scores. SATs have not been accepted since 2021. They require the following scores:

- For courses requiring A*A*A at A level: either four APs at grade 5 (including any subjects required for the course applied for) or three APs at grade 5 (including any subjects required for the course applied for) plus a score of 33 or above in the ACT or 1480 or above (out of 1600) in the SAT.
- For courses requiring A*AA at A level: either four APs at grade 5 (including any subjects required for the course applied for) or three APs at grade 5 (including any subjects required for the course applied for) plus a score of 32 or above in the ACT or 1470 or above (out of 1600) in the SAT.

- For courses requiring AAA at A level: either four APs at grade 5 (including any subjects required for the course applied for) or three APs at grade 5 (including any subjects required for the course applied for) plus a score of 31 or above in the ACT or 1460 or above (out of 1600) in the SAT.

NB: The optional essay for either the ACT or the SAT is not required. Neither Calculus AB and Calculus BC nor AP Physics C and AP Physics 1 can be counted as two separate subjects to meet an offer.

To meet the requirements of an offer, the SAT Total Score for the SAT Evidence-based Reading and Writing, and SAT Math sections must be from the same session. Oxford will not consider scores from multiple sessions (known as 'superscoring'). This also applies to scores for the ACT, so only the 'Highest Full Battery' score will be considered, not the ACT Superscore. Applicants are asked to enter all their scores for any tests taken when they complete their UCAS application, showing the relevant dates for each along with any pending test scores (details of any test they intend to take up until the end of Senior Year).

Applied General qualifications (including BTECs and T levels)

The majority of courses at Oxford will not accept qualifications such as BTECs, Cambridge Technical Diplomas, UAL Diplomas and the new T levels by themselves, though they can form part of an application alongside appropriate A levels. For example, for Engineering Science, the Advanced Diploma in Engineering (Level 3) is acceptable so long as it comes with A level Physics and a Level 3 Certificate in Maths for Engineering. You should consult the specific course pages to find out which combinations will make you an eligible applicant. A D grade (distinction) in an Applied General qualification would be considered by Oxford to be equivalent to an A at A level, and a D* in a BTEC National to an A* at A level.

Cambridge Pre-U

The Pre-U Diploma is deemed to be an acceptable entry qualification. It depends on the subject, but if you are made an offer it is likely to be in the following range: D2, D2, D3 and D3, D3, D3. If in doubt, you should check the precise requirements with the faculty to which you are applying. Oxford says that D2 is regarded as similar to an A* grade at A level and D3 to an A grade. It also says that applicants may study Pre-U Principal Subjects instead of A levels.

Extended Project Qualification (EPQ)

As with Cambridge, while Oxford sees the merit of the EPQ for the skills it develops, it will not make any offers based on it. However, if you have gained skills and experience from working on an EPQ, it is always worth discussing this in your personal statement. The EPQ demonstrates an independent approach to study and the research skills that Oxford sees as very important attributes in a student.

International Baccalaureate

IB students typically receive offers of 38–40 points, including core points; in addition, they need to attain 6s and 7s in higher level subjects. You should visit the course page for the subject for which you are applying for details of the individual requirements (www.ox.ac.uk/admissions/undergraduate/courses/course-listing).

The maths component of the IB has recently been revised. Students beginning the IB in 2019 (for first exams in 2021) will be able to choose between (i) Analysis and Approaches and (ii) Applications and Interpretations. Both options will be available at both standard and higher level. Oxford says that all courses that require maths will accept both options at HL, with the exception of chemistry. Chemistry applicants will need either option at HL or the Analysis and Approaches option at SL, depending on their choice of other subjects. Full details can be found here: www.ox.ac.uk/admissions/undergraduate/courses-listing/chemistry.

Irish Leaving Certificate

Republic of Ireland applicants who are taking the Irish Leaving Certificate would typically receive offers on the following basis:

* For courses with an A level entrance requirement of AAA: H2,H2,H2,H2,H2,H2 at Higher level.
* For courses with an A level entrance requirement of A*AA: H1,H1,H2,H2,H2,H2 at Higher level.
* For courses with an A level entrance requirement of A*A*A: H1,H1,H1,H1,H2,H2 at Higher level.

Scottish Highers and Advanced Highers

At the moment, the typical offer is AAAAB or AAAAA in Scottish Highers with the addition of two or more Advanced Highers. AAB is normally required if a student is in a position to study three Advanced Highers; if a student is not able to do this, he or she would normally be required to achieve AA in two Advanced Highers, as well as an A grade in a third Higher course studied in Year 6.

4| Money matters

This chapter will try to give you an idea of what it costs to study at Oxford or Cambridge. It is a common misconception that an Oxbridge education is more expensive than other universities.

Both universities are keen to ensure that no talented student should be barred from studying with them because of the cost, and they are aware that the financial backgrounds of their applicants are varied. There are generous bursary schemes available if you are facing financial difficulty – most colleges want to take the best students regardless of income and don't want money worries distracting you from your degree.

Accommodation in both cities is expensive compared with that in other regional universities, but many colleges provide accommodation for their students for all three or four years of their courses. For the year 2021–22, Oxford suggests budgeting between £5,895 and £7,110 for college accommodation for nine months (www.ox.ac.uk/students/fees-funding/living-costs). (Please note that the figures may be refreshed online at any time, and make sure to check the website above for the latest information.) Private accommodation varies, but it will be higher, see www.oxfordstudentpad.co.uk/Accommodation and www.ox.ac.uk/students/life/accommodation.

The latest figures on Cambridge's website (www.undergraduate.study.cam.ac.uk/fees-and-finance/living-costs) are for the year 2020–21; however, they only give a broad figure of £10,000 a year, noting that it may vary considerably depending on your lifestyle! College accommodation costs range from £3,600 to £6,000 (£4,200 to £6,300 for an en suite) for a 30-week residency.

If we translate these figures into monthly costs, then college accommodation in Oxford ranges from £655 to £790 per month and in Cambridge from £520 to £912. Cambridge advises consulting individual colleges to determine accurate accommodation costs but gives a rough figure of £4–£7 for a meal in college. Do note that some colleges will also require students to pay a yearly Kitchen Fixed Charge, which ranges from £195 to £575. The college websites can be found by visiting www.undergraduate.study.cam.ac.uk/colleges/collegecontacts. On top of this, of course, are additional course costs (dependent upon course) and transport.

If cost is a consideration, you should ensure that the college you choose offers accommodation for the whole of your course, as 'living in' is generally cheaper than 'living out'. Living expenses are generally in line with other universities in the south of England.

The cost of studying at Oxford or Cambridge

When you are studying at any university in the UK, you will have to take into account two main types of cost: your tuition fees and your living costs. Government loans are available for all students towards both types of cost and you should contact your local student finance office to see what is on offer. You do not need to pay either for your tuition fees or for your basic term-time living costs up front. It is worth visiting the relevant funding website for your country for more details:

England: www.gov.uk/student-finance

Wales: www.studentfinancewales.co.uk

Scotland: www.saas.gov.uk

Northern Ireland: www.studentfinanceni.co.uk.

Tuition fees

On 21 October 2021, the UK government announced that the tuition fee cap for UK undergraduate students (also known as Home students) for the academic year 2022–23 would remain at £9,250, including for those studying at Oxford and Cambridge. Students from the EU can expect to pay fees at the overseas rate that applies to students from the rest of the world. If you are a student from the EU, EEA or Switzerland who has been granted settled or pre-settled status under the EU Settlement Scheme, you may be eligible for the 'Home' rate if you meet the residence requirement. Please visit www.ox.ac.uk/admissions/undergraduate/fees-and-funding/tuition-fees/fee-status and www.undergraduate.study.cam.ac.uk/fees-and-finance/tuition-fees for more information.

For overseas students, tuition fees are considerably higher than for Home students. With the exception of Medicine, the annual cost of a course at Oxford starting in October 2022 ranges between £27,840 and £39,010. Cambridge's latest figures are for 2021, where (excepting Medicine), the annual cost at Cambridge is between £22,227 and £33,825. It would be reasonable to expect Cambridge's fees for 2022 entry to rise to be more in line with Oxford's figures. Humanities courses attract the lower fee, with Philosophy, Politics and Economics costing £29,500 at Oxford (2022 entry) and Philosophy costing £22,227 at Cambridge (2021 entry). The fee for Mathematics is £32,480 at Oxford (2022 entry) and £24,789 at Cambridge (2021 entry). Science courses are at the upper end, with Biology costing £39,010 at Oxford (2022 entry) and £33,825 at Cambridge (2021 entry). Medicine and Veterinary Medicine attract the considerably higher fee of £36,800/£48,600 (Oxford 2022 entry: the first figure is for the first three years and the second figure for the second three years) and £58,038 (Cambridge 2021 entry).

Visit www.ox.ac.uk/students/fees-funding/search/undergraduate and www.undergraduate.study.cam.ac.uk/international-students/fees for more information. Further general information on fees and costs can be found at www.gov.uk/student-finance/new-fulltime-students.

It should be borne in mind that students at Oxford and Cambridge benefit from far more teaching time and individual attention than the average student at other UK universities. In Oxford, tuition fees are reduced for students from some low-income families (see Table 4, below).

Table 4 Oxford bursary*

Household income	Annual Oxford bursary
£16,000 or less	£3,200
£16,001–£20,000	£3,000
£20,001–£22,500	£2,750
£22,501–£25,000	£2,500
£25,001–£30,000	£2,000
£30,001–£35,000	£1,500
£35,001–£37,500	£1,000
£37,501–£40,000	£800
£40,001–c.£42,875	£500

Source: www.ox.ac.uk/admissions/undergraduate/fees-and-funding/oxford-support.
The above is an example of figures for entry in October 2022 (as of 13 November 2021). Please note that the figures may be refreshed online at any time, and make sure to check the university's website (www.ox.ac.uk/admissions/undergraduate/fees-and-funding/oxford-support) for up-to-date information.

Living costs

All money available to students for living expenses is provided as a maintenance loan, to be paid back once students start earning £25,000 or more for those who studied in England, Wales and Scotland, and £19,895 for those who studied in Northern Ireland. Table 5 (opposite) shows the figures for what a student in England might receive; however, figures for students from different parts of the UK will vary slightly. For further details please refer to the UCAS website, www.ucas.com/student-finance-england/repaying-your-student-loan. Table 6 (opposite) provides an estimation of your living costs at the University of Oxford.

Table 5 Maintenance loan for living costs from September 2020

Full-time student	2020/21 academic year	2020/21 academic year
Living at home	Up to £7,747	Up to £7,987
Living away from home, outside London	Up to £9,203	Up to £9,488
Living away from home, in London	Up to £12,010	Up to £12,382
You spend a year of a UK course studying abroad	Up to £10,539	Up to £10,866

Source: www.gov.uk/student-finance/new-fulltime-students.

Table 6 Estimated living costs at the University of Oxford*

	Per month		Total for nine months	
	Lower range	Upper range	Lower range	Upper range
Food	£290	£410	£2,610	£3,690
Accommodation (including utilities)	£680	£810	£6,120	£7,290
Personal items	£135	£260	£1,215	£2,340
Social activities	£45	£120	£405	£1,080
Study costs	£45	£100	£405	£900
Other	£20	£55	£180	£495
Total	**£1,215**	**£1,755**	**£10,935**	**£15,795**

Source: www.ox.ac.uk/admissions/undergraduate/fees-and-funding/living-costs.
*The above is an example of figures for entry in October 2022 (as of 13 November 2021. Please note that the figures may be refreshed online, and make sure to check the university's website (www.ox.ac.uk) for up-to-date information.

Cambridge living costs are available to view at www.undergraduate. study.cam.ac.uk/fees-and-finance/living-costs, where you will find a breakdown of costs for accommodation, college meals, course costs and transport, food, learning costs and personal expenses. As with Oxford, there are government loans available to all UK students to cover living costs.

Financial support for UK and EU students at Cambridge

Cambridge offers an additional scheme to students, the Cambridge Bursary Scheme. The Cambridge Bursary Scheme provides bursaries for Home students each year. The scheme is for students whose household incomes are below a certain threshold. Any student who meets the eligibility criteria may be awarded a bursary. For 2021/22 entry, students whose household incomes were below £62,215 per annum were offered a sum of between £100 and £3,500 depending on the exact household income. For more information, visit www.cambridge students.cam.ac.uk/cambridgebursary.

Practicalities

At both universities, you may prefer to prepare your own food rather than eat in hall all the time. Most colleges have adequate kitchen facilities and you can buy fresh food from the local markets and super-markets quite cheaply. You will also need to budget a small amount each week to do your laundry. Most colleges have a laundry room with washing machines and tumble dryers and these cost approximately £3.

Transport

You won't need to spend money getting around the university as both are easily navigable by bike or on foot. For those outside of the centre, there are also many buses with cheap fares. However, most students cycle everywhere. This is by far the fastest and the cheapest way to travel. If you don't have a bike already you can buy one from one of the many second-hand bike shops in both cities for under £100. Alternatively, you could consider renting a bike; although you will pay more, the pack-age will include such things as free maintenance, lights and a lock. For Oxford, take a look at www.baintonbikes.com/bike-hire/oxford; for Cambridge, see www.citycyclehire.com/rental-info/students. There are many bike mechanics across both cities who will fix your bike for a fee. However, college porters usually have free bike repair kits and there are normally bike reps (students whom you can call on for help with mend-ing and servicing your wheels for absolutely no charge) at each college.

As with many UK cities, both Oxford and Cambridge have seen on-street e-bikes and e-scooters hire points. These facilities allow you to pick up an e-bike or e-scooter in one location and drop it off at a point near your destination.

Study materials

Most books that you'll need are available in college and university librar-ies, so your expenses should be limited to the usual items of stationery that you had at school. Unless you're specifically instructed to buy books by your faculty, it's probably best to wait until you arrive before spending lots of money unnecessarily.

You will probably want to buy a laptop, if you don't already own one.

Scientists may need to purchase lab coats and mathematicians may need to buy calculators. Again, you will be told by the college if you need any specific study materials for your course.

Case study: Kim, Oxford

'It can be difficult to manage your finances at any university and in life in general, but I have tried to work out a basic budget that helps me to make my money last longer. I tend to write down how much I spend or am likely to spend on clothes, food, books and socialising at the start of each term. I then assess how closely I have kept to my budget at the end of each term. Sometimes it is not as close as it could have been!

'I sell my books at the end of the academic year, so this allows me to recoup some of my costs. However, I try not to spend too much on books in the first place. I do this by making as much use of the college and faculty libraries, as well as the Bodleian Library, as possible. I tend to find everything I need there, especially if I do not leave everything until the last minute. My family are also very good at asking me about my required reading, so that I often get some of the books I need for birthday and Christmas presents.

'I go to the college bar when socialising, as not only are most of my friends based in college, so it is convenient, but because it is cheaper than the pubs in Oxford. If a big night out is being planned, I usually set a little extra money aside for that. I do not spend much on travel when I am in Oxford, as I can quite easily walk to most places I need to go to.

'I am lucky enough to get a regular part-time job during my vacations and since the terms are only eight weeks long I do manage to save a little bit during this time, which I can then use during term time.'

Case study: One parent's view on the cost of studying at Cambridge

'My daughter Alice certainly overspent in her first term as many students do when they first move away from home. This was more to do with inexperience in terms of budgeting than any necessary costs. After she started to keep a note of how much she was spending, particularly in coffee shops and restaurants, she was more aware and thus more careful with her student loan money.

'Now she describes herself as fairly average in terms of spending. She still treats herself occasionally but takes most of her meals at college and chooses Formal Hall for a special night out rather than more expensive restaurants. She and a friend have also taken to scouting charity shops as well as popular chains for clothes and share outfits between them as they are a similar build. This definitely reduced her outgoings.

'One area which has never been a problem is books. While some of my friends with children at other universities occasionally get panicked phone calls from their children in desperate need of £50–£100 for a textbook this has not happened to me. Alice can always find a copy of the books she needs in her college, her faculty or the university library.'

Scholarships, college awards and prizes

Oxford and Cambridge are two of the most well-endowed universities in the UK and provide generous support to students at both university and collegiate level throughout their studies. Similarly, there are academic scholarships and prizes available to students once they have commenced studying, which are often awarded at the end of the first year. Sources of funding may be available from your college and you should consult individual college websites for full details. These can include:

- prizes for academic and other achievements
- grants for study-related books and equipment
- travel grants
- grants and loans to help with unforeseen financial difficulties.

There are a number of university-wide academic scholarships available at Oxford and Cambridge. These include the following.

Oxford

- The **Bright Oceans Corporation Scholarship** covers course fees and provides an additional grant towards living costs for students ordinarily resident in China (excluding the Special Administrative Regions of Hong Kong and Macau) and studying an undergraduate course in the Mathematical, Physical and Life Sciences Division. NB: at the time of writing, it has not been confirmed whether it will be offered for 2022 entrants, so please check www.ox.ac.uk/admissions/undergraduate/fees-and-funding/oxford-support.
- The **Crankstart Scholarship** (formerly the Moritz-Heyman Scholarship) provides generous bursary support to students whose family household income is £27,500 per year or less: www.ox.ac.uk/admissions/undergraduate/fees-and-funding/crankstart.
- The **Oxford-Arlan Hamilton & Earline Butler Sims Scholarship** covers course fees and provides an additional grant towards living costs for UK residents of Black African or Black Caribbean heritage, who are from disadvantaged backgrounds: www.ox.ac.uk/admissions/undergraduate/fees-and-funding/oxford-support/oxford-arlan-hamilton-earline-butler-sims-scholarship.

- The **Palgrave Brown Scholarship** provides an annual grant towards living costs for students ordinarily resident and/or educated in Albania, Armenia, Azerbaijan, Belarus, Bosnia and Herzegovina, Bulgaria, Croatia, Czech Republic, Estonia, Georgia, Hungary, Kazakhstan, Kyrgyz Republic, Latvia, Lithuania, Macedonia, Moldova, Montenegro, Poland, Romania, Russia, Serbia, Slovakia, Slovenia, Tajikistan, Turkmenistan, Ukraine or Uzbekistan: www. ox.ac.uk/admissions/undergraduate/fees-and-funding/oxford-support/palgrave-brown-scholarship-non-uk.
- The **Palgrave Brown UK Scholarship** provides an annual grant towards living costs to students ordinarily resident or educated in Norfolk or Suffolk: www.ox.ac.uk/admissions/undergraduate/fees-and-funding/oxford-support/palgrave-brown-uk-scholarship.
- The **Reach Oxford Scholarship** is open to nationals of low-income countries (those that receive official development assistance from the Organisation for Economic Cooperation and Development (OECD)): www.ox.ac.uk/admissions/undergraduate/fees-and-funding/oxford-support/reach-oxford-scholarship.
- The **Simon and June Li Undergraduate Scholarship** covers course fees and provides an additional grant towards living costs for students ordinarily resident in Bahrain, Bangladesh, Brunei Darussalam, China, Hong Kong SAR, India, Indonesia, Iran, Iraq, Israel, Jordan, Kuwait, Lebanon, Malaysia, Myanmar, Nepal, Oman, Papua New Guinea, Pakistan, Philippines, Qatar, Saudi Arabia, Singapore, South Korea, Sri Lanka, Syria, Taiwan, Thailand, Turkey, United Arab Emirates, Vietnam or Yemen: www.ox.ac.uk/admissions/undergraduate/fees-and-funding/oxford-support/simon-and-june-li-scholarship.

Cambridge

- For information on Cambridge scholarships, visit www.cambridge trust.org/scholarships. You will be able to search for scholarships relevant to your country of origin, subject and college.

Individual colleges may also offer scholarships and bursaries generously provided by former students. Cambridge advises that individual colleges may have specific awards and grants, which are listed on the college websites (www.undergraduate.study.cam.ac.uk/fees-and-finance/financial-support).

Music awards and scholarships

Both universities are well known for the excellence and diversity of their music-making. One of the ways they maintain their high standards of musicianship is by offering music awards to students. Music award-holders are among the hardest-working students in the universities, as they have to juggle extensive musical commitments with their academic studies. The experience they gain is huge, though, and the opportunity to sing with, play in orchestras with or conduct some of the best young musicians in the country is unique. Many award-holders go on to careers in music.

If you're a talented musician, it is worth considering applying for a scholarship. At both universities you can apply for organ, choral or instrumental scholarships and there are some special awards for répétiteurs and chamber music. The way you apply is different from the normal route. The most important initial piece of information to be aware of is that applications for organ and choral scholarships have to be submitted by 1 September of the year in which you are applying.

Most colleges have open days where you can find out more about the awards and you are strongly advised to attend them to better understand the application process. You will also have the opportunity of meeting current music award-holders and visiting the colleges to see their facilities for music-making.

Auditions generally take place in September. An offer of a choral, organ or instrumental scholarship does not guarantee you a place at a college as you will still need to go through the normal admissions procedure and achieve the necessary grades.

Some colleges will not allow students studying certain subjects to be music scholars because the academic demands of their courses are too great. Check this information with the college before making a scholarship application.

Anyone wishing to apply for a music award needs to read the relevant university and college websites very carefully for full details of the awards and the application process. For more information visit:

- Cambridge: www.undergraduate.study.cam.ac.uk/finance/music-awards
- Oxford: www.ox.ac.uk/admissions/undergraduate/applying-to-oxford/choral-and-organ-awards.

Choral awards

In all, 14 colleges at Oxford and 27 colleges at Cambridge offer choral awards, covering the whole range of voices: sopranos, contraltos, countertenors, tenors, baritones and basses. The basic duty of choral scholars is to sing at chapel services, but their involvement in college and university music goes further than this, extending to solo work, chamber groups and choruses. These and several of the mixed-voice choirs undertake concerts, tours and recordings, with some of these activities falling within the vacation periods. A number of colleges offer singing lessons as part of the award.

Case study: Jack, Cambridge

'Being a choral scholar is one of the best experiences that Oxbridge has to offer. It's enormously enriching musically, is masses of fun and has some amazing perks. There are also choirs for all levels of commitment and ability: John's and King's do around seven services per week, Trinity do three, while some smaller colleges only do one. Shop around to find a choir that suits you!

'I'm a choral scholar at Trinity, and it has been the best part of my time at Cambridge. We sing three services and rehearse for around five hours per week. It seems a lot, but one of the best things about being a choral scholar is … well, the other choral scholars! We're all pretty firm friends, and this makes rehearsals fly by – there are also regular pub trips, film nights, etc. It's a fantastic group to be part of socially, and I'm sure all Oxbridge choirs are the same.

'This is without mentioning the rest of the perks of the job: free Feasts six or seven times a year, money off our college bill each term, free singing lessons with internationally renowned teachers, lots of drinks parties hosted by our amazing Chaplains and Directors of Music, all-expenses-paid tours abroad … (Canada last year and the USA and Australia in the next couple of years – guaranteed to be among the most fun weeks of your entire life).

'If you're interested in singing and interested in being a choral scholar, then the best thing to do is to get in touch with some of the Directors of Music at Oxford or Cambridge and arrange an informal meeting. They'll be able to give you advice as to which college might be best for you, what life as a choral scholar is like, and how to balance work–life commitments while at Oxbridge. Their email addresses will be on their college's website, and they are always happy to field any queries. It's worth mentioning also that you don't have to have been a chorister/sung your whole life; the majority of choral scholars haven't, and some of Cambridge's best singers only began singing in the sixth form at school. Neither should you feel hidebound to apply to your own college's choir – many people sing at colleges other than their own.

'For me, singing in Trinity Choir has been a real privilege. We get to work with some amazing musicians and at a really high standard while having enormous amounts of fun. Whether you are interested in singing seven services a week or one, it's a decision that you won't regret.'

Organ awards

Organ scholarships are offered by 22 Oxford and 23 Cambridge colleges. The organ scholar is responsible for supporting the director of music and in some cases running the chapel music where there is no music tutor involved, and also for playing a leading part in the college's musical life in general. The experience is invaluable for musicians interested in directing and organising musical activities across a wide spectrum. Colleges normally assist in the cost of organ lessons. Interviews for prospective organ scholars take place at the same time as the auditions and tests before the main interview period in December.

Applicants for organ awards are unique in that they may apply to both Oxford and Cambridge. However, they should note that their *choice* of course may prevent them from applying to both. For details on the restrictions, see www.undergraduate.study.cam.ac.uk/finance/music-awards/organ-scholarships/vacancies and www.ox.ac.uk/admissions/undergraduate/applying-to-oxford/choral-and-organ-awards/organ-awards/subject-availability-organ-awards.

Répétiteur scholarships

The répétiteur scholarship is open to pianists in Oxford who are interested in coaching singers. It is offered jointly by St Catherine's College, Oxford and New Chamber Opera. This offers the possibility of extensive experience as a répétiteur in the musical theatre (www.newchamberopera.co.uk/about/repetiteur-scholarship).

Instrumental awards

At Oxford, many colleges offer instrumental awards for which you can audition once you have begun your studies; for a list of colleges and requirements, visit www.ox.ac.uk/admissions/undergraduate/applying-to-oxford/choral-and-organ-awards/other-music-awards.

At Cambridge, the Instrumental Awards for Chamber Music Scheme is open to players of the following instruments: violin, viola, cello, flute, oboe, clarinet, bassoon, French horn, trombone, trumpet, tuba and piano. The award runs for one academic year and offers the opportunity for students to hone their chamber music performance skills. Successful applicants benefit from masterclasses, financial assistance with music lessons, recital opportunities and professional tuition for their ensemble. For more details on requirements and how to apply, visit: www.undergraduate.study.cam.ac.uk/finance/music-awards/instrumental-awards.

PART II

Your Application

5 | The early stages of preparation

Choosing the right course is the most important decision you will have to make during the whole application process. It is primarily your enthusiasm for your subject that will be attractive to the admissions tutors and interviewers and, if you are accepted, your love for your subject will sustain you through all the hard work you will undoubtedly have to do. When considering which course to take and when preparing for interview, reading is another, and absolutely essential, form of preparation. You need to read widely and in depth. Knowing the specifications of the subject you are studying is not enough. You should be able to think and talk about ideas beyond the scope of school work and above the level of your peers.

The importance of reading

Remember that the academics who teach at Oxford and Cambridge, and who interview prospective students, have dedicated their whole lives to their subject. They believe passionately in the importance of their research and expect you to do the same. If you have read around your subject this shows that you are dedicated and passionate and this will be very attractive to interviewers.

In addition, if you are accepted, the majority of your time as an undergraduate will be spent studying. Whereas students on an essay-based course at UCL, for example, may be asked to write four 2,500-word essays over the course of a 10-week term, Oxbridge students are expected, in some subjects, to write two essays a week, and sometimes more, making a total of around 16 essays per eight-week term. Students who study science subjects at Oxbridge will have a large amount of contact time per week. These hours are made up of lab sessions, supervisions or tutorials, seminars and lectures that fill up most of the week and may run into your weekends. There is little time off, and most of it is taken up studying for assignments and essays. You need to be excited by this work and find the pressure enjoyable rather than a burden.

The method of working at Oxbridge is very different from school. Students who study humanities subjects (English Literature and History, for example) typically have very few hours of contact time in the week: perhaps six to eight hours of lectures, tutorials or supervisions and one hour-long seminar per week. However, they are expected to work as many hours as the scientists. This requires them to be independent in their study practice. Humanities students need to be dedicated, focused and able to follow through their own research without getting distracted. Like the scientists, therefore, humanities students need to show that they are able to research independently.

Finally, in order to make the right choice, it is important to gather as much information about a course and its content as possible. Prospectuses for Oxford and Cambridge give detailed course guides, including information on course content and A level requirements, as well as some other equivalent qualifications. In addition, Oxford produces individual prospectuses for each subject. Read this information and the criteria very carefully, making sure your qualifications fulfil the requirements specified.

If you want to be really thorough, contact the individual faculty secretaries at the university. Remember that, while the college administers the teaching, it is the faculty (i.e. the subject department within the university) that controls the syllabus. The faculty secretary will have much more detail on course content than is available in the prospectuses. Information about faculty addresses, including website addresses, is available in the prospectuses.

When you talk with the faculty secretary, ask him or her for an up-to-date reading list for new undergraduates. This will list the books that students are expected to read before they come up to Cambridge or Oxford for the first time. If you dip into some of these books you will get an idea of the sort of information you will be tackling if you study the subject. In addition, if you have time to visit Cambridge or Oxford again, you could spend the afternoon in the university bookshop (Blackwell's in Oxford or Heffers in Cambridge). The staff at both bookshops will be very familiar with the texts used by undergraduates. Of course, if you know any current undergraduates at either university, discuss their work with them. It might also be an idea to read books on your subject from the Oxford University Press's (OUP) 'Very Short Introduction' series, which usually give a good overview.

Collecting this information will boost your confidence and reassure you about your subject decision. Remember that in order to argue your case at interview, and to cope with the workload if you get a place, you must be deeply committed to your subject.

Recommended reading

On the following pages is a list of suggested books and films that may help you to start your research. This list is not definitive and not officially endorsed by the Oxbridge faculties. As already stated, most faculties will have a recommended reading list on their websites and you should be familiar with this.

If you need further ideas, consult the relevant subject list below. Don't feel you must read every book on this list either. Dip into one or two to start with and see what particularly interests you. If your subject is not included here, or if you want to find out more, ask your teacher at your school or college for further guidance.

Anglo-Saxon, Norse and Celtic (Cambridge)

- Brink, S. and N. Price, eds, *The Viking World*, Routledge, 2011.
- Brownworth, L., *The Sea Wolves*, Crux Publishing, 2014.
- Campbell, J., E. John and P. Wormald, *The Anglo-Saxons*, Penguin, 1991.
- Charles-Edwards, T.M., *Wales and the Britons 350–1064*, OUP, 2014.
- Foster, S.M., *Picts, Gaels and Scots*, London, 1996.
- Higham, N.J. and M.J. Ryan, *The Anglo-Saxon World*, Yale, 2013.
- Mitchell, B., *An Invitation to Old English and Anglo-Saxon England*, Blackwell, 1994.
- O'Donoghue, H., *Old Norse-Icelandic Literature. A Short Introduction*, OUP, 2004.
- Price, N., *The Children of Ash and Elm*, Penguin, 2011.
- Sawyer, P., ed., *The Oxford Illustrated History of the Vikings*, OUP, 2001.

Archaeology (Cambridge)

- Bender, B. et al, *Stone Worlds*, Left Coast Press, 2007.
- Broodbank, C., *The Making of the Middle Sea*, Thames and Hudson, 2013.
- Darvill, T., *Prehistoric Britain* (2nd edn), Routledge, 2010.
- Diamond, J., *Collapse*, Allen Lane, 2005.
- Diamond, J., *Guns, Germs, and Steel: A Short History of Everybody for the Last 13,000 Years*, New York: Norton, 1998.
- Gamble, C., *Archaeology: The Basics*, Routledge, 2000.
- Gosden, C., *Archaeology & Anthropology*, Routledge, 1999.
- Hodder, I., *Archaeological Theory Today* (2nd edn), Polity, 2012.
- Jones, M., *Feast: Why Humans Share Food*, OUP, 2008.
- Kemp, B., *Ancient Egypt* (2nd edn), Routledge, 2005.
- Parker Pearson, M., *Stonehenge*, Simon and Schuster, 2013.
- Pascoe, B., *Dark Emu*, Broome: Magabala Books, 2018.
- Pauketat, T., *Cahokia*, Penguin, 2010.
- Rathje, W.L. and C. Murphy, *Rubbish! The Archaeology of Garbage*, University of Arizona Press, 2001.
- Renfrew, C., *Prehistory: The Making of the Human Mind*, Modern Library, 2009.

- Renfrew, C. and P. Bahn, *Archaeology: Theory, Methods, and Practice* (6th edn), Thames & Hudson, 2012.
- Rutherford, A., *A Brief History of Everyone Who Ever Lived*, Weidenfeld & Nicolson, 2016.
- Scarre, C., *Exploring Prehistoric Europe*, OUP, 1998.
- Scarre, C., *The Human Past* (2nd edn), Thames & Hudson, 2009.
- Van de Mieroop, M., *A History of the Ancient Near East* (2nd edn), Blackwell, 2006.
- Wenke, R., *Patterns in Prehistory* (4th edn), OUP, 1999.
- Wynn, T. and F. Coolidge, *How To Think Like a Neanderthal*, OUP, 2013.
- Yong, E., *I Contain Multitudes* (1st edn), Vintage, 2017.

Archaeology and Anthropology (Oxford)

Archaeology

See reading for Archaeology (Cambridge)

Social anthropology

- Fox, K., *Watching the English*, Hodder & Stoughton, 2007.
- Keesing, R. and A. Strathern, *Cultural Anthropology: A Contemporary Perspective*, Cengage Learning,2007.
- Monaghan, J. and P. Just, *Social and Cultural Anthropology: A Very Short Introduction*, OUP, 2000.

Biological anthropology

- Clack, T., *Ancestral Roots: Modern Living and Human Evolution*, Palgrave Macmillan, 2008.
- Lewin, R., *Human Evolution: An Illustrated Introduction*, Blackwell, 2005.

General books

- Barley, N., *The Innocent Anthropologist*, Waveland, 2000.
- Carrithers, M., *Why Human Beings Have Cultures*, OUP, 1992.
- Dunbar, R., *Gossip, Grooming and the Evolution of Language*, Faber, 1996.
- Engelke, M., *Think Like An Anthropologist*, Pelican, 2017.
- Fagan, B., *People of the Earth*, Longman, 2004.
- Harrison, G.A., *Human Biology*, OUP, 1992.
- Haviland, W., *Cultural Anthropology*, Harcourt Brace, 2003.
- Hendry, J., *An Introduction to Social Anthropology,* Macmillan, 1999.
- Keesing, R. and A. Strathern, *Cultural Anthropology: A Contemporary Perspective*, Harcourt Brace, 1998.
- Kuper, A., *The Chosen Primate*, Harvard University Press, 1996.
- Layton, R., *An Introduction to Theory in Anthropology*, CUP, 1998.

Architecture (Cambridge)

Also look at the reading list for History of Art.

* Bo Bardi, L., *Stones Against Diamonds*, Architectural Association Publications, 2012.
* Curtis, W., *Modern Architecture Since 1900*, Phaidon, 1982.
* Davies, C., *Thinking about Architecture: An Introduction to Architectural Theory*, Lawrence King Publishing Ltd., 2011.
* Gelernter, M., *Sources of Architectural Form: A Critical History of Western Design Theory*, Manchester University Press, 1995.
* Girouard, M., *Cities and People*, Yale University Press, 1985.
* Gombrich, E., *The Story of Art*, Phaidon, 1966.
* Gordon, J.E., *Structures – or Why Things Don't Fall Down*, Penguin, 1978.
* Hatherly, O., *A Guide to the New Ruins of Great Britain*, Verso, 2011.
* Kostoff, S., *A History of Architecture, Settings and Rituals*, OUP, 1995.
* Moore, R., *Why We Build*, Picador, 2013
* Pallasmaa, J., *The Eyes of the Skin*, Wiley, 2012.
* Perec, G., *Species of Space and Other Pieces*, Penguin, 2008.
* Sutton, I., *Western Architecture*, Thames & Hudson, 2000.
* Till, J., *Architecture Depends*, MIT Press, 2013.
* Vitruvius, P., *The Ten Books on Architecture* (various editions).

Biochemistry (Oxford)

Also look at the reading list for Biology.

* Campbell, M. and S. Farrell, *Biochemistry* (6th edn), Cengage Learning, 2008.
* Lewin, B. et al., eds, *Cells* (1st edn), Jones & Bartlett, 2007.
* Lodish et al., *Molecular Cell Biology* (8th edn), W.H. Freeman, 2016.
* Stryer et al., *Biochemistry* (6th edn), W.H. Freeman, 2004.
* Voet, D., J. Voet and C. Pratt, *Fundamentals of Biochemistry* (3rd edn), Wiley, 2008.

Biology (Oxford)

* Aydon, C., *Charles Darwin: His Life and Times*, Robinson, 2008.
* Barton, N. et al., *Evolution*, Cold Spring Harbour Laboratory Press, 2007.
* Burton, R., *Biology by Numbers*, CUP, 1998.
* Bynum, H. and W. Bynum, *Remarkable Plants*, Thames & Hudson, 2014.
* Chalmers, A.F., *What is This Thing Called Science?*, OUP, 1998.
* Collins, H.M. and T. Pinch, *The Golem* (2nd edn), CUP, 1998.
* Coyne, J., *Why Evolution is True*, OUP, 2009.
* Dawkins, R., *The Selfish Gene*, OUP, 1976.
* Dawkins, R., *The Greatest Show on Earth*, Black Swan, 2010.

- Dawkins, R. and H. Wong, *The Ancestor's Tale*, Weidenfeld & Nicolson, 2017.
- Freedman, D., R. Pisani and R. Purves, *Statistics* (3rd edn), W.W. Norton & Company, 1997.
- Gribbin, J., *Science: A History, 1543–2001*, Penguin, 2002.
- Jones, S., *Almost Like a Whale*, Black Swan, 2001.
- Jones, S., *Y: The Descent of Man*, Abacus, 2003.
- Kolbert, E., *The Sixth Extinction*, Bloomsbury Publishing, 2014.
- Lane, N., *Oxygen*, OUP, 2016.
- Lane, N., *Power, Sex, Suicide*, OUP, 2006.
- Medawar, P., *Advice to a Young Scientist*, Basic Books, 1981.
- Ridley, M., *Genome*, Fourth Estate, 2000.
- Ridley, M., *Nature via Nurture*, Harper Perennial, 2004.
- Southwood, R., *The Story of Life*, OUP, 2003.
- Sykes, B., *The Seven Daughters of Eve*, W.W. Norton & Company, 2002.
- Wagner, A., *Arrival of the Fittest*, Oneworld Publications, 2015.
- Wood, B., *Human Evolution: A Very Short Introduction*, OUP, 2005.

Physiology of organisms
- King, J., *Reaching for the Sun*, CUP, 1997.
- Widmaier, E.P., *Why Geese Don't Get Obese (And We Do)*, W.H. Freeman, 2000.

Although Oxford does not specifically require any of these resources to be read, it does recommend that prospective students read *New Scientist*, *National Geographic* or any other relevant materials to stimulate interest in the subject area.

Biomedical Sciences (Oxford)

General
- Ashcroft, F., *Life at the Extremes*, University of California Press, 2002.
- Black, J., C.A.R. Boyd, and D. Noble, eds, *The Logic of Life*, OUP, 1993.
- Calvin, W.H., and G.A. Ojemann, *Conversations with Neil's Brain: The Neural Nature of Thought and Language*, Basic Books, 1995.
- Dawkins, R., *The Selfish Gene*, OUP, 2006.
- Dawkins, R., ed., *The Oxford Book of Modern Science Writing*, OUP, 2009.
- De Kruif, P., *Microbe Hunters*, Kessinger Publishing Co, 2005.
- Glynn, I., *Elegance in Science*, OUP, 2010.
- Goldacre, B., *Bad Science*, Harper Perennial, 2009. (See also Ben Goldacre's columns for the *Guardian* at www.guardian.co.uk/profile/bengoldacre.)
- Greenfield. S., *The Human Brain: A Guided Tour*, Orion Publishing Group, 1998.

- Jones, S., *The Language of the Genes*, Harper Collins (Flamingo), 2000.
- Medawar, P., *Advice to a Young Scientist*, Perseus Books, 1989.
- Noble. N., *The Music of Life*, OUP, 2006.
- Sacks, O., *The Man Who Mistook his Wife for a Hat*, Picador, 2011.
- Sykes, B., *Blood of the Isles*, Corgi Books, 2007.
- Wishart, A., *One in Three*, Profile Books, 2007.

Biochemistry and Cell Biology
- Alberts, B. et al., *Molecular Biology of the Cell*, Taylor & Francis (Garland Publishing), 2008.
- Stryer, L., *Biochemistry*, W.H. Freeman & Co Ltd, 2006.

Neurophysiology
- Aidley, D., *The Physiology of Excitable Cells*, CUP, 1998.
- Bear, M., B. Connors and M. Paradiso, *Neuroscience: Exploring the Brain* (3rd edn), Lippincot, Williams and Wilkins, 2006.
- Kandel, E., J. Schwartz and T. Jessell, *Principles of Neural Science*, Elsevier, 2000.

Pharmacology
- Rang, H. et al., *Pharmacology*, Elsevier Health Sciences (Churchill Livingstone), 2007.

Physiology
- Boron, W. and E. Boulpaep, *Medical Physiology*, Elsevier Health Sciences (Saunders), 2008.
- Levy, M., B. Koeppen and B. Stanton, *Berne & Levy Principles of Physiology*, Elsevier, 2009.

Scientific Thought
- Keynes, R & D. Aidley, *Nerve and Muscle*, CUP, 2001.
- Medawar, P., *Induction and Intuition in Scientific Thought*, Taylor & Francis Routledge, 2008.
- Wolpert, L., *The Unnatural Nature of Science*, Faber & Faber, 2000.

Statistics
- Kirkwood, B., *Essentials of Medical Statistics*, Blackwell Science, 2003.

Chemistry (Oxford)

- Atkins, P. and J. de Paula, *Atkins' Physical Chemistry* (9th edn), OUP, 2010.
- Boyd, Robert N. and Robert T. Morrison, *Organic Chemistry*, Prentice Hall, 1992.
- Bryson, B., *A Short History of Nearly Everything*, Black Swan, 2004.
- Cotton, F.A. and G. Wilkinson, *Advanced Inorganic Chemistry* (5th edn), Wiley, 1999.

- Emsley, J., *Molecules at an Exhibition*, OUP, 1998.
- Keeler, J. and P. Wothers, *Why Chemical Reactions Happen*, OUP, 2003.
- Morrison, R.T. and R.N. Boyd, *Organic Chemistry* (6th edn), Prentice Hall, 1992.
- Rovelli, C., *Seven Brief Lessons on Physics*, Penguin, 2016.
- Stephenson, G., *Mathematical Methods for Science Students* (2nd edn), Pearson, 1978.

Oxford also suggests that students may wish to read *Chemistry World* magazine and look at other resources on the Royal Society of Chemistry (RSC) website (www.rsc.org/resources-tools).

Chemical Engineering (Cambridge)

- Azapagic, A. et al., *Sustainable Development in Practice*, Wiley, 2004.
- Duncan, T.M. and J.A. Reimer, *Chemical Engineering Design and Analysis: An Introduction*, CUP, 1998.
- Felder, R.M. and R.W. Rousseau, *Elementary Principles of Chemical Processes*, Wiley, 2003.
- Field, R., *Chemical Engineering*, Palgrave Macmillan, 1988.
- Freshwater, D., *People, Pipes and Processes*, IChemE, 1998.
- Solen, K.A. and J.N. Harb, *Introduction to Chemical Engineering*, Wiley, 2010.

The final book in this list by K.A. Solen and J.N. Harb is particularly recommended by Cambridge, as it states that many other published books are not of a suitable level for prospective students.

Classics

- Beard, M., *Confronting The Classics*, Profile, 2014.
- Beard, M., *SPQR*, Profile, 2016.
- Beard, M. and J. Henderson, *Classics: A Very Short Introduction*, Oxford, 1995.
- Beaton, R., *The Greeks*, Faber, 2021.
- Davies, J.K., *Democracy and Classical Greece* (2nd edn), Fontana, 1993.
- Goodman, M., *The Roman World 44 BC–AD 180*, Routledge, 1997.
- Graves, R., *The Greek Myths*, Penguin, 2000.
- Herodotus, *The Histories*, Penguin Classics, 2003.
- Homer, *The Iliad*, Penguin Classics, 2003.
- Homer, *The Odyssey*, Penguin Classics, 2003.
- Irwin, T., *Classical Thought*, OUP, 1989.
- Parker, R., *On Greek Religion*, Cornell University Press, 2013.
- Scullard, H.H., *From the Gracchi to Nero*, Routledge, 2010.
- Sophocles, *The Three Theban Plays*, Penguin, 2000.
- Ste Croix, G.E.M. de, *Class Struggle in the Ancient Greek World*, Duckworth, 1982.

- Thucydides, *History of the Peloponnesian War*, Penguin Classics, 2000.

Both Cambridge and Oxford recommend that candidates familiarise themselves with a range of prose texts including Thucydides' *History of the Peloponnesian War* (especially books 1–2), Plato, *Republic* and Tacitus *Annals* (especially books 1–4) if they have not already been covered in an A level course.

In addition, it is also recommended that prospective students visit websites with excellent links to materials about the ancient world, such as the British Museum or the BBC Radio 4 archives, for example for the programme *In Our Time* covering material from Ancient Greece and Ancient Rome. There are also many social media sites that can be joined, such as Classics Confidential, Classics Outreach and Classics International.

Computer Science

Applicants for computer science can expect to have their logical thinking tested in preparation for learning about coding and algorithms. Two excellent websites to help you develop your coding skills are https:// codeforces.com/problemset and https://open.kattis.com/problems.

- Bostrom, N., *Superintelligence*, OUP, 2016.
- Christian, B., and T. Griffiths, *Algorithms to Live By*, William Collins, 2016.
- Dewdney, K.A., *The New Turing Omnibus*, Palgrave Macmillan, 2003.
- Gleick, J., *The Information*, Fourth Estate, 2012.
- Hillis, D., *The Pattern on the Stone*, Basic Books, 2015.
- Isaacson, W., *The Innovators*, Simon and Schuster, 2015.
- Körner, T., *The Pleasures of Counting*, CUP, 1996.
- Levitin, A. and M. Levitin, *Algorithmic Puzzles*, OUP, 2011.
- Nisan, N., and S. Schocken, *The Elements of Computing Systems*, MIT Press, 2021.
- Petzold, C., *Code: The Hidden Language of Computer Hardware and Software*, Microsoft Press, 2000.
- Shasha, D. and C. Lazere, *Out of Their Minds*, Springer, 2008.
- Singh, S., *The Code Book*, Fourth Estate, 2002.

Earth Sciences (Geology) (Oxford)

- Alley, R., *The Two Mile Time Machine*, Princeton University Press, 2014.
- Alvarez, W., *T. Rex and the Crater of Doom*, Princeton University Press, 2015.
- Benton, M.J., *When Life Nearly Died*, Thames & Hudson, 2005.
- Broecker, W. and C. Langmuir, *How to Build a Habitable Planet*, Princeton University Press, 2012.
- Ince, M., *Rough Guide to the Earth*, Rough Guides/Penguin, 2007.

- Lamb, S. and D. Sington, *Earth Story*, BBC Books, 1998.
- Nield, D., *Supercontinent*, Granta Books, 2008.
- Redfern, M., *The Earth: A Very Short Introduction*, OUP 2003.
- Searle, M., *Colliding Continents*, OUP, 2017.
- Waltham, D., *Lucky Planet: Why Earth is Exceptional – and What that Means for Life in the Universe*, Icon Books, 2015.
- Zalasiewicz, J. and M. Williams, *The Goldilocks Planet: The 4 billion year story of Earth's climate*, OUP, 2012.

Economics

All students should read *The Economist* and one (or preferably) both of the *Times* and the *Financial Times*.

- Aghion, P., C. Antonin, and S. Bunel, *The Power of Creative Destruction*, Belknap Press, 2021.
- Akerlof, A. and R. Shiller, *Animal Spirits*, Princeton University Press, 2010.
- Ariely, D., *Predictably Irrational*, HarperCollins, 2009.
- Banerjee, A. and E. Duflo, *Poor Economics*, Penguin, 2021.
- Begg, D.K.H., S. Fischer and R. Dornbusch, *Economics* (latest edn), McGraw-Hill.
- Bourne, R., *Economics in One Virus*, Cato Institute, 2021.
- Buchholz, T., *New Ideas from Dead Economists* (4th edn), Plume Books, 2021.
- Carney, M., *Value(s)*, William Collins, 2021.
- Cassidy, J., *How Markets Fail*, Penguin, 2010.
- Chang, H.J., *Economics: The User's Guide*, Pelican Books, 2011.
- Chang, H.J., *23 Things They Don't Tell You About Capitalism*, 2011.
- Collier, P., *The Bottom Billion*, OUP, 2008.
- Collins, C., *The Wealth Hoarders*, Polity, 2021.
- Dasgupta, P., *Economics: A Very Short Introduction*, OUP, 2007.
- Davies, R., *Extreme Economies*, Black Swan, 2020.
- Dixit, A. and S. Skeath, *Games of Strategy* (2nd edn), Norton, 2009.
- Easterlin, R., *An Economist's Lessons on Happiness*, Springer, 2021.
- Ferguson, N., *The Ascent of Money*, Penguin, 2019.
- Haass, R., *The World: A Brief Introduction*, Penguin, 2021.
- Harford, T., *The Logic of Life*, Abacus, 2009.
- Harford, T., *The Undercover Economist*, Abacus, 2007.
- Heilbroner, R., *Worldly Philosophers*, Penguin, 2000.
- Lynn, M., *Bust*, Bloomberg Press, 2010.
- McKenzie, R., *Why Popcorn Costs So Much at the Movies*, Springer, 2008.
- Marshall, T., *Prisoners of Geography*, Elliott and Thompson Ltd, 2016.
- Mason, P., *Meltdown*, Verso, 2010.
- Mazzucato, M., *Mission Economy*, Allen Lane, 2021.
- Mlodinow, L., *The Drunkard's Walk*, Penguin, 2019.

- Philippon, T., *The Great Reversal*, Belknap Press, 2021.
- Raworth, K., *Doughnut Economics*, Random House Business, 2018.
- Ridley, M., *The Origins of Virtue*, Penguin, 1997.
- Sem, A., *Development as Freedom*, OUP, 2001.
- Shafik, M., *What We Owe Each Other*, Bodley Head, 2021.
- Thomas, M., *99%*, Apollo, 2019.
- Tooze, A., *Shutdown*, Allen Lane, 2021.

Engineering, Engineering Science

- Adams, J., *Flying Buttresses, Entropy and O-Rings: The World of an Engineer*, Harvard University Press, 1992.
- Allwood, J. and J. Cullen, *Sustainable Materials – With Both Eyes Open*, UIT Cambridge Ltd, 2012.
- Anderson, D and S. Eberhart, *Understanding Flight*, McGraw-Hill Professional, 2009.
- Ball, P., *Made to Measure*, Princeton University Press, 1999.
- Bloomfield, L., *How Things Work*, John Wiley & Sons, 2009.
- Cadbury, D., *Seven Wonders of the Industrial World*, Harper Perennial, 2004.
- Eberhart, M., *Why Things Break*, Three Rivers Press, 2005.
- Florman, S., *The Existential Pleasures of Engineering*, Souvenir Press Ltd., 1995.
- Forbes, P., *The Gecko's Foot*, Harper Perennial, 2006.
- Gordon, J. E., *The New Science of Strong Materials*, Penguin, 2008.
- Gordon, J. E., *Structures*, DaCapo Press, 2003.
- Lawlor, R., *Engineering in Society*, Royal Academy of Engineering, 2013. An e-book published by the Royal Academy of Engineering that is available as a free (pdf) download from the RAEng website.
- Levy, M and Salvadori, M., *Why Buildings Fall Down*, W.W. Norton & Company Ltd., 1994.
- MacKay, D., *Sustainable Energy – Without the Hot Air*, UIT, 2008.
- McCarthy, N., *Engineering: A Beginner's Guide*, Oneworld Publications, 2009.
- Maxfield, C., *Bebop to the Boolean Boogie*, Newnes (Elsevier), 2009.
- Petroski, H., *Invention by Design*, Harvard University Press, 1998.
- Petroski, H., *To Engineer is Human*, Vintage Books, 1992.
- Petroski, H., *Small Things Considered*, Random House, 2004.
- Petroski, H., *Pushing the Limits*, Vintage Books, 2005.
- Petroski, H., *Design Paradigms: Case Histories of Error and Judgment in Engineering*, CUP, 1994.
- Petroski, H., *Success Through Failure*, Princeton University Press, 2008.
- Petroski, H., *The Essential Engineer*, Knopf Publishing Group, 2010.
- Salvadori, M., *Why Buildings Stand Up*, W.W. Norton & Company Ltd., 1991.

- Spufford, F., *The Backroom Boys*, Faber & Faber Ltd., 2004.
- Tennekes, H., *The Simple Science of Flight*, MIT Press, 2009.
- Tremayne, D, *The Science of Formula 1 Design*, J.H. Haynes & Co. Ltd., 2009.
- Vincenti, W.G., *What Engineers Know and How They Know It*, Johns Hopkins University Press, 1993.
- Vogel, S., *Cats' Paws and Catapults*, W.W. Norton & Company, 2000.

English

Your personal statement should identify your knowledge and appreciation of authors outside those of the English A level syllabus. It is sensible also to display an interest in different genres and periods; a student who only referred to twentieth-century American literary texts would not be overly impressive. You should not simply be reeling names off but explaining why your chosen authors mean so much to you. Also, if you display an interest in the work of an author it is only sensible to have read more than one work by him or her and to have considered the cultural context in which he or she wrote.

- Auerbach, E., *Mimesis: The Representation of Reality in Western Literature*, Princeton Classics Edition, 2013.
- Barry, P., *Beginning Theory* (4th edn), Manchester University Press, 2017.
- Bate, J., *The Soul of the Age*, Viking, 2008.
- Beard, M., *Women & Power: A Manifesto*, Profile, 2018.
- Butler, J., *Gender Trouble*, Routledge Classics, 2006.
- Culler, J., *Literary Theory: A Very Short Introduction*, OUP, 2011.
- Culler, J., *Structuralist Poetics*, Routledge, 2002.
- Daiches, D., *Critical Approaches to English Literature*, Kessinger, 2007.
- Davis, P., *Shakespeare Thinking*, Bloomsbury 2009.
- Davis, P., *Why Victorian Literature Still Matters*, Wiley-Blackwell, 2008.
- Eagleton, T., *How to Read Literature*, Yale University Press, 2019.
- Eagleton, T., *Literary Theory: An Introduction*, University of Minnesota Press, 1983.
- Eagleton, T., *The English Novel: An Introduction*, Blackwell Publishing, 2005.
- Ferguson, M., M.J. Salter and J. Stallworthy, eds, *The Norton Anthology of Poetry*, W.W. Norton & Company, 2004.
- Gilbert, S. and S. Gunbar, *The Madwoman in the Attic*, Veritas Paperbacks, 2020.
- Griffiths, E., *If Not Critical*, OUP, 2018.
- Guerin, W.L. et al., *A Handbook of Approaches to Literature*, OUP, 2010.
- Kerrigan, J., *Revenge Tragedy: From Aeschylus to Armageddon*, Clarendon Press, 1997.

- Lodge, D., *The Language of Fiction*, RKP, 1966.
- Lodge, D., *The Modes of Modern Writing*, Bloomsbury Revelations, 2005.
- Nowottny, W., *The Language Poets Use*, Athlone Press 1962.
- Nuttall, A.D., *A New Mimesis*, Methuen, 1983.
- Nuttall, A.D., *Why Does Tragedy Give Pleasure?*, OUP, 2001.
- Ricks, C., *Beckett's Dying Words*, OUP, 1990.
- Storr, W., *The Science of Storytelling*, William Collins, 2020.
- Tanner, T., *Prefaces to Shakespeare*, Harvard University Press, 2012.
- Young, T., *Studying English Literature: A Practical Guide*, CUP, 2008.
- Wood, J., *How Fiction Works*, Vintage 2010.

Geography

General

- Bonneuil, C. and J-B. Fressoz, *The Shock of the Anthropocene*, Verso, 2016.
- Berners-Lee, M., *There is No Planet B*, CUP, 2021.
- de Blij, H., *Why Geography Matters More than Ever*, OUP, 2012.
- Cloke, P., M. Crang and M. Goodwin, *Introducing Human Geographies* (3rd edn), Routledge, 2013.
- Criado Perez, C., *Invisible Women*, Vintage, 2019.
- Dodds, K., *Geopolitics: A Very Short Introduction*, OUP, 2007.
- Dorling, D., *Do We Need Economic Inequality?*, Polity, 2017.
- Dorling, D. and C. Lee, *Geography: Ideas in Profile*, Profile, 2016.
- Goudie, A. and H. Viles, *Landscapes and Geomorphology: A Very Short Introduction*, OUP, 2010.
- Green, D., *How Change Happens*, OUP, 2018.
- Harari, Y.N., *Sapiens*, Penguin, 2014.
- Harari, Y.N., *Homo Deus*, Penguin, 2016.
- Harvey, D., *Rebel Cities*, Verso, 2019.
- Heffernan, O., 'Climate research is gaining ground,' *Nature Climate Change* 6, 2016.
- Hoare, P., *The Sea Inside*, Fourth Estate, 2013.
- Jones, R., *Violent Borders*, Verso, 2014.
- Klein, N., *This Changes Everything*, Penguin, 2014.
- Koser, K., *International Migration: A Very Short Introduction*, OUP, 2007.
- Maslin, M., *Global Warming: A Very Short Introduction*, OUP, 2008.
- Matthews, J. and D. Herbert, *Geography: A Very Short Introduction*, OUP, 2008.
- Mayne, A., *Slums*, Reaktion Books, 2017.
- Middleton, N., *Deserts: A Very Short Introduction*, OUP, 2009.
- Oppenheimer, C., *Eruptions that Shook the World*, CUP, 2011.
- Platt, E., *The Great Flood*, Picador, 2019.
- Purseglove, J., *Taming the Flood*, William Collins, 2017.
- Redfern, M., *The Earth: A Very Short Introduction*, OUP, 2003.

- Roberts, N., *The Holocene* (3rd edn), Wiley, 2014.
- Rogers, A., N. Castree and R. Kitchin, *A Dictionary of Human Geography*, OUP, 2013.
- Rosling, H., *Factfulness*, Sceptre, 2018.
- Rosling, H., *How I Learned to Understand the World*, Macmillan USA, 2020.
- Sassen, S., *Expulsions*, Harvard University Press, 2015.
- Spiegelhalter, D. and M. Blastland, *The Norm Chronicles*, Profile, 2013.
- Thomas, C., *Inheritors of the Earth*, Penguin, 2017.
- Tortell, P. (ed), *Earth 2020*, Open Books, 2020.
- Trouet, V., *Tree Story*, Johns Hopkins University Press, 2020.
- Wulf, A., *The Invention of Nature*, Hodder & Stoughton, 2016.

Physical Geography

- Barry, R.G., R.J. Chorley and T. Chase, *Atmosphere, Weather and Climate*, Routledge, 2013.
- Francis, P. and C. Oppenheimer, *Volcanoes*, OUP, 2004.
- Gaston, K. and J. Spicer, *Biodiversity* (2nd edn), Blackwell, 2004.
- Gregory, K.J., *The Earth's Land Surface*, Sage, 2010.
- Huggett, R.J., *Fundamentals of Biogeography* (2nd edn), Routledge, 2004.
- Lomolino, M.V., B.R. Riddle, R.J. Whittaker and J.H. Brown, *Biogeography* (4th edn), Sinauer Associates, 2010.
- Masselink, G. and M.G. Hughes, *An Introduction to Coastal Processes and Geomorphology*, Hodder Arnold, 2003.
- McIlveen, R., *Fundamentals of Weather and Climate* (2nd edn), OUP, 2010.
- Thomas, D.S.G., ed., *Arid Zone Geomorphology* (3rd edn), Wiley-Blackwell, 2010.
- Townsend, C.R., M. Begon and J.L. Harper, *Essentials of Ecology* (3rd edn), Blackwell, 2008.

Human Geography

- Anderson, J., *Understanding Cultural Geography*, Routledge, 2009.
- Clifford, N., S. Holloway, S. Rice and G. Valentine, eds, *Key Concepts in Geography* (2nd edn), Sage, 2009.
- Coe, N., P. Kelly and H. Yeung, *Economic Geography: A contemporary introduction* (2nd edn), Wiley-Blackwell, 2013.
- Flint, C., ed., *The Geography of War and Peace*, OUP, 2005.
- Gough, J., A. Eisenschitz and A. McCulloch, *Spaces of Social Exclusion*, Routledge, 2006.
- Held, D., ed., *A Globalizing World? Culture, Economics, Politics* (2nd edn), Routledge/OUP, 2004.
- Murray, W.E., *Geographies of Globalization*, Routledge, 2006.

Historical Geography

- Davis, M., *Late Victorian Holocausts: El Niño Famines and the Making of the Modern World Economy*, Verso, 2000.

- Graham, B. and C. Nash, eds, *Modern Historical Geographies*, Prentice Hall, 2000.
- Pomeranz, K., *The Great Divergence*, Princeton University Press, 2000.

Society Environment and Development

- Adams, W.M., *Green Development* (2nd edn), Routledge, 2001.
- Allen, T. and A. Thomas, eds, *Poverty and Development into the 21st Century*, OUP, 2000.
- Lawson, V., *Making Development Geography*, Hodder Arnold, 2007.

History

The key piece of advice for would-be Oxbridge historians is to ensure that you have read widely around your A level topics. You need to show an awareness of recent historical debate and to understand different interpretations of the same events. The books listed below either deal with historiography or are particularly well written and deserve attention.

- Bartlett, R., *The Making of Europe: Conquest, Colonization and Cultural Change, 950–1350*, Penguin, 1994.
- Blanning, T., *Pursuit of Glory: Europe 1648–1815*, Penguin, 2008.
- Burleigh, M., *Earthly Powers*, Harper Perennial, 2006.
- Cannadine, D., *In Churchill's Shadow*, Penguin, 2003.
- Cannadine, D., *Victorious Century*, Penguin, 2018.
- Colley, L., *The Gun, the Ship and the Pen*, Profile, 2021.
- Davies, C.S.L., *Peace, Print and Protestantism 1450–1558*, Paladin, 1977.
- Elton, G., *The Practice of History*, Wiley-Blackwell, 2001.
- Evans, R.J., *In Defence of History*, Granta, 2001.
- Ferguson, N., *Civilization*, Penguin, 2011.
- Ferguson, N., *Doom: The Politics of Catastrophe*, Allen Lane, 2021.
- Finlay, V., *Fabric*, Profile, 2021.
- Graeber, D. and D. Wengrow, *The Dawn of Everything*, Allen Lane, 2021.
- Hobsbawm, E., and T. Ranger, eds, *The Invention of Tradition*, CUP, 1983.
- Hobsbawm, E., *On History*, Weidenfeld and Nicolson, 1997.
- Judt, T., *Postwar: A History of Europe since 1945*, Vintage, 2010.
- Mazower, M., *Dark Continent*, Penguin, 1999.
- Morris, M., *The Anglo-Saxons*, Hutchinson, 2021.
- Nasar, S., *Grand Pursuit*, Fourth Estate, 2012.
- Oliver, N., *The Story of the World in 100 Moments*, Bantam Press, 2021.
- Pagden, A., *The Enlightenment and Why it Still Matters*, OUP, 2013.
- Sanghera, S., *Empireland*, Viking, 2021.
- Worden, B., *Roundhead Reputations*, Penguin, 2002.

Students would also be advised to search out relevant articles in the *London Review of Books*, *Literary Review* and *History Today*.

History of Art

- Baxandall, M., *Painting and Experience in Fifteenth-Century Italy: A Primer in the Social History of Pictorial Style*, OUP, 1988.
- Beard, M. and J. Henderson, *Classical Art: From Greece to Rome*, OUP, 2001.
- Berger, J., *Ways of Seeing*, Penguin, 1972.
- Boardman, J., ed., *Oxford History of Classical Art*, OUP, 1993.
- Camille, M., *Gothic Art: Glorious Visions*, Pearson, 1996.
- Campbell, S.J. and M.W. Cole, *A New History of Italian Renaissance Art*, Thames & Hudson, 2012.
- Clark, T.J., *The Painting of Modern Life*, Thames & Hudson, 1995.
- Crow, T., *The Rise of the Sixties*, Laurence King, 1996.
- Crow, T., *Modern Art in the Common Culture*, Yale University Press, 1998.
- Elsner, J., *Imperial Art and Christian Triumph*, OUP, 1998.
- Gombrich, E.H., *The Story of Art*, Phaidon, 1995.
- Greenhalgh, M., *The Classical Tradition in Art*, Duckworth, 1978.
- Hall, J., *Dictionary of Subjects and Symbols in Art*, John Murray, 1974.
- Harbison, C., *The Mirror of the Artist*, Pearson, 1995.
- Haskell, F., *History and its Images*, Yale University Press, 1993.
- Hockney, D., *Secret Techniques*, Thames & Hudson, 2006.
- Honour, H. and J. Fleming, *A World History of Art* (7th edn), Laurence King, 2005.
- Johnson, G.A., *Renaissance Art: A Very Short Introduction*, OUP, 2002.
- Kemp, M., *Behind the Picture*, Yale University Press, 1997.
- Nochlin, L., *Women, Art and Power and Other Essays*, Thames & Hudson, 1989.
- Pevsner, N., *An Outline of European Architecture*, Thames & Hudson, 2009.
- Pollitt, J.J., *Art and Experience in Classical Greece*, CUP, 1972.
- Pollock, G., *Vision and Difference*, Routledge, 2003.
- Summerson, J., *Architecture in Britain, 1530–1830*, Pelican History of Art, 1993.
- Summerson, J., *The Classical Language of Architecture* (several edns).
- Vasari, G., *Lives of the Artists*, selected lives trans. by G. Bull, Penguin, 2 vols., 1965 & 1987.
- Watkin, D., *A History of Western Architecture*, Laurence King Publishing, 2015.
- White, J., *The Birth and Rebirth of Pictorial Space* (several edns).

Another useful resource is BBC Four, which broadcasts a wide range of high-quality and engaging documentaries that provide a useful background for the aspiring art historian, such as *The Art of China* by Andrew Graham Dixon, *The History of Art in Three Colours* by Dr James Fox and *The Power of Art* by Simon Schama.

Human, Social and Political Sciences (HSPS) (Cambridge)

Politics and International Relations

- Achen, C. and L. Bartels, *Democracy for Realists*, Princeton University Press, 2016.
- Adhiambo Owuor, Y., *Dust*, Knopf Publishing Group, 2013. (Fiction)
- Atwood, M., *The Handmaid's Tale*, Vintage, 1985. (Fiction)
- Blyth, M., *Austerity: The History of a Dangerous Idea*, OUP, 2013.
- Ellsberg, D., *The Doomsday Machine*, Bloomsbury Press, 2017.
- Fraser, N., *Fortunes of Feminism*, Verso, 2013.
- Lebron, C., *The Making of Black Lives Matter*, OUP, 2017.
- Mabanckou, A., *Black Moses*, The New Press, 2017. (Fiction)
- Mair, P., *Ruling the Void*, Verso, 2013.
- Marozzi, J., *Baghdad*, Allen Lane, 2014.
- Mishra, P., *Age of Anger*, Allen Lane, 2017.
- Moyn, S., *The Last Utopia*, Harvard University Press, 2010.
- Penn Warren, R., *All The King's Men*, Penguin, 2001 (1946). (Fiction)
- Runciman, D., *How Democracy Ends*, Profile Books, 2018.
- Sassen, S., *Expulsions*, Belknap, 2014.
- Scott, J., *Two Cheers for Anarchism*, Princeton University Press, 2012.
- Welsh, J., *The Return of History*, Anansi, 2017.
- Williams, J., *Stand out of our Light*, CUP, 2018.
- Vitalis, R., *White World Order, Black Power Politics*, Cornell University Press, 2015.

Social Anthropology

- Abu-Lughod, L., *Veiled Sentiments: Honor and Poetry in a Bedouin Society*, University of California Press, 1986.
- Astuti, R., et al, *Questions of Anthropology*, OUP, 2007.
- Cohen, J., *Eating Soup without a Spoon: Anthropological Theory and Method in the Real World*, University of Texas Press, 2015.
- Engelke, M., *Think Like an Anthropologist*, Pelican, 2017.
- Eriksen, T.H., *Small Places, Large Issues* (4th edn), Pluto Press. 2015.
- Holmes, S., *Fresh Fruit, Broken Bodies: Migrant Farmworkers in the United States*, University of California Press, 2013.
- King, L., *Euphoria*, Picador, 2015.
- Robbins, J., *Becoming Sinners* (Vol. 4), University of California Press, 2004.
- Shah, A., *Nightmarch*, Hurst, 2018.
- Wacquant L.J.D., *Body & Soul*, OUP, 2004.

Sociology

- Alexander, J.C. and K. Thompson, *A Contemporary Introduction to Sociology*, Paradigm Publishers, 2008.
- Bauman, Z., *Thinking Sociologically* (2nd edn), Wiley-Blackwell, 2001.
- Bhambra, G., *Connected Sociologies*, Bloomsbury, 2014.

- Connell, R.W., *Gender* (2nd edn), Polity, 2009.
- Crompton, R., *Class and Stratification* (3rd edn), Polity Press, 2008.
- Giddens, A. and P. Sutton, *Sociology* (7th edn), Polity, 2013.
- Goldstone, J. ed., *Revolutions: Theoretical, Comparative, and Historical Studies*, Harcourt Brace College Publishers,1994.
- Hill Collins, P., *Black Feminist Thought*, Routledge, 2000.
- Noble, S. and B. Tyne, *The Intersectional Internet*, Peter Lang, 2016.
- Sennett, R., *The Culture of the New Capitalism*, Yale, 2006.
- Sennett, R., *Together*, Yale University Press, 2012.
- Smith, A., *Nationalism* (2nd edn), Polity Press, 2013.
- Surak, K., *Making Tea, Making Japan: Cultural Nationalism in Practice*, Stanford University Press, 2012.
- Wilkinson, R. and K. Pickett, *The Spirit Level*, Penguin, 2010.
- Yuval-Davis, N.,*The Politics of Belonging*, Sage, 2011.

Law
- Appleton, C., *Life after Life Imprisonment*, OUP, 2010.
- Berlins, M. and C. Dyer, *The Law Machine*, Penguin, 2000.
- Bingham, T., *The Rule of Law*, Penguin, 2011.
- Lord Denning, *The Discipline of Law*, OUP, 1979.
- De Schutter, O., *International Human Rights Law: Cases, Materials, Commentary*, CUP, 2010.
- Griffith, J.A.G., *The Politics of the Judiciary*, Fontana, 2010.
- Grove, T., *The Juryman's Tale*, Bloomsbury, 2000.
- Grove, T., *The Magistrate's Tale*, Bloomsbury, 2003.
- Holland, J.A. and J.S. Webb, *Learning Legal Rules*, OUP, 2010.
- Klarman, M.J., *Brown v. Board of Education and the Civil Rights Movement*, OUP, 2007.
- McBride, N., *Letters to a Law Student*, Longman, 2010.
- McLeod, I., *Legal Method*, Palgrave Macmillan, 2011.
- Pritchard, J., *The New Penguin Guide to the Law*, Penguin, 2004.
- Shaw, M., *International Law*, CUP, 2008.
- Smith, A.T.H., *Glanville Williams: Learning the Law*, Sweet & Maxwell, 2010. (This is a popular introductory book. It will not give you any specific, substantive legal knowledge, but it will provide you with useful information ranging from how to read cases to what the abbreviations mean.)
- Vidal, J., *McLibel: Burger Culture on Trial*, Pan Books, 1997.
- Waldron, J., *The Law*, Routledge, 1990.

Linguistics
- Aitchison, J., *The Linguistic Mammal*, Routledge, 2011.
- Akmajian, A., *Linguistics: An Introduction to Language and Communication*, MIT Press, 2001.
- Deutscher, G., *The Unfolding of Language*, Arrow, 2006.
- Deutscher, G., *Through the Language Glass*, Arrow, 2011.

- Fromkin, V. et al., *An Introduction to Language*, Thomson/Heinle, 2003.
- Holmes, J. and N. Wilson, *An Introduction to Sociolinguistics*, Routledge, 2017.
- Matthews, P., *Linguistics: A Very Short Introduction*, OUP, 2003.
- Pinker, S., *The Language Instinct*, William Morrow and Company, 1994.
- Radford, A., *Linguistics: An Introduction*, CUP, 1999.

Management Studies

- Dixit, A. and B. Nalebuff, *Thinking Strategically*, W.W. Norton & Company, 1991.
- Handy, C., *Understanding Organisations* (4th edn), Penguin, 1993.
- McCraw, T.K., *Creating Modern Capitalism*, Harvard Business School Press, 1998.
- Pfeffer, J., *The Human Equation*, Harvard Business School Press, 1998.
- Pfeffer, J. and R. Sutton, *Hard Facts, Dangerous Half-Truths and Total Nonsense,* Harvard Business School Press, 2006.
- Tedlow, R., *New and Improved*, McGraw-Hill, 1996.

Materials Science (Oxford)

- Ball, P., *Bright Earth: The Invention of Colour*, Vintage Books, 2008.
- Ball, P., *Made to Measure*, Princeton University Press, 1999.
- Cotterill, R., *The Material World*, CUP, 2008.
- Gordon, J.E., *The New Science of Strong Materials – or Why You Don't Fall Through the Floor*, Penguin, 2008.
- Martin, J.W., *Materials for Engineering*, Woodhead Publishing Ltd., 2006.
- Miodownik, M., *Stuff Matters*, Viking, 2013.
- Molotch, H., *Where Stuff Comes From*, Routledge, 2005.

Mathematics

- Bellos, A., *Alex's Adventures in Numberland*, Bloomsbury, 2011.
- Clegg, B., *A Brief History of Infinity*, Robinson, 2003.
- Conway, J. and R. Guy, *The Book of Numbers*, Copernicus, 1998.
- Courant, R. and H. Robbins, *What is Mathematics?*, OUP, 2007.
- Devlin, K., *The Millennium Problems*, Basic Books, 2003.
- du Sautoy, M., *The Music of the Primes*, Harper Perennial, 2004.
- du Sautoy, M., *Finding Moonshine (Symmetry)*, Harper Perennial, 2009.
- Eastaway, R., *Why Do Buses Come in Threes?*, Portico, 2005.
- Ellenberg, J., *How Not to be Wrong*, Penguin, 2015.
- Gleick, J., *Chaos*, Vintage, 1997.
- Gowers, T., *Mathematics: A Very Short Introduction*, Oxford Paperbacks, 2002.
- Hardy, G.H., *A Mathematician's Apology*, Stellar Editions, 2016.

- Hoffman, P., *The Man Who Loved Only Numbers*, Fourth Estate 1999.
- Hollingdale, S., *Makers of Mathematics*, Dover, 2009.
- Körner, T., *The Pleasures of Counting*, CUP, 1996.
- Maor, E., *e: The Story of a Number*, Princeton University, 1998.
- Petzold, C., *The Annotated Turing*, Wiley Publishing, 2008.
- Rooney, A., *The Story of Mathematics*, Arcturus, 2014.
- Seife, C., *Zero*, Souvenir Press, 2000.
- Simmons, G., *Calculus Gems*, McGraw Hill, 2007.
- Singh, S., *Fermat's Last Theorem*, Fourth Estate, 2002.
- Stewart, I., *Seventeen Equations that Changed the World*, Profile, 2013.
- Stewart, I., *Letters to a Young Mathematician*, Basic Books, 2006.
- Stewart, I., *From Here to Infinity*, OUP, 1990.
- Stewart, I., *The Great Mathematical Problems*, Profile, 2014.
- Szpiro, G., *The Secret Life of Numbers*, Henry Joseph, 2006.

Medicine

- Asimov, I., *New Guide to Science*, Penguin, 1993.
- Bryson, B., *A Short History of Nearly Everything*, Black Swan, 2004.
- Calvin, W.H. and G.A. Ojemann, *Conversations with Neil's Brain: The Neural Nature of Thought and Language*, Basic Books, 1995.
- Greenfield, S., *The Human Brain*, Weidenfeld & Nicolson, 1997.
- Goldacre, B., *Bad Pharma*, Fourth Estate, 2012.
- Goldacre, B., *Bad Science*, Fourth Estate, 2008.
- Jeffreys, D., *Aspirin*, Bloomsbury, 2005.
- Konner, Dr M., *The Trouble with Medicine*, BBC Books, 1993.
- Medawar, P.B., *Advice to a Young Scientist*, Basic Books, 1981.
- Noble, D., *The Music of Life: Biology Beyond Genes*, OUP, 2008.
- Nuland, S., *How We Die*, Vintage, 1997.
- Nuland, S., *How We Live*, Vintage, 1998.
- Revill, J., *Everything You Need to Know about Bird Flu*, Rodale, 2005.
- Ridley, M., *Genome*, Fourth Estate, 2000.
- Sacks, O., *The Man Who Mistook His Wife for a Hat*, Picador, 2011.
- Seedhouse, D. and L. Lovett, *Practical Medical Ethics*, Wiley-Blackwell, 1992.
- Thomas, L., *The Youngest Science*, Penguin, 1995.
- Watson, J., *DNA: The Secret of Life*, Arrow, 2004.
- Weatherall, D.J., *Science and the Quiet Art*, W.W. Norton & Company, 1995.
- Wilham, Dr D., *Body Story*, Channel 4 Books, 1998.

Modern Languages

French: reading
- Simone de Beauvoir, *L'Invitée*.
- Samuel Beckett, *En attendant Godot*.

- Albert Camus, *Caligula* or *La Chute*.
- Marie Cardinal, *La Clé sur la Porte*.
- Marguerite Duras, *Moderato Cantabile*.
- André Gide, *La Porte étroite*.
- Guy de Maupassant, *Bel-Ami*.
- Patrick Modiano, *Dora Butler*.
- Molière, *Le Misanthrope*.
- Marcel Proust, *Du Côté de chez Swann*.
- Jean Racine, *Phèdre* or *Bérénice*.
- Alain Robbe-Grillet, *La Jalousie*.
- François de La Rochefoucauld, *Maximes*.
- Jean-Paul Sartre, *La Nausée*.
- Stendhal, *Le Rouge et le Noir*.
- Voltaire, *Candide* or *Micromegas* (short story).

French: poetry
- Charles Baudelaire, *Les Fleurs du Mal* (see in particular 'L'albatros').
- Victor Hugo, *Les Rayons et les Ombres* (see in particular 'Fonction du poète').
- Francis Ponge, *Le Parti Pris des Choses*.

French: Literary theory/Criticism
- Roland Barthes, 'L'effet de réel' (*Communications* 11, March 1968).
- Jean-Paul Sartre, *Qu'est-ce que la littérature*.
- Jean Starobinski, 'Racine et la poétique du regard' (*L'œil Vivant*).

French: films
Jean Renoir, François Truffaut, Robert Bresson, André Téchiné, Eric Rohmer, Louis Malle and Agnès Varda are important figures in French cinema. Xavier Nolan is a young, interesting director from Quebec. Read the following texts if possible:

- Bresson, *Notes Sur le Cinématographe*.
- Truffaut, *Les Films de Ma Vie*.

German: reading
- Heinrich Böll, *Die verlorene Ehre der Katharina Blum*.
- Bertolt Brecht, *Der kaukasischer Kreidekreis*; *Mutter Courage*.
- Friedrich Dürrenmatt, *Die Physiker*; *Der Besuch der alten Dame*.
- Max Frisch, *Andorra*.
- Günther Grass, *Die Blechtrommel*; *Katz und Maus*.
- Franz Kafka, *Die Verwandlung*; *Sämtliche Erzählungen*.
- Thomas Mann, *Tonio Kröger*; *Der Tod in Venedig*.
- Bernhard Schlink, *Der Vorleser*.
- Patrick Süskind, *Das Parfum*; *Die Taube*.

German: art

Taschen books are readily available and cheap. Read in English or German. Books are available on the following subjects:

- Bauhaus
- Expressionism
- Wiener Werkstätte.

German: films

Films about the Second World War:
- *Das Boot*
- *Europa, Europa*
- *Die Fälscher*
- *Heimat*
- *Sophie Scholl*
- *Der Untergang.*

Films about the former East Germany:
- *Goodbye Lenin!*
- *Der Himmel über Berlin*
- *Das Leben der Anderen*
- *Sonnenallee*
- *Der Tunnel.*

Italian: reading

- Italo Calvino, *Se una notte d'inverno un viaggiatore.*
- Natalia Ginzburg, *Lessico famigliare.*
- Giuseppe Tomasi di Lampedusa, *Il gattopardo.*
- Primo Levi, *Se questo è un uomo.*
- Luigi Pirandello, *Sei personaggi in cerca d'autore.*
- Leonardo Sciascia, *A ciascuno il suo.*
- Italo Svevo, *La coscienza di Zeno.*

Italian: films

- *Il Gattopardo.*
- *Ladri di Bicilette.*
- *Roma, città aperta.*
- *Il vangelo secondo Matteo.*

Russian: reading

- Anna Akhmatova, *Requiem.*
- Iosif Brodsky, *Collected Poems in English 1972–1999.*
- Mikhail Bulgakov, *The Master and Margarita.*
- Ivan Bunin, *Life of Arseniev.*
- Anton Chekhov, *Uncle Vanya.*
- Fyodor Dostoevsky, *The Brothers Karamazov; Notes from the Underground.*

- Nikolai Gogol, *Taras Bulba*; *Diary of a Madman*.
- Mikhail Lermontov, *A Hero of our Time*.
- Boris Pasternak, *Doctor Zhivago*.
- Alexander Pushkin, *Eugene Onegin*.
- Aleksandr Solzhenitsyn, *One Day in the Life of Ivan Denisovich*.
- Leo Tolstoy, *Anna Karenina*.
- Ivan Turgenev, *A Month in the Country*.

Spanish: reading
- *Lazarillo de Tormes*.
- Leopoldo Alas, *La Regenta*.
- Pedro Calderón de la Barca, *La Vida es Sueño*.
- Pio Baroja, *El árbol de la Ciencia*.
- Camilo José Cela, *La Familia de Pascual Duarte*; *La Colmena*.
- Miguel de Cervantes, *El Quijote*.
- Julio Cortázar, *Rayuela*.
- Miguel Delibes, *Cinco Horas con Mario*.
- Rafael Sánchez Ferlosio, *El Jarama*.
- Carmen Martín Gaite, *Lo Raro es Vivir*.
- Juan Goytisolo, *Señas de Identidad*.
- Mario Vargas Llosa, *La Tía Julia y el escribidor*.
- Federico García Lorca, *Poeta en Nueva York*; *La Casa de Bernarda Alba*.
- Carlos Marcial, *El Surrealismo y Cuatro Poetas de la Generación del 27: Ensayo Sobre Extensión y Límites del Surrealismo en la Generación del 27*.
- Javier Marías, *Corazón Tan Blanco*.
- Gabriel García Márquez, *Cien Años de Soledad*.
- Luis Martin-Santos, *Tiempo de Silencio*.
- Ana María Matute, *Olvidado Rey Gudú*.
- Eduardo Mendoza, *La Ciudad de los Prodigios*.
- Pablo Neruda, *Confieso Que he Vivido*.
- Fernando de Rojas, *La Celestina*.
- Miguel de Unamuno, *La Tía Tula*.

Spanish: films
- Pedro Almodóvar, *Todo Sobre mi Madre*.
- Jaime Chávarri, *Las Bicicletas son Para el Verano*.
- Víctor Erice, *El Espíritu de la Colmena*.
- Alejandro González Iñárritu, *Amores Perros*.
- Carlos Saura, *Cría Cuervos*; *La Caza*; *Elisa, Vida Mía*.

Music
In addition to reading you should become familiar with the Dover scores of string quartets and symphonies by Haydn, Mozart and Beethoven. Aim to get to know several quartets and symphonies by all three composers.

- Aldwell, E. and C. Schachter, *Harmony and Voice Leading* (3rd edn), Wadsworth Publishing Co., 2002.
- Bohlman, P., *World Music: A Very Short Introduction*, OUP, 2002.
- Caplin, W.E., *Classical Form: A Theory of Formal Functions for the Instrumental Music of Haydn, Mozart, and Beethoven*, OUP, 1998. (This will be invaluable, not only for your analysis studies but also for your understanding of classical-period harmony.)
- Clayton, M., T. Herbert and R. Middleton, eds, *The Cultural Study of Music: A Critical Introduction*, Routledge, 2003.
- Cook, N., *A Guide to Musical Analysis*, OUP, 1994.
- Cook, N., *Music: A Very Short Introduction*, OUP, 2000.
- Ledbetter, D., ed., *Continuo Playing According to Handel*, Clarendon Press, 1990.
- Morris, R.O. and H. Ferguson, *Preparatory Exercises in Score Reading*, OUP, 1931.
- Parker, R., ed., *The Oxford Illustrated History of Opera*, OUP, 1994.
- Ross, A., *The Rest is Noise*, Fourth Estate, 2008.
- *The New Harvard Dictionary of Music*, Harvard University Press, 1986; or *The Grove Concise Dictionary of Music*, Macmillan, 1988. (Both are useful reference books.)

Harmony and counterpoint
Play and study the following.

- *The Chorale Harmonisations of J.S. Bach*. Recommended edition: Breitkopf and Härtel, ed. B.F. Richter; less good but adequate: Chappell, ed. Albert Riemenschneider.
- 'Fugal Expositions' by J.S. Bach in *The Well-Tempered Clavier* (the '48'). Recommended edition: Associated Board, ed. Richard Jones.
- *Schubert Lieder*. Recommended edition: Dover (either *Schubert's Songs to Texts by Goethe* or *Complete Song Cycles*). The lieder of Beethoven, Mendelssohn and Schumann are also recommended for your attention.
- *Renaissance polyphony*. Listen to some of the many fine recordings of the music of Palestrina and his contemporaries (the Gimell and Hyperion labels are a rich source).

Natural Sciences (Cambridge)
See the reading lists for Biology, Chemistry, Computer Science, Earth Sciences (Geology), Materials Science and Physics.

Philosophy

- Ayer, A.J., *The Central Questions of Philosophy*, Penguin, 1976.
- Blackburn, S., *Being Good*, OUP, 2004.
- Blackburn, S., *Think*, OUP, 2001.
- Blackburn, S., *The Big Questions*, Quercus, 2009.

- Buckingham, W. et al., *The Philosophy Book*, DK Publishing, 2017.
- Conee, E. and T. Sider, *Riddles of Existence*, OUP 2014.
- Cottingham, J., *Western Philosophy: An Anthology*, Blackwell Philosophy Anthologies, 2008.
- Crane, T., *The Mechanical Mind* (3rd edn), Routledge, 2015.
- Davies, B., *An Introduction to the Philosophy of Religion* (3rd edn), OUP, 2004.
- Descartes, R., *Discourse on the Method and the Meditations* (many translations).
- Grayling, A., *The History of Philosophy*, Penguin, 2020.
- Guttenplan, S., J. Hornsby and C. Janaway, *Reading Philosophy: Selected Texts with a Method for Beginners*, Wiley-Blackwell, 2002.
- Hodges, W., *Logic* (2nd revised edn), Penguin, 2001.
- Hollis, M., *Invitation to Philosophy*, Wiley-Blackwell, 1997.
- Hospers, J., *An Introduction to Philosophical Analysis* (4th edn), Routledge, 1997.
- Hume, D., *An Enquiry Concerning Human Understanding*, OUP, 2008.
- Kenny, A., *A Brief History of Western Philosophy*, Blackwell, 1998.
- Mill, J.S., *On Liberty* (many editions), available with *Utilitarianism*, etc. in J.S. Mill, *On Liberty and Other Essays*, Oxford World's Classics, Oxford Paperbacks.
- Nagel, T., *What Does it All Mean?*, OUP, 2004.
- Papineau, D., *Philosophical Devices*, OUP, 2012.
- Patton, M. and K. Cannon, *The Cartoon Introduction to Philosophy*, Hill and Wang Inc., 2015.
- Priest, G., *Logic*, OUP, 2000.
- Russell, B., *The Problems of Philosophy*, OUP, 1997.
- Sainsbury, R.M., *Paradoxes*, CUP, 1988.
- Scruton, R., *A Short History of Modern Philosophy*, Routledge, 2001.
- Shand, J., *Philosophy and Philosophers*, Acumen, 2014.
- Warburton, N., *Philosophy: The Classics*, Routledge, 2006.
- Williamson, T., *Doing Philosophy*, OUP, 2018.
- Wolff, J., *An Introduction to Moral Philosophy*, W.W. Norton and Co., 2020.

Physics

- Bryson, B., *A Short History of Nearly Everything*, Black Swan, 2004.
- Culleme, J.P. and A. Machacek, *The Language of Physics*, OUP, 2008.
- Feynman, R.P., *Six Easy Pieces*, Penguin, 1998.
- Feynman, R.P., *Six Not So Easy Pieces*, Penguin, 1999.
- Gribbin, J., *In Search of Schrödinger's Cat – Quantum Physics and Reality*, Black Swan Books, 1991.
- Hawking, S., *A Brief History of Time*, Bantam Press, 1988.
- Rovelli, C., *Seven Brief Lessons on Physics*, Penguin, 2016.

For those with an interest in engineering

- Gordon, J.E., *Structures, or Why Things Don't Fall Down*, DaCapo Press, 2003.
- Gordon, J.E., *The New Science of Strong Materials*, Penguin, 1991.
- Petroski, H., *Invention by Design*, Harvard University Press, 1998.

PPE (Oxford)

See the readings for Philosophy and Economics.

Politics

- Bingham, T., *The Rule of Law*, Penguin, 2013.
- Curtis, M., *The Ambiguities of Power: British Foreign Policy Since 1945*, Zed, 1995.
- Elliott, F. and J. Hanning, *Cameron*, HarperCollins, 2012.
- Ford, R., and T. Bale, *The British General Election of 2015*, Palgrave Macmillan, 2021.
- Giddens, A., *The Politics of Climate Change* (2nd edn), Polity Press, 2011.
- Gonzalez, M., *BLM: The Making of a New Marxist Revolution*, Encounter, 2021.
- Hanson, V.D., *The Dying Citizen,* Basic Books, 2021.
- Hasan, M. and J. Macintyre, eds, *The Milibands and the Making of a Labour Leader*, Biteback, 2011.
- Heffernan, R. et al., eds, *Developments in British Politics 9*, Palgrave Macmillan, 2011.
- Joyce, H., *Trans: When Ideology Meets Reality*, Oneworld, 2021.
- Kahl, C. and T. Wright, *Aftershocks*, St Martin's Press, 2021.
- McCormick, J., *Contemporary Britain*, Palgrave Macmillan, 2012.
- McCormick, J., *European Union Politics*, Palgrave Macmillan, 2011.
- Rajan, R.G., *Fault Lines*, Princeton University Press, 2011.
- Rodrik, D., *The Globalization Paradox*, OUP, 2012.
- The Secret Barrister, *Fake Law*, Picador, 2017.
- Sumption, J., *Trials of State*, Profile, 2020.
- Vieira, M.B. and D. Runciman, *Representation*, Polity Press, 2008.
- Woolf, J., *An Introduction to Political Philosophy*, OUP, 2006.

Psychology

General

- Banister, P., E. Burman, I. Parker, M. Taylor and C. Tindall, *Qualitative Methods in Psychology: A Research Guide*, Open University Press, 1994.
- Bentall, R. and A.T. Beck, *Madness Explained: Psychosis and Human Nature*, Penguin, 2004.
- Carter, R., *Mapping the Mind*, University of California Press, 2010.
- Clegg, F., *Simple Statistics: A Course Book for the Social Sciences*, CUP, 1990.

- Colman, A. M., *A Dictionary of Psychology*, OUP, 2003.
- Coolican, H., *Introduction to Research Methods and Statistics in Psychology*, Psychology Press, 1997.
- Damasio, A., *Self Comes to Mind*, Vintage Books, 2010.
- Dennett, D.C., *Consciousness Explained*, Penguin, 1993.
- Eysenck, M. W. and M. T. Keane, *Cognitive Psychology: A Student's Handbook*, Psychology Press, 2010.
- Freud, S., *The Psychopathology of Everyday Life* (various editions).
- Gazzaniga, M.S., R.B. Ivry and G.R. Mangun, *Cognitive Neuroscience* (4th edn), W.W. Norton & Company, 2014.
- Goldacre, B., *Bad Science*, Fourth Estate, 2008.
- Goleman, D., *Emotional Intelligence*, Bloomsbury, 1996.
- Greenfield, S., *The Private Life of the Brain*, Penguin, 2002.
- Gross, R.D., *Psychology: The Science of Mind and Behaviour*, Hodder, 2010.
- Harris, P., *Designing and Reporting Experiments in Psychology* (2nd edn), Open University Press, 2002.
- Hayes, N., *Foundations of Psychology: Introductory Text* (3rd edn), Cengage Learning EMEA, 2000.
- Hewstone, M., F. Fincham and J. Foster, *Psychology: British Psychology*, Wiley, 2005.
- Hogg, M. and G. Vaughan, *Social Psychology: An Introduction*, Prentice Hall, 2010.
- Hrdy, S., *Mothers and Others: The Evolutionary Origins of Mutual Understanding*, Harvard University Press, 2011.
- James, W., *The Principles of Psychology* (Vol. 1), Dover, 1890.
- Kahneman, D., *Thinking, Fast and Slow*, Farrar, Straus and Giroux, 2011.
- LeDoux, J., *Synaptic Self*, Penguin, 2003.
- Milgram, S., *Obedience to Authority: An Experimental View*, Pinter & Martin Ltd, 2010.
- Murphy, G.L., *The Big Book of Concepts*, MIT Press, 2004.
- Nolen-Hoeksema, S., B. Fredrickson, et al, *Atkinson and Hilgard's Introduction to Psychology*, Cengage Learning, 2009.
- Northedge, A., J. Thomas, A. Lane and A. Peasgood, *The Sciences Good Study Guide*, The Open University, 1997.
- Parker, I., *Qualitative Psychology*, Open University Press, 2005.
- Pease, A., *Body Language*, Sheldon Press, 1997.
- Pinker, S., *The Better Angels of Our Nature*, Viking, 2011.
- Pinker, S., *The Language Instinct*, Penguin, 1995.
- Pinker, S., *How the Mind Works*, Penguin, 1997.
- Ramachandran, V.S. and S. Blacksee, *Phantoms in the Brain: Human Nature and the Architecture of the Mind*, Fourth Estate, 1999.
- Redman, P., *Good Essay Writing: A Social Sciences Guide* (2nd edn), The Open University/Sage, 2001.
- Ridley, M., *Nature via Nurture*, Harper Perennial, 2004.

- Sacks, O., *The Man Who Mistook his Wife for a Hat*, Picador, 2011.
- Schaffer, H.R., *Key Concepts in Developmental Psychology*, SAGE, 2006.
- Slater, L., *Opening Skinner's Box*, Bloomsbury Publishing, 2005.
- Winston, R., *The Human Mind*, Chartered Institute of Personnel and Development, 2006.
- Zimbardo, P., *The Lucifer Effect*, Rider, 2008.

Biology/Evolutionary Psychology
- Dawkins, R., *The Blind Watchmaker*, Penguin Group, 2006.
- Greenfield, S., *The Private Life of the Brain*, Penguin, 2000.
- Pinker, S., *The Blank Slate*, Book Club Associates, 2002.
- Rose, S., *The 21st Century Brain*, Vintage, 2006.
- Toates, F., *Biological Psychology: An Integrative Approach* (2nd edn), Pearson Education, 2006.

Consciousness
- Blackmore, S., *Consciousness: An introduction*, Hodder and Stoughton, 2003.
- Carter, R., *Consciousness*, Weidenfeld & Nicolson, 2002.
- Velmans, M., *Understanding Consciousness*, Routledge, 2000.

Biological psychology
- Bear, M.F., B.W. Connors and M.A. Paradiso, *Neuroscience: Exploring the brain* (3rd edn), Lippincott Williams and Wilkins, 2006.
- Crossman, A.R. and D. Neary, *Neuroanatomy: An Illustrated Colour Text* (2nd edn), Churchill Livingstone, 2000.
- Pinel, J.P.J. and M. Edwards, *A Colorful Introduction to the Anatomy of the Human Brain*, Allyn and Bacon, 1998.
- Ramachandran, V.S. and S. Blacksee, *Phantoms in the Brain: Human Nature and the Architecture of the Mind*, Fourth Estate, 1999.
- Toates, F., *Biological Psychology: An Integrative Approach* (2nd edn), Pearson Education, 2006.

Cognitive psychology
- Andrade, J., ed., *Working Memory in Perspective*, Psychology Press, 2001.
- Damasio, A., *Descartes' Error: Emotion, Reason and the Human Brain*, Vintage Books, 1994.
- Eysenck, M., *Principles of Cognitive Psychology* (2nd edn), Psychology Press, 2001.
- Harris, P., *Designing and Reporting Experiments in Psychology* (2nd edn), Open University Press, 2002.
- Ramachandran, V.S. and S. Blacksee, *Phantoms in the Brain: Human Nature and the Architecture of the Mind*, Fourth Estate, 1999.
- Styles, E.A., *The Psychology of Attention*, Psychology Press, 1997.

Social psychology

- Hepburn, A., *An Introduction to Critical Social Psychology*, Sage, 2003.
- Stainton-Rogers, W., *Social Psychology: Experimental and Critical Approaches*, Open University Press, 2003.
- Stevens, R., *Sigmund Freud: Examining the Essence of his Contribution*, Palgrave Macmillan, 2008.

> **TIP!**
>
> *The Psychologist*, the monthly publication of the British Psychological Society, has back issues freely available on its archive at https://thepsychologist.bps.org.uk.

Theology

General

- Armstrong, K., *The Case for God*, Vintage, 2010.
- Dawkins, R., *The Blind Watchmaker*, Penguin, 2006.
- Dawkins, R., *The God Delusion*, Black Swan, 2007.
- McGrath, A., *The Dawkins Delusion*, SPCK Publishing, 2007.
- Shortt, R., *Rowan's Rule*, Hodder, 2014.

Biblical

- Bellis, A. Ogden, *Helpmates, Harlots and Heroes*, Westminster/John Knox Press, 2007.
- Clines, D., *The Theme of the Pentateuch*, Sheffield Academic Press, 1997.
- Lambek, M., ed., *A Reader in the Anthropology of Religion*, Wiley-Blackwell, 2008.
- Painter, J., *The Quest for the Messiah*, Abingdon Press, 1994.
- Vermes, G., *The Changing Faces of Jesus*, Penguin, 2001.

History and doctrine

- St Augustine, *City of God* (various editions).
- St Augustine, *The Confessions* (various editions).
- Duffy, E., *The Stripping of the Altars*, Yale University Press, 2005.
- Gunton, C.E., *The One, the Three and the Many*, CUP, 1993.
- McCulloch, D., *Silence: A Christian History*, Allen Lane, 2013.
- McGrath, A., *Modern Christian Thought*, Wiley-Blackwell, 1995.
- McGrath, A., *Reformation Thought* (4th edn), Wiley-Blackwell, 2012.

Further resources

In addition to the suggestions above, remember to:

- read around your subject in the press
- search for podcasts and videos
- check out blogs and online articles
- if possible, discuss your reading with friends, family and teachers.

Case study: Pippa, Oxford

'When I am asked how best to prepare for Oxbridge, two things spring to mind: read and debate as much as you possibly can. I set myself the target of reading at least one book or journal article which was not set by my A level teacher every week throughout sixth form. I cannot say I achieved this every single week, but it was an excellent target to aim for. It definitely meant I had read far more by the time I walked into my Oxford interview than had I simply told myself I would do it "when I had time". There is never enough time; you need to make time.

'In terms of debating, I mean more than just going to a debating society (though that is an excellent thing to do too!). I tested my ideas and thoughts about history, and particularly the historical periods I was studying at A level, with as many people as possible – even calling in favours from friends regarding connections they had to specialists in the field. I managed to secure an informal chat with a scholar who worked on 17th-century England and she helped me to identify alternative points of view, weaker areas of my knowledge and ways that I might tackle questions on them. This gave me a great deal of confidence as it allowed me to accept that there was no "right" answer and that the way I approached thinking about a question mattered more than having a huge store of knowledge. She also reassured me that the interviewer would keep asking questions until they found an area where I had a lack of knowledge in order to see what I would do next. When that happened in my actual interview, I was expecting it and made extra effort to explain my train of thought. I'm sure that helped secure my place.'

6 | Experience to support your application

Everything about your Oxbridge application needs to be convincing if you are to present yourself in the best possible light. We have already discussed the importance of being able to show that you have read around your subject and that you have delved far beyond the standard exam texts in your desire to find out more about your subject. But what else can you do that will set your application apart?

Work experience is essential if you think you want to study a vocational subject such as medicine, and it is important that you explore how you are going to organise this well in advance. It is naïve to think that you can arrange work experience at short notice; you will need to ask the advice of your parents, friends and school to help you arrange something worthwhile and you must plan ahead. Ideally you will have arranged several stints of relevant work experience. Be aware, however, that both Cambridge and Oxford are very academically focused.

It is important to keep your eyes and ears open to relevant events that you could attend in your area, newspaper articles that relate to your subject, blogs, radio programmes and any other sources of information that might give your application an additional dimension. A whole range of companies have in the past offered gap-year programmes; for example, the big four accountancy firms (PricewaterhouseCoopers, KPMG, Deloitte, Accenture), as well as IBM, the Bank of England and Rothschild. There is also The Year in Industry (www.etrust.org.uk/the-year-in-industry), which specialises in a broad range of year-long gap-year placements.

Increasingly, Oxbridge admissions officers talk in terms of 'super-curricular' activities that support your application, rather than extra-curricular. If you have done something to investigate and explore your interests beyond the school curriculum and if these activities are relevant to your degree course, this could provide substantial evidence that you are really committed to your subject area. This could be something that shows that you have really engaged with your subject. However, the main criterion remains academic excellence in the case of both universities.

Gap years

There has been much debate recently about the value of gap years. You'll need to decide whether to make an application for deferred entry (this is when you apply while doing your A levels, two years in advance of your first term at university) or to apply a year after your school friends do, while you are on your year out. When making this decision you should ring your college of choice to discuss its preferences.

Can I take a gap year and defer my entry?

Some Cambridge and Oxford colleges don't like making offers to deferred entrants for some courses, simply because this means they have to commit a place before they have met competing applicants for the following year. In this case, colleges encourage you to wait a year and apply while on your gap year. If you ask their advice and make the most of your time out, you will find that most colleges are happy for you to have a gap year. In allowing yourself time to mature you may even make a better application and become a more attractive candidate. You should be aware, however, that if you apply pre-A level and ask for a gap year, you may be swaying your odds of being offered a place against you. It is always best to check with the college to which you are thinking of applying as to its policy before deciding on deferred entry or not.

Cambridge states that around 6% of students take a gap year before starting their studies. It acknowledges that a year out can be a very useful time in which to improve skills, earn money, travel and generally gain maturity and self-reliance. It asks that you state on your UCAS application if you wish to defer entry. You'll almost certainly be asked about your plans at interview, so you need to be prepared to talk about what you hope to do and achieve in your gap year.

If you're applying for Mathematics, most colleges have a preference for immediate entry as the skills you acquire in A level study can be quickly forgotten. However, if you're applying for engineering, many colleges generally prefer applicants to take a year out, to gain some experience in industry. You will not be able to defer entry for the graduate course in Medicine.

Oxford's view is broadly similar. If you do opt to take a gap year, it is important that you choose to do something worthwhile which, ideally, emphasises your enthusiasm for the subject. Some mathematics and science tutors do not encourage deferred entry, again because they are concerned to keep your mathematical skills 'on the boil'. They will, however, consider applications in certain special circumstances, e.g. where a candidate sponsored by industry is spending a year in a laboratory. Note that if you are applying to read History of Art or Fine Art at Oxford, you will not be able to apply for deferred entry.

It's important to understand that each college has a different point of view about gap years and you must check the college's website to ensure that you know what its opinion is or contact someone in the college if you are still not sure. It is a good idea to explain your gap-year plans on your application form.

Work experience

What kind of work experience is best?

Any kind of work experience will be useful. Just getting used to the routine of working in an office, shop, restaurant or factory can come as quite a shock. Getting to work on time, dressing appropriately, getting on with your work colleagues, coping with boredom as well as stress are all valuable lessons in life skills.

Ideally, though, you should try to find work experience that relates to the subject you hope to study at university. Experience within the work environment is particularly important if you want to study a vocational subject, such as Law or Medicine. It is often only in a work situation that one can fully understand the stresses, responsibilities and pleasures that go along with a particular career, and only then can you really commit. Work experience can provide admissions tutors with strong evidence that candidates are committed, determined and have thought through their applications carefully. It can also provide you with a goal that keeps you motivated even through the toughest periods of study.

Apart from giving a real idea of where you might be in five years' time, work experience can expose you to ideas relating to the subject you are about to study in exciting ways. For example, if you want to study a science subject at Oxford or Cambridge, you might try to get a week during school holidays helping or observing at a laboratory where the scientists are working on something you are particularly interested in. You will be able to sit in on lab meetings and hear for yourself the problems that they face and the solutions they come to. You can also ask them personally for reading suggestions. No one will be as ahead of the game as they are, and this will give you some really exciting things to discuss at interview.

If you are really serious about studying and learning, find a way to get more information within the work environment. This will not only give you greater knowledge and confidence, it will also show the admissions tutors that you are really interested.

Work experience and the Covid-19 pandemic

Measures taken to combat the spread of Covid-19 in 2020 and 2021 required people to observe lockdowns and socially distance, and so the possibility of normal work experience disappeared in many areas. This did, however, accelerate the development of online work environments in which students could gain many of the benefits remotely.

Some online courses provide general 'life skills'. A popular one has been Barclays' Life Skills Virtual Work Experience: https://barclays lifeskills.com/i-want-virtual-work-experience/school. Forage provides a number of work experience programmes that give students the chance to learn career skills from Fortune 500 companies: www. theforage.com. Speakers For Students is a charity that aims to help students whose backgrounds mean they have traditionally struggled to access work experience, and claims to work with over 700 employers: www.speakersforschools.org/experience-2/vwex.

Medical students are arguably those who will miss out most from work experience. Brighton and Sussex Medical School has put together an excellent site to help such students gain experience online: https:// bsmsoutreach.thinkific.com/courses/VWE. Doctalk has a five-day virtual work experience programme where you shadow NHS doctors: https://learn.thedoctalk.co.uk/courses/doctalk-virtual-work-experi-ence. Premed allows you to watch live content from operating theatres and interviews with doctors: www.premedprojects.co.uk/premed-projects-live-tv. Although it does not identify itself as a virtual work experience site, it is also worth mentioning the Royal College of General Practitioners' Observe a GP website which contains lots of videos on the life of a GP: www.rcgp.org.uk/training-exams/discover-general-practice/observe-gp.aspx.

Those hoping to study law should look at The Lawyer Portal, which has put together a list of companies offering virtual work experience: www. thelawyerportal.com/free-guides/law-work-experience/virtual-work-experience-for-law-students.

The design practice Halliday Fraser Munro has put together a work experience programme for those interested in design: https://workex-perience.hfm.co.uk.

How do I organise my work experience?

It's never too early to start planning your work experience, and the really ambitious student will aim to organise several sessions. It may be diffi-cult in the current economic climate to persuade companies to let you join them, but if you are persistent and imaginative you will find openings.

First, do your research. Search online to find out about companies and institutions that operate in your field of study. What about think tanks and other, more academic organisations or publishing houses that pro-duce literature for your chosen subject?

Next, find someone in your chosen organisation to contact. Never send a letter to a company or organisation without finding an appropriate person to address it to; the more senior, the better. Letters that are sent without a specific recipient usually end up in the accounts department!

Write a winning introductory letter. Say exactly what you're looking for in terms of job opportunities, when you want to join and what you feel you can offer the company.

Attach the perfect CV. Make sure it is brief, accurate, with no typing errors or grammatical or spelling mistakes.

Include a couple of references. You might include one from a teacher at your school and one from another responsible adult who has been impressed by your resourcefulness or past endeavours.

Email a few days after you've posted your letters. Quite often, your email will go straight to the relevant person if you type their full name with a stop in the middle and then their company name, e.g. joe.brown@ multinational.com. It is worth a try!

Follow up. If you haven't had a response, phone a week later and ask if they received your application. Be very polite. Good luck!

Case study: Julia, Oxford

'I have always been very interested in archaeology and anthropology, but in the years preceding my university application I had mostly just read about the subject. However, in my first year of A levels, as I was deciding that the subject was one that I definitely wanted to study at university, I thought it would be best for me to get some practical experience to see whether it was definitely for me. I also knew that the practical element was important.

'During that summer, I returned to my home country of China. My town is an ancient one with a great deal of history and tradition, so before I returned I wrote to my local cultural museum to see whether they needed any English-speaking volunteers. Fortunately, I was a good fit for the museum, as I could help with the many English-speaking tourists. I was really in my element.

'I also entered a competition for a travel fund that my college was running. I wrote about a special project I wanted to do, working in a village in Cambodia, observing the customs of the local ethnic group and reporting back on these. I was awarded a sum of money to pay for some of my costs and in return I had to write up some of my findings for the college magazine.

'I found both of these experiences to be very rewarding and they really helped to prepare me for my course at university.'

Events in your subject area

If you want to study a humanities subject, keeping up to date with current affairs and events in your subject area is perhaps even more important than work experience. If you are really passionate about your subject, and dedicated to getting a place at Oxford or Cambridge, you should be constantly on the look-out for local events that are relevant to the subject that you want to study. Local libraries often host talks by renowned authors, the Royal Institution and the Science Museum in London host regular science lectures, the Royal Geographical Society organises regular discussions with eminent geographers and the Royal Academy of Arts has an ongoing art history lecture series. In addition, the universities in your area may hold lectures that could interest you. Speak to your teachers for ideas or go online to search for relevant events.

At the time of writing, many institutions are closed because of the Covid-19 restrictions. You should investigate what online existence they have. Some museums and galleries will allow you to conduct virtual tours. They will also have videos of talks by experts and may even be hosting live talks that you can join online. The same will be true of academic societies and universities. Oxford has an events page: www.ox.ac.uk/events-list, as does Cambridge: www.admin.cam.ac.uk/whatson/index.shtml. Another excellent resource is the Open Lectures website: www.open-lectures.co.uk. You should also be developing your knowledge of your subject by using other familiar online resources: podcasts, blogs, social media, journals and newspapers, and so on. Both Oxford and Cambridge have excellent collections of online videos and podcasts: https://podcasts.ox.ac.uk and https://sms.cam.ac.uk.

Case study: Rachel, Cambridge

'Having been educated in London, I made the most of every opportunity to visit art galleries and exhibitions. At first this was not only because I was genuinely interested in furthering my knowledge about history of art, but because I was aware that it would enhance my profile for my personal statement. The more places I visited, however, the more I enjoyed the visits in themselves, so that this side of my preparation for university became a pleasure in itself.

'On family trips to Europe, I began to make a point of visiting art galleries and museums, such as the Musée D'Orsay in Paris and the Rijksmuseum in Amsterdam. These experiences really focused my mind on my chosen university degree course, History of Art. My other subject areas, English literature and ancient history, really complemented my History of Art A level and my teachers helped me by always encouraging me to make links between the subjects.'

---

7 | The UCAS application and the personal statement

So you are finally ready to apply. The next stage is arguably the one that causes students the most anxiety – until they are invited to interview, of course! Your UCAS application will need to be submitted by the closing date for all Oxbridge applications of 6pm on 15 October. Let's go through the practicalities step by step.

Step one: preparing your UCAS application

The online form will be the same as for every other university: through the Universities and Colleges Admissions Service (UCAS). The UCAS form is a long document that is completed online and sent to all five of your chosen universities. It asks you to include details of your school(s), exam grades, employment experience, your choices of university and a personal statement: a 4,000-character written document that outlines the reasons for your choice of subject.

We will look more closely at what makes a winning personal statement later in this chapter.

You will need to specify a campus code in your 'courses' section. For most universities, this will be 'main site', but for collegiate universities such as Cambridge and Oxford, you need to state the college you wish to apply to from the list, or select 'Open' if you are not concerned about naming a specific college.

Step two: references

You will need to tell your school or college as soon as possible that you wish to apply to Oxbridge. If it has had lots of candidates who have applied before, the staff will be aware of what the colleges are looking for from the academic reference. If your school has little experience of making Oxbridge applications, the universities will probably be aware of this anyway and base their decision more on your personal statement and grades. But it is worth reminding your referees of the early deadline and making sure they'll have your reference ready on time. It is also worth remembering that although it may only be one person, such as a Personal Tutor or Director of Studies, who will be writing your reference, they will be talking to all of your subject tutors, so it is in your best interests to keep them all very happy and impressed with your work.

You will also need to confirm that your school has submitted the Extenuating Circumstances Form to Cambridge, if you are eligible to apply through this scheme (see page 24).

Step three: external tests

You must check the deadlines for any special tests that you may be required to sit, such as the BMAT or the LNAT (Law National Admissions Test). Oxford admissions tests and pre-interview subject tests for Cambridge will take place on the same day (Wednesday, 2 November 2022). See Chapter 9 for more information.

Step four: supplementary questionnaires

Cambridge

Once you've submitted your UCAS form, you will receive an acknowledgement almost immediately from Cambridge by email, along with its Supplementary Application Questionnaire (SAQ), which will require completion by the following week. The following link gives some very helpful advice about completing the SAQ, which can be a bit daunting for some students: www.undergraduate.study.cam.ac.uk/applying/saq/faq. The link also contains the phone number for the admissions office and they are very happy to help students who have queries about how to complete the form.

The SAQ is filled out online, costs nothing to send and gives Cambridge more information about you and your application. If you do not have access to email you can contact the Cambridge admissions office for a paper version. The initial email will give you all the information you need in order to complete the form correctly, as well as a deadline (usually a week after the UCAS deadline: 22 October).

The SAQ includes the following eight sections.

1. **Application type.** This section asks questions about your application, such as whether you have applied for an organ scholarship, if you are taking a gap year or whether you are including the Extenuating Circumstances Form.

2. **Photograph.** You will need a passport-sized colour photograph of yourself, preferably in digital format, which can then be uploaded onto the form.

3. **Personal details.** This covers information about you and your own situation, such as where you live, what your first name is, etc.

4. **BMAT number.** This is for applicants for Medicine. You need to put your BMAT number here so that Cambridge can access your results when you sit the BMAT.

5. **Education.** In this section, you will need to provide information about your class sizes and the topics you have covered (up to the time of application in your A levels). You will also need to specify if you've received extra help if you are taking the STEP/AEA.

6. **Qualifications.** In this section, you need to give details of your AS and/or A level modules (for any qualifications sat under the 'legacy' modular specifications), or their equivalents, and your marks.

7. **Additional information.** This is where you can add an additional personal statement and inform the university of anything else they feel they should know about you.

8. **Submission.** In this final section, you are asked to confirm the visa status you entered on your UCAS application and then to submit the whole SAQ.

Some students will need to upload one or both of a High School Transcript and a University Transcript. The former is a record of academic achievement for those who have not yet been to university. There may be various reasons why you need to upload one, the most common being that you have taken fewer than six IGCSEs/GCSEs in the last three years before your application. The latter is a similar record for those who are studying at university or have studied at university. For more information, see www.undergraduate.study.cam.ac.uk/applying/transcripts.

The additional personal statement provides an opportunity for you to explain to the admissions tutor what it was about the course that made you apply to Cambridge and to give any reasons for applying to a particular college. Do not overthink this small section – it will not be the deciding factor! While it's a good idea to be able to say something, Cambridge are clear that even if you don't put anything down, it will in no way disadvantage your application.

Remember, however, not to duplicate anything you have said on the UCAS form. While your UCAS personal statement will be seen by every institution you apply to, the SAQ is for the admissions tutors at Cambridge only. This means that you can discuss particular elements of the course content or programme at Cambridge without putting any other university off. Make the most of this and explain why its course and teaching staff are perfect for you, and why you will fit in particularly well there.

Remember also that by mentioning your areas of special academic interest you will encourage predictable questions at interview, making it easier to prepare thoroughly.

Oxford

Your chosen college at Oxford will usually be fairly swift in confirming that it has received your application and it will write requesting any further information it requires. If you have made an open application, the college to which you have been allocated will respond.

Oxford only requires additional forms for the following.

1. Candidates for **choral or organ awards.** In both cases, you need to have completed and submitted the application form by 1 September – a full six weeks before the Oxbridge UCAS deadline! For more information, visit www.ox.ac.uk/admissions/undergraduate/applying-to-oxford/choral-and-organ-awards.
2. Graduate applicants for the **accelerated medical course.** The form needs to be completed and submitted by the same date as the UCAS application: 15 October. For more information, visit www.medsci.ox.ac.uk/study/medicine/accelerated/application-procedure.

Step five: submitting written work

Another way in which admissions tutors decide whether or not to interview you – if you are applying for an essay-based subject – is by looking at a sample of your written work. This is something that you need to consider once you have submitted your application form(s). By looking at your work, the admissions tutors will be able to assess your ability to research, organise information, form opinions and construct a coherent and cogent argument in writing. These are essential skills to have when studying an essay subject at Oxbridge, and the admissions tutors need to see that you have these skills, and the potential to improve.

Normally the work that you send will have been written as part of your A level course. It would not normally be expected to be more than 2,000 words. Make sure that you send a particularly good example of your work. Normally, this should be original work which has been marked by your teachers, but not corrected or re-written based on your teachers' feedback.

Do not, however, submit anything that could not have been written by you. Plagiarism will be very obvious to admissions tutors and could potentially get you into some tricky situations at interview, since submitted written work is often discussed then.

> 'The submitted essay is often used as the starting point for discussion in the interview. The essay can show us whether the candidate has the ability to argue and has academic confidence.'
>
> Admissions tutor, Cambridge

At Cambridge, each college has a different policy on written work, but you are more likely to be asked to send in work if you are applying to read an arts or social sciences subject. For example, to study HSPS at Selwyn College you will be required to submit two relevant and recently marked pieces of work. The college will contact you directly if it requires work from you. Table 7 (pages 101–105) indicates for which subjects individual colleges have most recently required submission of written work.

The Oxford prospectus gives clear instructions about what you need to send and when. Remember to inform your teachers in advance that you will need to send marked work. There are a number of courses at Oxford that require you to submit written work, and you should check the course page at www.ox.ac.uk/admissions/undergraduate/courses/course-listing to see if it is the case with your subject. At the time of writing the following subjects require written work to be submitted:

- Archaeology and Anthropology
- Classical Archaeology and Ancient History
- Classics
- Classics and English
- Classics and Modern Languages
- Classics and Oriental Studies
- English Language and Literature
- English and Modern Languages
- Fine Art (portfolio submission)
- History
- History (Ancient and Modern)
- History and Economics
- History and English
- History and Modern Languages
- History and Politics
- History of Art
- Modern Languages
- Modern Languages and Linguistics
- Music
- Oriental Studies
- Philosophy and Modern Languages
- Philosophy and Theology
- Religion and Oriental Studies
- Theology and Religion.

As with Cambridge, Oxford says that you should submit marked written work that you have completed over the course of your school or college studies. Each piece of written work should be no more than 2,000 words and should be submitted together with an accompanying written work cover sheet, which is available from the University of Oxford website.

Table 7 Subjects requiring written work for Cambridge colleges

Course	Christ's	Churchill	Clare	Corpus Christi	Downing
Anglo-Saxon, Norse and Celtic	Yes	Yes	Yes	Yes	Yes
Archaeology	Yes	Yes	No	Yes	No
Architecture	Yes	Yes	Yes	Yes	Yes
Asian and Middle Eastern Studies	Yes	Yes	Yes	Yes	Yes
Chemical Engineering	No	No	No	No	No
Classics	Yes	Yes	Yes	No	Yes
Computer Science	No	No	No	No	No
Economics	No	No	No	No	No
Education	Yes	Yes	No	n/a	Yes
Engineering	No	No	No	No	No
English	Yes	Yes	Yes	Yes	No
Geography	Yes	Yes	No	No	No
History	Yes	Yes	No	Yes	Yes
History and Modern Languages	Yes	Yes	No	Yes	Yes
History and Politics	Yes	Yes	No	Yes	Yes
History of Art	Yes	Yes	Yes	Yes	Yes
Human, Social and Political Sciences	Yes	Yes	No	Yes	Yes
Land Economy	Yes	n/a	No	n/a	No
Law	No	No	No	No	No
Linguistics	No	Yes	No	Yes	Yes
Management Studies (Part II course)	No	No	No	No	No
Manufacturing Engineering (Part II course)	No	No	No	No	No
Mathematics	No	No	No	No	No
Medicine	No	No	No	No	No
Modern and Medieval Languages	Yes	Yes	No	Yes	Yes
Music	Yes	Yes	Yes	Yes	Yes
Natural Sciences	No	No	No	No	No
Philosophy	Yes	Yes	No	No	Yes
Psychological and Behavioural Sciences	No	Yes	No	Yes	No
Theology, Religion and Philosophy of Religion	Yes	n/a	Yes	Yes	Yes
Veterinary Medicine	No	No	No	No	No

Table 7 Subjects requiring written work for Cambridge colleges (continued)

Course	Emmanuel	Fitzwilliam	Girton	Gonville & Caius
Anglo-Saxon, Norse and Celtic	Yes	Yes	Yes	Yes
Archaeology	Yes	Yes	No	Yes
Architecture	Yes	Yes	Yes	Yes
Asian and Middle Eastern Studies	No	Yes	No	Yes
Chemical Engineering	No	No	No	No
Classics	Yes	Yes	Yes	Yes
Computer Science	No	No	No	No
Economics	No	No	No	No
Education	No	Yes	n/a	Yes
Engineering	No	No	No	No
English	No	Yes	Yes	Yes
Geography	No	No	Yes	Yes
History	No	Yes	Yes	Yes
History and Modern Languages	No	Yes	Yes	Yes
History and Politics	No	Yes	Yes	Yes
History of Art	Yes	Yes	n/a	No
Human, Social, and Political Sciences	No	No	No	Yes
Land Economy	n/a	Yes	No	No
Law	No	No	No	No
Linguistics	Yes	No	No	Yes
Management Studies (Part II course)	No	No	No	No
Manufacturing Engineering (Part II course)	No	No	No	No
Mathematics	No	No	No	No
Medicine	No	No	No	No
Modern and Medieval Languages	No	No	No	Yes
Music	Yes	Yes	Yes	Yes
Natural Sciences	No	No	No	No
Philosophy	No	Yes	No	No
Psychological and Behavioural Sciences	No	No	No	No
Theology, Religion, and Philosophy of Religion	Yes	Yes	Yes	Yes
Veterinary Medicine	No	No	No	No

Homerton	Hughes Hall	Jesus	King's	Lucy Cavendish	Magdalene	Murray Edwards	Newnham
Yes	Yes	Yes	Yes	Yes	Yes	Yes	Yes
Yes	No	No	No	Yes	Yes	Yes	Yes
Yes	n/a	Yes	Yes	Yes	Yes	Yes	Yes
Yes	Yes	No	Yes	Yes	Yes	Yes	Yes
No	No	No	No	No	No	No	No
Yes	Yes	Yes	Yes	Yes	Yes	Yes	Yes
No	No	No	No	No	No	No	Yes
No	No	No	No	No	No	No	n/a
Yes	Yes	No	n/a	Yes	No	n/a	n/a
No	No	No	No	No	No	No	No
Yes	Yes	Yes	Yes	Yes	Yes	Yes	Yes
No	Yes	No	Yes	Yes	No	No	Yes
Yes	Yes	Yes	Yes	Yes	Yes	Yes	Yes
Yes	Yes	Yes	Yes	Yes	Yes	Yes	Yes
Yes	Yes	Yes	Yes	Yes	Yes	Yes	Yes
Yes	Yes	Yes	Yes	Yes	Yes	Yes	Yes
Yes	Yes	Yes	Yes	Yes	Yes	Yes	Yes
No	Yes	No	n/a	Yes	No	Yes	No
No	No	No	No	No	No	No	No
No	Yes	No	No	Yes	No	Yes	No
No	No	No	No	No	No	No	No
No	No	No	No	No	No	No	No
No	No	No	No	No	No	No	No
No	No	No	No	No	No	No	No
Yes	No	No	Yes	Yes	Yes	Yes	No
Yes	Yes	Yes	Yes	Yes	Yes	Yes	Yes
No	No	No	No	No	No	No	No
No	Yes	No	No	Yes	Yes	n/a	No
No	Yes	No	No	Yes	Yes	Yes	No
Yes	Yes	Yes	Yes	Yes	Yes	Yes	Yes
No	No	No	No	No	No	No	No

Table 7 Subjects requiring written work for Cambridge colleges (continued)

Course	Pembroke	Peterhouse	Queens'	Robinson	Selwyn
Anglo-Saxon, Norse and Celtic	Yes	Yes	Yes	Yes	Yes
Archaeology	Yes	Yes	n/a	Yes	Yes
Architecture	Yes	Yes	Yes	Yes	Yes
Asian and Middle Eastern Studies	Yes	Yes	No	Yes	No
Chemical Engineering	No	No	No	No	No
Classics	Yes	Yes	Yes	Yes	Yes
Computer Science	No	No	No	No	No
Economics	No	No	No	No	No
Education	Yes	n/a	No	No	Yes
Engineering	No	No	No	No	No
English	Yes	Yes	Yes	Yes	Yes
Geography	No	n/a	Yes	No	No
History	Yes	Yes	Yes	Yes	Yes
History and Modern Languages	Yes	Yes	Yes	Yes	Yes
History and Politics	Yes	Yes	Yes	Yes	Yes
History of Art	Yes	Yes	Yes	n/a	No
Human, Social and Political Sciences	Yes	Yes	No	No	No
Land Economy	Yes	n/a	No	No	No
Law	No	No	No	No	No
Linguistics	Yes	Yes	No	No	Yes
Management Studies (Part II course)	No	No	No	No	No
Manufacturing Engineering (Part II course)	No	No	No	No	No
Mathematics	No	No	No	No	No
Medicine	No	No	No	No	No
Modern and Medieval Languages	Yes	Yes	No	Yes	Yes
Music	Yes	Yes	Yes	Yes	Yes
Natural Sciences	No	No	No	No	No
Philosophy	No	Yes	n/a	Yes	No
Psychological and Behavioural Sciences	Yes	n/a	No	Yes	No
Theology, Religion and Philosophy of Religion	Yes	Yes	Yes	Yes	Yes
Veterinary Medicine	No	No	No	No	No

Sidney Sussex	St Catharine's	St Edmund's	St John's	Trinity	Trinity Hall	Wolfson
Yes	Yes	Yes	Yes	Yes	Yes	Yes
Yes	No	Yes	No	Yes	Yes	Yes
Yes	n/a	Yes	Yes	Yes	Yes	Yes
Yes	Yes	Yes	Yes	Yes	Yes	Yes
No	No	No	No	No	No	No
Yes	Yes	Yes	Yes	Yes	Yes	Yes
No	No	No	No	No	No	No
No	No	No	No	No	No	n/a
n/a	n/a	Yes	No	n/a	n/a	Yes
No	No	No	No	No	No	No
Yes	Yes	Yes	Yes	Yes	Yes	Yes
No	No	Yes	No	Yes	Yes	Yes
Yes	Yes	Yes	Yes	Yes	Yes	Yes
Yes	Yes	Yes	Yes	Yes	Yes	Yes
Yes	Yes	Yes	Yes	Yes	Yes	Yes
Yes	n/a	Yes	Yes	Yes	Yes	Yes
Yes	Yes	Yes	Yes	Yes	Yes	Yes
No	No	Yes	No	No	Yes	Yes
No	No	Yes	No	No	No	Yes
Yes	n/a	Yes	Yes	No	Yes	Yes
No	No	No	No	No	No	No
No	No	No	No	No	No	No
No	No	No	No	No	No	No
No	No	No	No	No	No	No
Yes	Yes	Yes	Yes	Yes	Yes	Yes
Yes	Yes	Yes	Yes	Yes	Yes	Yes
No	No	No	No	No	No	No
Yes	Yes	Yes	No	Yes	Yes	Yes
Yes	No	Yes	No	No	Yes	No
Yes	No	Yes	Yes	Yes	Yes	Yes
No	No	No	No	No	No	No

Step six: await the call for interview!

See Chapter 10 for advice on interviews.

How to write your personal statement

This part of the application process can be tortuous if you allow yourself to overcomplicate matters. The quest for the 'perfect personal statement' is like searching for the Holy Grail. There's no such thing; or, if there is, you will have died of exhaustion before you find it. Before you start you might want to remind yourself of what admissions tutors are looking for.

Oxford personal statement advice

The admissions tutors will be looking carefully at your personal statement to gauge whether you are the sort of person who has plenty of potential and evident enthusiasm for your subject. They do not want to see you list achievements or to work systematically through your A levels (or equivalent) identifying things that interested you and skills you have learned. They want to see evidence of engagement with the subject that goes beyond what you have studied at school or college through reading and relevant super-curricular activities. You should ensure your personal statement really is personal and therefore convey what has interested you in the course for which you apply. In the same vein, you should avoid stock phrases and clichés. For more advice, see www.ox.ac.uk/admissions/undergraduate/applying-to-oxford/guide/ucas-application.

Cambridge personal statement advice

There is no 'one size fits all' approach to the ideal personal statement. A personal statement is your 'shop window' for displaying, first and foremost, your academic potential. The admission tutors will want to see evidence of someone who is interested in ideas and able critically to evaluate them, and someone who can think independently but be flexible enough to recognise when to change one's mind. They will also be looking for enthusiasm for the chosen course. Promising applicants will have read beyond the limits of the standard requirements for the subjects they are studying at A level (or equivalent). Finally, the emphasis on independent study at Cambridge means that applicants should show

how they are self-motivated and able to manage their time well, such as by showing how they can balance the academic and personal sides of their life. For more advice, see www.undergraduate. study.cam.ac.uk/writing-a-great-personal-statement.

Think of things from the admissions tutor's point of view. Most candidates will present with excellent grades, predicted or actual, and glowing references from their teachers. They may also have taken specific admission tests or submitted written work. The personal statement is one more element that the staff can use to judge whether or not a candidate will be suitable for their courses. Most admissions tutors are keen to stress that all candidates' applications are viewed 'in the round'. Be assured that they are not expecting your personal statement to be a literary masterpiece or a work of stunning originality. They want to hear about you, and, in particular:

- what interests you about your chosen subject (and why)
- why you want to study the subject(s) you've applied for
- what activities you have undertaken that show how you have gone beyond the syllabus, such as reading, listening to podcasts, attending lectures and exhibitions, and so on
- activities you've participated in that have added to your knowledge of your subject, such as entering maths or essay competitions, performing in plays, and so on.

The admissions tutors are looking for academic potential. Your personal statement should convey a deep intellectual fascination with your subject with evidence of good reading around and beyond your current studies. A simple but important principle to bear in mind is, 'show, don't tell'. You need to show the admissions tutor that you are a thoughtful individual interested in your subject. This is not done by telling them that you are a thoughtful individual interested in your subject. You need to show that there is more to you than this. To this end, do not simply tell the admissions tutor the contents of what you have read or (worse) listing what you have read, as that doesn't indicate you have anything interesting to say about it. You need to show the tutor the questions that interest you by *reflecting* on what you have read (or seen, or heard, etc.) and the thoughts that your reflections generated. Work experience and what you have learned from it should be stated if relevant, especially for more vocational courses such as Medicine. There should be no clichés in your personal statement and it should be a minimum of 80% academic content. You can mention your interests but Oxford and Cambridge do say explicitly that they are not looking for individuals with a wonderful range of extra-curricular activities. While there are many clubs, societies, sports and so on that the universities hope people will become involved with, they are clear that you are mainly there to study!

How to get started — some dos and don'ts

Do take time to submit something that is well written; i.e. the grammar and spelling should be correct, and you should write in sentences rather than a list. Ask your teacher or someone you trust to read it through carefully for mistakes.

Do go into detail. It's better to write in detail about a few topics than try to cite lots of interesting topics in a cursory way. Use examples to demonstrate your understanding of your subject so far and your desire to explore it further.

Do justify everything that you put down on paper. 'I found going to lectures at the LSE fascinating' only raises the question 'Why?'

Don't be tempted to just list the books that you have read; explain how reading them enriched your learning or excited you and made you want to read around your subject. Similarly, please don't tell them that you've read the obvious choices; when the twentieth Economics applicant says that they've enjoyed *Nudge*, even the most well-disposed tutor will marvel at a student's lack of imagination.

Don't feel you have to trace your interest in your subject back to your childhood. It is hard to believe the student who says that they have been interested in macroeconomics since before they could properly walk.

Don't go overboard with exuberant language. Avoid saying that you have a passion for topic X, that you never cease to think about the question of Y, that you find the issue of Z simultaneously awe-inspiring, breathtaking and something without the study of which your life would be irreparably incomplete. Once again, show, don't tell. Show how interested – and interesting – a person you are through a clear statement of what fascinates you and the thoughts you have.

Don't use long, convoluted sentences that are hard to follow; the admissions tutor may lose concentration before he or she reaches the end of the paragraph. Your writing should be clear, concise and precise.

Don't lie. You will be found out. If you are lucky enough to be called for interview you will be asked about your personal statement, and although you may not remember that you said that you read and enjoyed Nietzsche's *Twilight of the Idols*, the tutor interviewing you will. Be warned!

Don't be tempted to spend too much time listing your achievements outside school. No more than a fifth of your personal statement should be devoted to non-academic matters. Always try to demonstrate the relevance of your outside experience to your chosen subject; some of it may not be directly relevant but you are likely to have acquired useful, transferable skills that can be highlighted.

Don't simply tell the admissions tutors the contents or conclusions of things you've read. They will want to hear your thoughts on what you have read. They are looking for people with whom they can have an academic discussion rather than people who can just grasp the ideas in what they are reading.

Don't feel you have to be an expert. You are not supposed to show them that you have a comprehensive knowledge of all of Shakespeare's works. You are applying to join an institution where you can mix with the best and learn much more. There would be no point in applying if you'd covered everything already!

Don't mechanically work through your A level courses identifying something that has interested you and something that might be relevant to the course you are applying for. If you are applying to read English literature and one of your A levels is Biology, there may well be no interesting connection between the two. This doesn't mean that you can't make reference to the knowledge or skills that Biology has given you. This said, avoid platitudinous remarks: writing that A level Philosophy has 'given me critical skills and helped me write better essays' is unlikely to impress.

Another important consideration is the fact that your personal statement needs to be no more than 4,000 characters including spaces; this is a strict limit and so you need to ensure that you stay within it.

Many schools who are very successful at getting their students into Oxbridge adopt a fairly formulaic approach to writing personal statements. This is certainly one way of making your life a little easier and it might help you on your first draft. But remember, the key to writing your personal statement is that it should be personal; if you allow lots of people to read yours, you will receive lots of different opinions on its strengths and weaknesses. This can be confusing, to say the least. In the end, the best advice is to decide what you want to say and say it with conviction, in your own words, not those of your parents, teachers or other advisers. A typical personal statement takes time and effort to get right; don't expect perfection after one draft.

A final note on the pandemic. If the pandemic inspired your choice of course, then it may be relevant to make reference to it. Otherwise, you are advised not to talk about it. A very great number of you will have been affected by the pandemic, emotionally, physically and the impact on your education. If your circumstances are particularly grave, then consider writing to the college (Oxford) or completing an Extenuating Circumstances Form (Cambridge).

A model Oxbridge personal statement

There are no hard and fast rules about how to structure your personal statement. Below, however, is an example of how a well-organised statement might be written, with a synopsis, paragraph by paragraph. Below each synopsis is an example of a paragraph written by a candidate who did get a place at Oxford to study History (Ancient and Modern). Read the example carefully, but **do not copy it**.

The **first paragraph** should explain what sparked your interest in your chosen subject and why you wish to study it at university.

My interest in history and ancient history began, perhaps unusually, in the genre of historical novels, and the more general histories of those such as Norwich and Goldsworthy. These originally caught my imagination with their sweeping narratives of the Roman military world, and the world of late antiquity. This swiftly sparked an interest in more specific and more scholarly works, such as Syme's *The Roman Revolution*, which made me think differently about my assumptions of the power of individuals; in this case Augustus' role as the product of a talented new ruling class, rather than as a lone genius, as well as Scullard's *From the Gracchi to Nero*, on the challenges that Rome faced internally, as she externally became a superpower, and the necessary changes that the fall of the republic would later bring about.

In **paragraph two** you could discuss your particular interests in relation to your university subject choice. This is your chance to write about specific ideas you have developed as a result of reading beyond your A level syllabus.

What perhaps fascinates me the most is the way in which history, particularly in the distant past, is perceived by the succeeding generations of scholars, either through a difference of opinion in scholarly debate, or as a natural result of their environment. For example, Gibbon's demonisation of the Byzantine Empire, despite hardly being based in historical fact, is easy to understand in the context of the founding of the European world empires and the Enlightenment. Another example of this is the illusion of the founding of nations during the Dark Ages, and the tendency of historians to link the kingdoms of the Dark Ages with the modern states they were to form later on. Christopher Wickham's discussion of this phenomenon, in his *The Inheritance of Rome*, interested me immensely, as it made me question the blind belief I had shown before when reading the narrative history of this period. Perhaps in a less orthodox way, I was also heavily influenced by Terry Jones' protestations at the misinterpretation of Celtic culture in his study *Barbarians*. Though clearly it is difficult to make assertions about an empire without trusting your sources to some degree, it is nevertheless hugely interesting to read history from a contrary viewpoint.

The **third paragraph** can start to incorporate your personal experiences and how these have shaped your academic interests and choice of university subject.

Another stimulating part of studying both history and ancient history is the way in which one can see how different cultures have left their mark on a particular place. A good example of this, particularly in an ancient context, is in Tunisia, where the Phoenicians, the Carthaginians, the Romans, the Vandals, the Byzantines and the Arabs have all left their mark in the numerous sites, which are fascinating in the context of both ancient and modern history. To follow this up, therefore, independently, I undertook a week-long trip, in which I covered a route retracing Cato's last march, as well as looking at the ruins of Jugurtha's capital at Beja, which has since seen many conquerors, the Byzantine fortress at Kelibia, the remarkable Arabic city of Kairouan, and the Roman ruins at Dougga. One piece of extended work which I have done this summer has been on the Jugurthine war, and the other was on Justinian's capture of Africa from the Vandals. I have also used my trip to supplement my research, as well as to develop much further my knowledge of post-Almohad Tunisian history.

The **fourth paragraph** can include a brief summary of your extra-curricular activities. It was noted above that the admissions tutors are not really that interested in this section. However, you will be a member of the college for three or four years and if you do have something else to offer, it is worth putting down.

Outside of the academic sphere, my main passion is music. I play the double bass to grade seven standard, and have recently started the jazz double bass, as well as enjoying collecting vinyl records. I have also attended many Model United Nations meetings, which I have enjoyed and have excelled in, particularly those set in historical situations. I am also interested in journalism, in which I have done work experience, and I would hope to contribute to magazines at university. My reading, though mostly focused on history, also encompasses literature, and I am particularly interested in the great American novel, having been moved by the works of Fitzgerald, Hemingway and Capote, as well as the works of Leo Tolstoy, Maxim Gorky and Fyodor Dostoevsky.

Examples of successful Oxbridge personal statements

Through many revised editions of this book one of the things that students have said they found most useful are examples of really good personal statements. What follows, therefore, is a set of excellent personal statements recently collected. It is important to stress that it's worth reading not just the one specific to your subject. I hope that you can see several common factors that have impressed Oxbridge tutors.

- They explain clearly why the student wants to study the subject they have applied for.
- There are no spelling mistakes or grammatical errors.
- They show that the candidate has the ability to think logically, critically and independently.
- They show enthusiasm and clear motivation through their detailed examples of how the student has explored their subject beyond the A level syllabus – by extra reading, through work experience or through attendance on extra-curricular courses.
- They show that the student has the skills necessary for studying at a university where the tutorial system reigns; that they are organised, committed and able to put forward a point of view and justify it.
- They show that the candidate is the sort of person the tutors would like to teach.
- If the student has gap-year plans, they relate them to the chosen area of study.

It is a useful exercise once you have finished a first draft to see how many of the above qualities your personal statement encompasses.

History – Oxford (3,981 characters, with spaces)

The many differing depictions of Anne Boleyn sparked my interest in History. I could not equate Philippa Gregory's murderous, incestuous, cruel Anne with the Anne who argued with Cromwell because she wanted the proceeds of the Reformation to go to charitable causes. Reading Susan Bordo's *The Creation of Anne Boleyn*, I was struck by how historians could take the same source material yet create such different depictions of her depending on their perspective. For example, Nicholas Sander, a Catholic propagandist, depicted Anne as a seductive monster with six fingers and warts, while Protestants such as John Foxe and Alexander Ales portray her as a heroine of the Reformation. Bordo's analysis of early female historians, such as Elizabeth Benger, resonated with me as I had studied late 19th-century women in Pre-U History and led my school's Feminist Society. The more domestic-focused work of these female historians was trivialised as gossip and sentimental, while male historians were praised for investigating domestic life; one of the many ways women were kept out of the intellectual sphere. While Bordo is clear that both sides lack nuance, her fondness for Anne is apparent, and in revealing the myriad Annes created by historians, Bordo makes her own: one that is imperfect, but intelligent and a proto-feminist, defying the establishment.

I found Bordo's analysis of how history is created compelling, and it led me to read Margaret MacMillan's *The Uses and Abuses of History*. I was especially interested by her argument that history has come to represent something larger than ourselves: a new religion in an increasingly secular world. I could see this reflected in how history has overtaken religion to justify monumental decisions, such as the US using the memory of the failure of appeasement and the universal legitimacy of the Second World War to warrant the invasion of Iraq. I have long been interested in the role of religion in pre-industrial life, having spent the summer after my GCSEs visiting gothic cathedrals in Northern France. What must have been a striking juxtaposition between people's everyday lives and these stupendous, heavenly buildings impressed on me the centrality of religion to life in 12th- and 13th-century Christendom.

Interested in pre-industrial life, and having studied Maths and Physics at A level, I was intrigued by Peter Laslett's quantitative approach to history in *The World We Have Lost*. He uses statistics to reveal the intricacies of pre-industrial life, and corrects misinterpretations, such as girls married in their early teens, when in fact the mean age in 1619–60 was 23.58. This was a novel way of approaching history for me, and one I found particularly insightful. Having studied only late modern history at Pre-U, his revelations about the early modern era were entirely new to me, and are something I would like to explore further at university. I was also struck by Laslett's approach to class. He rejects the Marxist view of a rising capitalist class in conflict with the feudal aristocracy, and posits the idea of a one-class society with the power concentrated with the gentry and aristocracy. However, in my opinion, Laslett sees the Industrial Revolution as too drastic a transformation. I felt that his view of the post-industrial proletariat as stuck in overwhelming poverty too pessimistic, when, by the end of the 19th century, they were gaining political representation, and now had enough power to be considered a class. This interest in class and my enjoyment of studying 19th-century British and German politics led me to begin a further A level in Politics. I have so far enjoyed understanding the adaptation of the late 19th-century political system into the one we have today.

Outside of my studies, I edited the school history magazine on Transnationalism, from which I learnt valuable skills of teamwork and leadership while coordinating a team of article writers.

English – Oxford (3,709 characters, with spaces)

Virginia Woolf envisioned reading as 'atoms as they fall upon the mind'. There are myriad approaches to every text. Some judge Proust's *In Search of Lost Time* to be illusory; others applaud his belletrism. *Mrs Dalloway* has been read as a paean to time and consciousness, and as a study of inter-war London. It is our intimacy with words that forms the molecules of interpretation, and it is the thrill of creating new matter – new shivers and sympathies – that inspires me to study literature at degree level.

Maupassant said, 'the trouble with happiness is that it writes white; it doesn't show up on the page'. Tribulation, suffering even, propels narrative. This is exemplified in Ian McEwan's *Atonement*, in which Briony's narrative searches for redemption. In St Aubyn's *Melrose* quintet, a childhood trauma is revisited in the guises of addiction and betrayal. Larkin presents many iterations of death, from ambulances to investigative priests. From these readings, I have accepted the demonic notion that literature favours suffering. Only in Larkin's last poem, 'Aubade', is death no longer an abiding shadow: it all but consumes the text.

While musing on Larkin's response to mortality, I uncovered Edward Said's book on 'late style' – the influence of oncoming death on an artist's work. Dissatisfied with Said's limited scope, and finding Edith Wharton's work apposite to my studies, I devised my Extended Project title, 'Do Edith Wharton's late works constitute a "late style"?' In arguing for her 'late style', I found her shift into scandalous material chimed with my exploration into literary representations of the obscene. Like Elisabeth Ladenson in *Dirt for Art's Sake*, it strikes me that one generation's 'dirt' can be another generation's 'art'. Once judged vulgar, Chaucer's *Canterbury Tales*, Donne's erotic lyrics, and Flaubert's *Madame Bovary* became checkpoints in the development of literary style, and were crucial in sublimating sexuality into society. I particularly admire Defoe's *Roxana*, where the self-lacerating narration skews the reader's judgement of the anti-hero's sin. My independent research has filled me with excitement for the scholarly discipline of university.

Harold Bloom called Shakespeare 'the inventor of the human'. *King Lear* is a true testament to this, a dramatisation of the human psyche. I am most moved by The Fool in the play, who is a living paradox: a loving, filial figure to Lear and the agent of his psychological ruin. D.H. Thomas' presentation of the hallucinogenic in 'The White Hotel' is a stimulating touchstone for comparison with *King Lear*. Although Thomas prefers lurid, psychedelic lyricism to

The Fool's doggerel, both texts suffer, or celebrate, linguistic collapse to penetrate the kaleidoscopic subconscious. Patrick Hamilton depicts the same solipsistic delirium in 'Hangover Square', though the latter is a marked stylistic contrast: spasmodic, staccatoed surges supply the rhythmic thrum of the narrative.

This year, aside from winning my school's English Prize, I completed grade 8 LAMDA with distinction, delighting in the mordant criticism of bureaucracy in Kafka's *The Trial*. To make the most of my gap year, I am studying an A level in Classical Civilisation. As the foundation stones of the Western literary canon, I am impressed by the detailed patchwork of countless universal traditions in *The Iliad*, all of which prevail today and reemerge often in neoclassicism. It is this so-called 'deathlessness' of English literature, made indelible in history through the minds of its readers, which fuels my enthusiasm for work experience in publishing this year, and excites me for my continued study of literature.

Engineering – Oxford (3,988 characters, with spaces)

When I think of the breakthroughs in technology that have happened in my lifetime it is thrilling to think about the projects I will work on. My interest in disruptive technologies led me to read Diamandis' *The Future is Faster Than You Think*, which considers ten rapidly growing technologies and their interconnection for the design and production of advanced machines. I believe upcoming technologies, such as hyperloop and eVTOLs will change our lives as much as the internet has. After reading this book, I became fascinated in the interplay of different disciplines in engineering and decided I wanted to study engineering.

In my studies, I enjoy taking a practical approach to learning new mathematical concepts and applying them to solve problems. I find mechanics fascinating because all the concepts and formulae can be used to create a visual model of the experimental observations by pioneering physicists. I came third in my school in the UKMT Maths Challenge and won gold in the BPhO Senior Physics Challenge. As I wanted to learn programming skills and the engineering side of drones, I built a small drone using Raspberry Pi and Pix Hawk. Preventing the excess vibration between the drone's parts that risked damaging the electronic components was challenging. To solve it, I used my physics knowledge of hysteresis loops to develop a shock absorber. I also wrote some basic code; for example, using Mav Proxy to connect the Raspberry Pi and the Pix Hawk flight controller. It was my first attempt at programming, and by adopting a 'use this to ...' approach analogous to that outlined in many mathematics books, I was able to successfully conclude my project. In fact, my challenge was to understand the specific purposes of externally developed codes for my project and organise them in a correct, overarching structure for the drone to work effectively.

My interest in Mechatronics pushed me to complete a Coursera course on UAVs in which I learnt advanced physics, such as the physics of oppositely spinning rotors that enable roll, yaw and pitch. After reading an article published by the Oxford Robotics Institute about the application of Lidar to map forests and retrieve DBH data to monitor tree growth, I learnt how advances in computer vision and sensor technologies can lead to the automatic control of machines by feeding data to operate software that optimises paths such as 'route inspection algorithm'. I also learned how an engineering field like sensors and semiconductors, which might seem distant to robotics, was crucial for further advancement.

My purchase of a 3D-printed shock absorber encouraged me to explore the future of additive manufacturing. I read an E&T Journal and a MIT report on its forecasted impact for the $100bn manufacturing industry. I have also researched 3D printing technologies, such as direct metal laser sintering and selective laser melting methods. These made me appreciate new ethical challenges posed by 3D printing. The advancement of this technology to the stage of manufacturing artificial organs and weapons will present big issues on the regulation of illegal activities, and the protection of intellectual properties. It will also be interesting to see how tech giants like Amazon, who operate on a massive traditional supply chain, will adapt to the increasing demand and potential offered by 3D printing.

I have a strong work ethic thanks to my intense Korean education, but I also enjoy being part of a community. I play in the school football team which has enhanced my teamwork and communication skills. I always strive to get out of my comfort zone and challenge myself. Moving to England from South Korea and adapting to a new country and school during the pandemic was challenging, and I am motivated to face more challenges with the same enthusiasm. I am confident I can become a versatile and fast adapting engineer who will contribute to the rapidly changing fourth industrial revolution.

Natural Sciences – Cambridge (3,912 characters, with spaces)

I see physics as an all-encompassing field covering every natural phenomenon imaginable. I have already been introduced to so many fascinating aspects; from the quantum world, governed by the electromagnetic, weak and strong forces, through to stars and galaxies that are constantly shaped by gravity. This inspires me to look deeper into both Newtonian and Relativistic mechanics.

The language of physics is mathematics so it is obviously a crucial area of study and one that I very much enjoy. It gives me a chance to challenge myself, tackling the toughest questions. I enjoy the sense of achievement which comes from solving a difficult question, even more so when I find a mathematically eloquent solution. Studying further maths gives me more time to develop my abilities; providing an understanding of complex numbers, matrices and advanced calculus.

In chemistry, I tend towards the physical side and being one of the select few chosen to take part in a day of practical work in an undergraduate lab at the University of Leeds was a great experience. We used spectroscopes to study the hydrogen spectra to calculate the Rydberg constant as well as studying the links between temperature and rate of reaction. This provoked me to research the kinetic theory of gases for a maths project.

Since starting A levels I've done as much as I can to drive my passion for physics. I contacted Dr J. Collins, who has been mentoring me since. Over the last year he has suggested reading material, such as The Feynman Lectures, and assisted me with problems. During the year I have attended lectures; one about radio astronomy by Dr T. O'Brian and another about dark matter given by Dr S. Paling, which inspired me to read the thought provoking *A Brief History of Time*. I attended the Physics Master Class at Cambridge in early 2013; it gave me my first deepened insight into the world of quantum mechanics which was broadened by working through sections of Cavendish Quantum Mechanics Primer. In the summer I completed a week of work experience at the University of York, undertaking experiments ranging from measuring the specific heat capacity of liquid nitrogen through to measuring the charge/mass ratio of an electron using a cathode ray tube. Talking to both theoretical and experimental researchers demonstrated to me the current problems being tackled by physicists.

At school, I, along with three other students, ran the STEM club. We worked with lower school students with the aim of inspiring them to take on physics through GCSE and beyond. The club consisted of fun practical work and we pushed the students to ask questions and think about why and how something happens. This is something I feel passionately about, as physics is seen by some to be one of the least popular sciences and this is something that I would like to help change.

Outside of school, I currently work as a tutor at Explore Learning, tutoring children from the ages of 5 to 14 in maths and English. Sharing my passion for maths is extremely rewarding. It is helping me to develop my communication skills, working with young people of a range of ages and abilities. I also have many hobbies, the main of which is photography. Although it is essentially a creative hobby, the practical understanding of how a camera works will always create the best results. I have been lucky enough to reach the final of the RSPCA Young Photographer Awards and win the AMP Awards photography competition, as well as being in a business team which organised the event. I have been playing the trumpet since the age of 10 and have played in the school bands throughout my school life.

I am driven simply by, in the words of Feynman, the pleasure of finding things out. I look to build on the concepts that I have been briefly introduced to and then to continually develop my understanding of the physical world throughout the rest of my life. It will be a genuine pleasure to be a part of the era of scientific development.

Economics – Cambridge (3,992 characters, with spaces)

During my volunteer week in Chiang Mai, when I helped out at a community kitchen, I witnessed how extreme deprivation led boys and girls to learn nothing but basic selling by evoking the compassion of tourists. By the definitions of Economics, it was their choice. But what choices had they made?

Reading *Globalization and Its Discontents Revisited*, by Joseph Stiglitz, inspired me to reshape the world around me using economic scope. My research about New Trade Theory led me to rethink economic relationships in the East Asia. Witnessing the dynamics of the EU, I think a complete economic integration – an EU in East Asia – may be the solution to the limitations of export-led growth models. This raised the question of how to solve a lack of fiscal integration in the EU. If Germany is draining wealth from Spain and Greece due to lack of fiscal compensation, it seems plausible as applied to Korea's relationship with other countries in the Asian union. I realised that extracting key concepts from ongoing social issues and applying them to other real-life situations is a key aspect of economics as a social science. My assumption that a monetary union such as the EU is a unitary system of geo-economic organisation was challenged by reading *Euro* by Stiglitz, where the concept of the 'divisibility of the euro' was introduced. This caused me to reconsider assumptions that may have been entrenched in my mind and improved my intellectual malleability. I further noticed that encompassing a broader perspective was necessary for social experiments in the world around me; for this reason, I started to read *The Economist* and the *Financial Times*. I was impressed by the growing use of technology to overcome the traditional limitations of social science. By researching, I found a branch of Economics, Neuroeconomics, that deals with decision-making and information processing. The notion that fMRIs can be used to quantify the decision-making process and to build better economic devices to help people to make wiser decisions was a radical one.

This motivated me to conduct my own experiment this summer. I tried to build incentives for students who often avoided studying with different descriptions of tasks, rewards and punishments. I carefully observed their behaviour, anchored and framed by my wording, varying under different cognitive sequences of a fundamentally identical incentive system. A systematic approach acquired from studying Further Maths helped me to filter the relevant data, and to achieve a silver certificate in UKMT. Although I struggled to theorise a precise explanation on why there are changes in the outcomes, my constant effort brought me to understand and apply a wider range of behavioural economics to students' decision-making, thus helping them to achieve successful results. This gives a lesson on the value of Economics as a tool to improve people's decision-making and their living standard. At the same time, the challenge crystallises my academic passion to further expand my economic understanding in university.

My unique experience in various fields have developed my character. I have contributed to two projects as part of launching a new brand and service which involved unfamiliar contracts. learned the value of creative thinking in a multi-dimensional business environment to solve problems, while keeping to deadlines with limited resources. I developed resilience and cultural adaptability during military service when I participated in joint military exercises with the US Army and UN forces. Practical knowledge learned from these experiences was significant when completing three A levels in a year. An insight I can offer to my colleagues as a mature student, is that theory alone does not suffice. I look forward to bringing my enthusiasm for Economics to university. In the longer term, I hope to contribute to changing the lives of people around me and perhaps bringing the kids in Chiang Mai a more affluent life.

Archaeology and Anthropology – Oxford (3,796 characters, with spaces)

I became convinced of my interest in Archaeology last year, when I attended a lecture on 'Art and Iconoclasm in the Islamic World'. I was enthused by the inclusion of Islamic coins; in particular how during the reign of Caliph Abd Al-Malik the coinage used was changed to reflect the religious nature of the state. Previously it had used Byzantine currency minted by Justinian II, which was subsequently replaced by an Arabic inscription and an image of the Caliph. This shift, with its expression of the Umayyad's values and beliefs, led me to consider how material culture reflects the ideas and values held within society. My next step was to join the Royal Numismatic Society, which gave me access to a fascinating portfolio of resources. I read *An Introduction to the Study of Ancient and Modern Coins* by Akerman which categorises and explains the history of coinage and inspired me to take up coin collecting.

I relished studying Art History. I most enjoyed analysing architecture and sculpture that predates the general canon of Western art. Engaging with 'The Younger Memnon', a bust of Ramesses II, was particularly memorable. The highly stylised depiction and size show power and authority, and the two-tone granite of the statue reflects the dual role of the pharaoh as head of state and the church. Moreover, on the breast of the statue there is a large hole that was created in 1798 when Napoleon and his men were unable to transport the colossal figure. Close observation and analysis such as this fires my enthusiasm to study Archaeology. For example, I am captivated by the way in which the architectural tradition within Venice reflects the values and history of the city. St Mark's Basilica, the most important church in the city, prominently displays onion domes and ogee arches, demonstrating the

Islamic influence. The pinnacles and tracery highlight Northern European influence, while the intense gilding and the prominent display of *spolia* illustrate the obvious Byzantine element to the church. Through this analysis, the history and principles of the city become clear.

My interest in Anthropology developed differently. Through my study of Economics, I became interested in the way in which financial institutions have evolved to accommodate our increasingly complex and globalised society. This encouraged a broader interest in Institutional Anthropology. I was drawn towards the work of Goffman, who in his collection of essays on asylums, sought to define and categorise institutions into five groups. I have found this assessment of society interesting, and I have since become a member of the Royal Anthropological Institute to further my understanding of the science. I recently attended a memorable lecture on negotiating knowledge through documentation, where the lecturer spoke extensively about his fieldwork in Papua New Guinea.

My experiences outside of school have also increased my desire to study Anthropology. Over the last two years I gained a qualification in British Sign Language, which allowed me to volunteer at the Frank Barnes School for Deaf Children, where lessons are conducted in a bilingual learning environment. Reading *Linguistic Anthropology* by Nancy Hickerson led me to fully consider the way that languages have evolved; I found this book very engaging and I look forward to being able to further interact with Linguistic Anthropology as a result of my study of Spanish. In addition to this, I founded and led a society at my former school, Record Society, where students and teachers were invited to speak about musical topics of importance to them.

I eagerly anticipate the challenge of attending a demanding and stimulating course, and I look forward to nurturing my curiosity for Archaeology and Anthropology in my undergraduate studies.

Personal statement advice from a student

Here is some very useful advice from a student who has successfully applied to both Oxford and Cambridge for two very different degrees. Flora read Geography at St Anne's College, Oxford followed by Medicine on a graduate-entry programme at Wolfson College, Cambridge.

- Think about how you can make your personal statement stand out from the others.

- Don't try and pack it with too much information. Tutors like to see your thought process and how you critically analyse things. Explore issues rather than just writing a sentence about it.
- Whatever examples you do provide in your personal statement, make sure you are comfortable and familiar with them as there is a high chance they will bring it up in your interview (and not in the way you may expect them to!) – know the basics!
- Think outside of the box – try to approach scenarios or problems in a unique, interesting and thoughtful way.
- The tutors have to read so many personal statements – make yours thought-provoking and fun – engage the reader!
- Think about how you can link different examples together to make it fluid and interconnected.
- It sounds obvious, but really think about why you want to study your chosen course. What is it about that subject that engages you? What are you passionate about? What does the Oxford/Cambridge course offer that attracts you to it? Look at what modules are on offer, etc. Reflect on your own life (whether academic or personal) and think about why that course is suited to you.

Case study: Jamie, Oxford

'When applying for any arts subject at Oxbridge it is important to know your personal statement well. It isn't necessarily going to form the entirety of your interview, if it features at all you're incredibly lucky and the tutors will most likely only base the first few questions on your personal statement in order to put your mind at ease. Despite this, developing the ideas that you introduced in your personal statement – and trust me, with PPE they will have been very brief introductions indeed – is still good practice. The tutors in their questions, whether they be on the philosophy of Hamlet or how you would advise ISIS (yes, someone did get that question!), are testing to see how you think – you will not have ever seen anything like the materials they will give you at interview, but it's fine because no one else will have either. That's why developing your personal statement is so important; it offers a base from which you can leap off in your interview. It also helps you hone those all-important thinking skills. It is pointless trying to anticipate the questions that can come up in interview, but at least if you are well grounded on your personal statement you have something to fall back on and have some knowledge that may be applicable.

'As for the personal statement itself there are some very clear dos and don'ts, the first being do not cite *The Prince* by Machiavelli, as everyone who has ever applied for a politics-based course has had that idea before you (including me). As well as this, starting a personal statement with the words "the interconnections between politics, philosophy and economics" has been done before (again by me). Other than that, there are not many specifics to worry about with your personal statement.'

The UCAS application

These are the steps you need to take, and when to take them, to apply through UCAS.

1. Go to www.ucas.com/students to register. UCAS should be open to students applying for 2023 entry in May 2022. In order to do this you will need an email address and will be asked to choose a password. Your password should be easy to remember and ideally one that you don't use for other accounts. If you have a school email address, use it to register. After inputting some basic personal details you will be given your username and UCAS application number which is to be used in all correspondence with UCAS and the universities. Once you have chosen four security questions, in case you lose your details and have to contact UCAS directly, you'll be asked to log in to your application. If you are applying through a school or college then you will have a buzzword to enter (ask your UCAS adviser if you don't know what it is). This will associate your application with that school or college which will allow your reference to be uploaded by them.

2. The entire application is done online. You can complete it in stages, save, and come back to it. There are 'help' buttons by the side of most fields that need to be completed in case you get stuck.

3. Fill in the 'Personal details' section, which includes your name, address and date of birth. Some of this information will already be there from when you registered. You will also need to supply details of how your tuition will be funded, any special needs or impairments and any criminal convictions. You will also have the option of giving a parent, guardian or adviser nominated access to your application. This means that they can speak to UCAS on your behalf in case you are away or ill at crucial times, such as results day.

4. Next is an 'Additional information' section for applicants from the UK. You will need to provide information about your ethnic origin, national identity and occupational background. There are optional questions about your religious beliefs, sexual orientation and gender status. It is important to note that the information gathered here is not sent to the universities before they have made their offers, so it won't influence your application at all. It is just statistical information that universities can make use of afterwards. You will also have the opportunity in this section to provide details of your parents' education, whether you've been in care and widening participation activities such as summer schools. This information will be submitted to the universities to help them compile a fuller picture of you. Visit the UCAS website for more information (www.ucas.com/contact-us).

5. Fill in the 'Student Finance' section, which is where you have to select your fee code. Once again the help buttons will help to explain the options available if you are uncertain. If you are a British national your local authority will be your fee payer.

6. The next section is where you enter your university choices. You can apply to either Oxford or Cambridge but not both. Choose the correct university code from the drop-down menu (CAM C05 for Cambridge or OXF O33 for Oxford). You also need to add what UCAS calls the 'campus code', which is the college code. A drop-down list will appear again. You will also need to choose the subject and select which year of entry you are applying for.

7. The next section asks you for details of your education. You need to write down every GCSE and A level (or equivalent qualification) you have taken and what grade you got under the heading of the school in which you took them. If you are applying post-A level, you need to write down all of your module grades.

8. The next section is 'Employment'. This does not ask you about work experience but about paid employment. It is worth writing down even the most insignificant jobs you have done – washing dishes at the local restaurant, for example – since admissions tutors will value the commitment and maturity you will have shown when holding down a job.

9. Next is the 'Personal statement'. This is your chance to show the admissions tutors how you write and how informed you are about your subject. You should write this in a Word document, spell check it and read it through carefully; then, when it is ready, copy and paste it into the UCAS form. You have a maximum limit of 4,000 characters for your personal statement, including spaces, and the application form will automatically tell you if you have exceeded that limit and by how much.

10. Finally, send the application in the first week of October to be completed by your teachers. Your teachers may need some time to write the reference, so don't delay. If you are applying to UCAS as an individual, for example, a mature student not applying through a school or college, you will need to provide the contact details of your chosen referee (this would usually be your employer) so that they can log in to your application and fill in the reference page separately; see Chapter 8 for more details. The application fee for 2022 entry is £22 if you're applying to just one university or £26.50 for multiple courses. This must be paid by credit card (your school may have a policy of paying this for you so you need to check before you part with any money). Your teacher, Personal Tutor or Director of Studies will then be able to open your application on the advisers' part of the UCAS site. They will read it to check everything is correct and will then write their reference and your predicted grades.

11. Your teacher or adviser then needs to submit your UCAS application by 6pm on 15 October.

8 | Non-standard applications

This chapter deals with 'non-standard' applications from international students and mature students.

International students

International students are welcome at both Oxford and Cambridge and are valued members of the student population. At Cambridge, there are currently over 22,000 students (undergraduate and postgraduate) at the University, including around 9,000 international students from around 150 different countries reading undergraduate courses.

At Oxford, there are currently around 24,000 students (undergraduate and graduate) with around 10,900 students from over 160 different countries.

If you've read the previous chapters in this book, you will know that both universities offer a distinctive form of undergraduate education. Students apply for a three- or four-year degree in one to three subjects and they study those subjects exclusively. English universities typically do not have 'general education' or 'core curriculum' degrees that, for example, require humanities students to do science courses. The important admissions criterion is excellent academic promise. Oxford and Cambridge select on academic ability and academic potential, evinced by secondary school results (examination results and/or predicted grades), a personal statement, an academic reference and, if required, an admissions test or written work.

Teaching is by the tutorial/supervision system. Students attend lectures and seminars, and have practical laboratory sessions in the sciences, but the heart of the Oxbridge teaching method is a weekly meeting with the student's tutor – typically a leading academic – and one or two other students to engage in an intensive exchange of ideas about the week's work.

All Oxford and Cambridge undergraduates live, eat and study in one of the universities' residential colleges or permanent private halls. These small communities of typically 30–70 academics and 300–500 students from across disciplines are the focus for teaching and for social and sporting life.

Both universities are research intensive, where academics are conducting cutting-edge research in every subject. The collegiate system allows academics and students across subjects and year groups and from different cultures and countries to come together to share ideas.

Oxford and Cambridge qualifications are recognised and valued around the world. Graduates will go on to further study and/or to work in a range of professions in some of the best companies and organisations in the world.

In order to study at Oxford or Cambridge your level of English must be of a high standard. This is measured by your performance in various different examinations, including:

- the IELTS (International English Language Testing System), in which you need a score of at least 7.0 in each section (speaking, listening, writing and reading) and an overall score of 7.5. Oxford offers a lower score of at least 6.5 in each component and 7.0 overall for the following subjects: Computer Science, Mathematics, Mathematics and Computer Science, Mathematics and Statistics. For information about the IELTS exam and where and when it can be taken, visit www.ielts.org
- the TOEFL Internet Based Test (IBT) in which, for Cambridge, you normally need a minimum overall score of 110 with 25 or above in each element. For Oxford, you need a minimum of 110 with minimum component scores of 22 (Listening), 24 (Reading), 25 (Speaking) and 24 (Writing), except for those subjects mentioned above that require a lower IELTS score, for which you need a minimum of 100 but with the same minimum component scores of 22 (Listening), 24 (Reading), 25 (Speaking) and 24 (Writing)
- for Oxford, an English Language GCSE at grade B or grade 6. For Cambridge, you will need to enquire with your college admissions office. Please note that Oxford does not accept IGCSE English First or Second Language
- the Cambridge Certificate in Advanced English, in which, for Cambridge, you need a minimum overall score of 193, with no element lower than 185. For Oxford, you need a minimum overall score of 191 with no element lower than 185, except for those subjects mentioned above that require a lower IELTS score, for which you need a minimum overall score of 185 with no element lower than 176
- the Cambridge Certificate of Proficiency in English, in which, for Cambridge, you need a minimum overall score of 200 with no element lower than 185. For Oxford, the requirements are exactly the same as for the Cambridge Certificate in Advanced English above
- for European students a high grade in English taken as part of a leaving examination (for example the European Baccalaureate or the Abitur) may be acceptable.

For Oxford applicants it is worth noting that the following situations would exempt you from having to meet the English language requirements:

studying the International Baccalaureate (as long as it is taught in English); studying the Singapore Integrated Programme (SIPCAL); or being educated full-time in English for the duration of the two most recent years prior to the 15 October application deadline, and staying in full-time education taught in English in your country until the end of the academic year. Cambridge is also willing to consider the SIPCAL.

The level of English proficiency required depends a great deal on which subject you wish to study. If you want to apply for an essay-based subject (any of the arts or social science subjects, including Economics, PPE, Psychology, History and English Literature), your written work must be fluent. On the other hand, English Language is much less important for the study of Mathematics. (See www.ox.ac.uk/admissions/undergraduate/applying-to-oxford/for-international-students/ELR and www.undergraduate.study.cam.ac.uk/international-students/english-language-requirements for further details.)

How much does it cost?

As an international student there are three costs you'll need to consider. These are your tuition fees, college fees and living expenses.

You will have to prove that you can finance yourself for your entire course as it's not possible for you to work during the academic session to pay your way through university. Colleges ask for financial guarantees and proof is also required when applying for a visa.

Following the UK's departure from the EU, EU nationals will no longer be eligible to pay fees at the Home rate and will instead pay the same fees as overseas/international students. The only exceptions to this are Irish nationals living in the UK or Ireland, who will continue to pay the Home rate. This will mean a considerable increase in fees for EU nationals as the overseas rate is much higher than the Home rate. As detailed in Chapter 4, the basic Home rate for students is £9,250 with the international rate at Oxford varying between £27,840 and £48,600 and at Cambridge varying between £22,227 and £58,038. (See page 49 for more details.) For more information go to the following websites.

Cambridge:
- international students: www.undergraduate.study.cam.ac.uk/international-students
- financial issues for international students: www.undergraduate.study.cam.ac.uk/international-students/international-fees-and-costs.

Oxford:
- Student Information and Advisory Service: www.ox.ac.uk/students/new/international
- official site, including entrance requirements, international qualifications, etc.: www.ox.ac.uk/admissions/undergraduate/applying-to-oxford/for-international-students

* fees for international students: www.ox.ac.uk/students/fees-funding/search/undergraduate.

College fees

At Cambridge, all overseas-fee status students, and those Home students who are not eligible for tuition fee support (e.g. because they are taking a second degree), normally have to pay college fees in addition to university tuition fees and their living expenses. The college fee covers the cost to your college of providing a range of educational, domestic and pastoral services and support. At Cambridge, for the academic year 2021–22, the fees are £11,328 (for full details for each college, visit www.undergraduate.study.cam.ac.uk/files/publications/undergraduate_tuition_fees_2022-23.pdf). At Oxford, there is no separate college fee.

Living expenses

Your living expenses may be higher than for a UK student, for instance if you have to stay in Oxford or Cambridge or the UK during the vacations. The Oxford website suggests that between £14,190 and £20,520 will be needed for a calendar year (these figures include accommodation). It provides a breakdown on these figures at www.ox.ac.uk/students/fees-funding/living-costs.

The Cambridge website (www.undergraduate.study.cam.ac.uk/international-students/international-fees-and-costs) advises that the minimum resources needed per year are estimated to be approximately £11,230 (figure for 2020–21). Of course, many international students are likely to spend more money travelling to and from their home countries.

Making an application

Oxford and Cambridge require international students to complete a UCAS application in the same way as Home students. Cambridge requires most international applicants to pay an administration fee of £60. There are exceptions for those applying from low-income countries. For full details, see www.undergraduate.study.cam.ac.uk/international-students/international-applications.

Overseas applicants must go through the same stages as non-overseas applicants: submitting a UCAS form, taking aptitude tests or admissions assessments, submitting written work, and so on. They should check the conditions for overseas applications imposed by their chosen university, course and college to see whether there are exceptions.

The interview

The Covid-19 pandemic that is still affecting the UK at the time of writing has meant that both Oxford and Cambridge have been conducting all interviews online. It is unclear what will happen in 2022 and 2023.

It is very much to be hoped that things will have returned to normal, but it is possible that, even if they have, Oxford and Cambridge will continue to interview some or all applicants online. What you will find below are the policies both universities have followed in recent years. You will need to check the universities' websites nearer to the time to get the latest details.

Shortlisted applicants to Oxford from the EU, the non-EU EEA countries Norway, Iceland and Liechtenstein, and from Switzerland must be present in person for the interview. Colleges may decide to conduct virtual interviews with students from outside these countries. You should be aware, though, that you have no entitlement to such an arrangement and they may therefore request that you be present in person. The one course exception is Medicine, for which all applicants must be present in person irrespective of country of residence.

Cambridge's policy with EU countries, the non-EU EEA countries and Switzerland follows Oxford's: shortlisted applicants must be present in person for an interview. For students outside of these countries, Cambridge holds a series of overseas interview schemes. For 2019 entry, Cambridge conducted interviews in Canada (Toronto), PR China (Shanghai), Hong Kong, India (Mumbai), Malaysia (Kuala Lumpur), Singapore and the USA (New York, via video-conferencing software) for those applicants who were unable to travel to Cambridge. However, it is always worth checking with the colleges to which you are applying, as colleges have the right to choose their own interview policy and may require shortlisted applicants to be present in person. For full details, visit: www.undergraduate.study.cam.ac.uk/international-students/overseas-interviews.

Admissions tests

Pre-interview aptitude tests and admissions assessments will take place on the same day for students overseas. For students applying for a course that has an at-interview assessment, then, if this is also a course for which remote interviewing is possible, you will sit the test at the same time as your remote interview. For full details see www.ox.ac.uk/admissions/undergraduate/international-students/test-arrangements-international-students and www.undergraduate.study.cam.ac.uk/international-students/overseas-interviews.

Mature students

A mature student at Oxford or Cambridge is classed as anyone over 21 at the start of October in their first year. Both universities welcome applications from mature students and, like everyone else who wishes to join these highly selective institutions, candidates will need to demonstrate academic ability and a firm commitment to study.

Your work experience and life skills will be considered to be relevant to your application but you must have also undertaken some type of formal academic qualifications within the three years before you apply. You will need to prove to your tutors that you will be able to cope with the demands of academic study and that you have sufficient study skills to commit to an undergraduate degree course. Many different academic qualifications are acceptable. For further information on the qualifications you would need to apply, please consult the universities' websites. Mature students, too, must submit their application through UCAS.

Cambridge

Mature applicants to Cambridge can apply to all colleges, of which three are for mature students only: Hughes Hall, St Edmund's and Wolfson. Students applying to a non-mature-student college or making an open application must submit their application by the usual 15 October 2022 deadline. The three mature-student colleges have an additional second application round for which the deadline is 8 March 2023, but only for some courses. The conditions for the 2022 cycle have not yet been published, but for the 2021 application cycle, applicants for the following courses at the mature-student colleges had to submit them by the 15 October deadline:

- Architecture
- Chemical Engineering
- Computer Science
- Engineering
- History of Art
- Medicine
- Graduate Course in Medicine
- Law*
- Music
- Natural Sciences
- Philosophy
- Veterinary Medicine

(*Wolfson requires students to submit applications to read law in the first round; Hughes Hall and St Edmund's allow students to apply in either round.)

Applicants for the following courses must take the relevant pre-interview assessment:

- Chemical Engineering
- Computer Science
- Engineering
- Medicine
- Natural Sciences
- Veterinary Medicine

Applicants for Economics, English and Land Economy will not take the standard pre-interview assessments, but a common format written assessment at interview instead. However, if you are an overseas student applying for Economics, English or Land Economy and wish to be considered for interview, or if you're a mature student applying to a standard-age college, you must take the required pre-interview assessment, for which you must be registered in advance. See www.undergraduate.study.cam.ac.uk/why-cambridge/support/mature-students/mature-student-applications for more detail.

Oxford

At Oxford, the application process for mature students is the same as for other students. Mature students can apply to any college that offers their course, but can also apply to Harris Manchester College or Wycliffe Hall, which are graduate only. (Note that Wycliffe Hall only offers the BA in Theology and Religion and the BA in Philosophy and Theology.) Mature applicants must sit the admissions tests, though may be exempt from submitting written work if they have been out of education for a while; applicants are advised to contact the college to which they are applying to discuss the matter. See www.ox.ac.uk/admissions/undergraduate/applying-to-oxford/mature-students for more information.

International mature students

Mature students from outside the UK should check carefully the information for international students. In particular, if they are planning to bring their family, they should examine the conditions under which their dependants will be eligible for a visa. See www.ox.ac.uk/students/visa/before/family and www.internationalstudents.cam.ac.uk/dependant-visas.

Mature students can get information and advice from the admissions offices, as well as details about events and activities run by the universities for prospective mature applicants. See the following websites for more information:

* www.ox.ac.uk/students/new/mature
* www.undergraduate.study.cam.ac.uk/why-cambridge/support/mature-students
* www.ucas.com/undergraduate/applying-university/mature-undergraduate-students.

Transfer and second-degree students

Oxford does not accept transfer students under any circumstances and Cambridge would only consider them under exceptional circumstances. However, you can apply to take a second undergraduate degree at both universities, and there is the option to apply to shorten your time by entering the course in the second year.

At Cambridge, such students are known as 'affiliate students'. They cannot make open applications and they cannot apply for Architecture, History and Modern Languages or History and Politics. Individual colleges may have their own further restrictions. Furthermore, only Lucy Cavendish, St. Edmund's and Wolfson colleges consider affiliate applications for Medicine and Veterinary Medicine. For more details, visit www.undergraduate.study.cam.ac.uk/why-cambridge/support/mature-students/second-undergraduate-degrees.

At Oxford, such students are known as those with 'senior status'. Hertford, New College, St Hilda's and Somerville do not offer senior status, and individual colleges may not offer it for all their courses. Applicants for Fine Art and Law with Law Studies in Europe may not apply for senior status. For more information, visit www.ox.ac.uk/admissions/undergraduate/applying-to-oxford/second-undergraduate-degree.

Lady Margaret Hall Foundation Year

The Lady Margaret Hall Foundation Year has been designed to enable students from under-represented backgrounds to have a chance of higher education at the University of Oxford. The development of academic skills is emphasised and each year a small number of students are given the chance to make an application to LMH for degree courses.

Students eligible to apply for the Foundation Year must meet the following criteria:

- have attended a UK state school for their entire school career
- have Home fee status
- come from a household with a combined income below £42,875
- belong to socio-economic groups 4–8 (calculated based on parental occupations) OR belong to socio-economic group 3 AND have parents with no qualification at undergraduate degree level or higher (or equivalent).

Further details on the application process can be found at the website www.lmh.ox.ac.uk/prospective-students/foundation-year and www.lmh.ox.ac.uk/prospective-students/foundation-year/lmh-foundation-year-students/what-foundation-year/eligibility.

PART III

Tests, Interviews & Beyond

9 | Succeeding in written tests

Applicants to Oxford and Cambridge will typically have excellent GCSE grades and be expected to achieve top A level grades. Admissions tutors need a lot more to work with to determine which students will be offered places. This chapter aims to give an account of the various written tests students face prior to or during their interviews, including the deadlines for registering for the exams; when and where the tests are sat; details about the structure of the tests, including knowledge requirements; sample questions; and useful links for more information and practice.

The majority of courses at both universities require applicants to sit admissions tests. They should take place in your school. If your school is not a registered examination centre or if you are applying as an independent candidate, you will need to find a centre where you can sit them (visit www.admissionstesting.org/find-a-centre for help). All of Oxford's tests take place around the start of November, a month before the interviews begin. Applicants for Cambridge will either sit their test at the same time as Oxford applicants or during the December interview period. The Oxbridge tests aim to measure the natural intelligence and academic potential of the candidate and, in doing so, widen access. Since it is often difficult to revise for the Oxbridge written tests, students have to rely on their innate intellectual ability to complete them. In theory, students whose schools have provided less preparation should not be disadvantaged, although it can help to have at least some understanding of what the tests entail.

The style of testing also differs from what many school leavers will be used to. Whereas A levels often test factual recall, the Oxbridge written exams look for analytical and critical capabilities. It should be noted, therefore, that these tests are likely to be much harder than anything you will have experienced at school. This is taken into consideration, and admissions tutors do not expect students to achieve 100%.

The following university websites provide links to all the tests you would be required to take for certain subjects:

- www.ox.ac.uk/admissions/undergraduate/applying-to-oxford/ guide/admissions-tests
- www.undergraduate.study.cam.ac.uk/applying/admissions-assessments.

Testing happens at various stages during the application process. Some tests are sat around the beginning of November at your school. The date for 2022 is 2 November. The results of these tests can then play a part in determining whether you are called to interview. Some tests take place when you go up for interview in early December. The results are then used, alongside your interview performance, your personal statement, your school references and your exam grades, to decide whether you should be made a conditional offer.

Don't let taking these tests put you off applying. If you are serious about wanting a place at a top university, you should be able to do well without masses of additional tuition or extra work. It is very important, however, to go online and get full details of what the tests entail and to do some practice papers if they are offered.

Oxford admissions tests

The schedule of tests for 2023 entry should be as shown below.

1 August 2022

- LNAT registration begins. For Oxford, you must register for the test from 15 September and the deadline for sitting it is 15 October.

1 October 2022

- Deadline date for registering for the BMAT. If you register between 2 October and 6pm on 15 October, you will pay a late fee.

15 October 2022

- 6pm is the final deadline for registering for Oxford admissions assessments and Cambridge pre-interview assessments.
- Closing date for all UCAS applications to Oxford and Cambridge.
- Closing date for applications for the accelerated medical course.

2 November 2022

- BMAT: Aptitude Test for Biomedical Sciences and Medicine. (NB If you are applying for the graduate Medicine course, you have the option of taking the BMAT in September.)
- CAT: Admissions test for Classics. Students applying for the joint courses Classics and English, Classics and Modern Languages or Classics with Oriental Studies are also required to take the test.
- ELAT: Aptitude Test for English Language and Literature. Students applying for the joint courses Classics and English or English and Modern Languages must also take the ELAT. Students applying for History and English do not need to sit the ELAT.
- HAT: Aptitude Test for History, History (Ancient and Modern). Students applying for the joint courses History and Economics,

History and English, History and Modern Languages or History and Politics must also take the test.

- MAT: Aptitude Test for Mathematics and for Computer Science. Students applying for the joint courses Computer Science and Philosophy, Mathematics and Computer Science, Mathematics and Philosophy or Mathematics and Statistics must also take the MAT.
- MLAT: Aptitude test for all Modern Languages courses. Students applying for the joint courses Classics and Modern Languages, English and Modern Languages, European and Middle Eastern Languages, History and Modern Languages, Modern Languages and Linguistics or Philosophy and Modern Languages must also take the MLAT.
- OLAT: Aptitude Test for oriental studies for students whose course combinations include Arabic, Hebrew, Jewish Studies, Persian or Turkish as part of one of the following courses: Oriental Studies, Classics and Oriental Studies, European and Middle Eastern Languages, and Religion and Oriental Studies.
- PAT: Aptitude Test for Physics, Engineering Science and Materials Science. Students applying for the joint course Physics and Philosophy must also take the PAT.
- Philosophy Test: Admissions Test for Philosophy and Theology. If you are applying for Modern Languages and Philosophy, check on the Oxford website which papers are required for your course.
- TSA: Thinking Skills Assessment for Experimental Psychology, Geography, Human Sciences, PPE (Philosophy, Politics and Economics) and PPL (Psychology, Philosophy and Linguistics). Applicants for Economics and Management and for History and Economics sit Section 1 of the TSA only.

If you are applying for Fine Art or Music and are called to interview, you will be asked to complete a practical test at interview. Applicants for Law with Law Studies in Europe applying for the French, German, Italian or Spanish options may be given an oral test in the relevant foreign language at interview.

There are no written tests for Archaeology and Anthropology, Biochemistry, Biological Sciences, Classical Archaeology and Ancient History, Earth Sciences (Geology), History of Art or Theology and Religion.

Cambridge admissions tests

Cambridge has common-format tests, which students must either take pre-interview (for 2022, the date is 2 November) or at interview (if shortlisted for interview). There are no common-format assessments for Mathematics and Music. Students applying for Mathematics are required to take the Sixth Term Examination Paper (STEP) in June; this is either one or two three-hour mathematics exams taken at the end of the A level exam period to test advanced problem solving and mathematical ingenuity rather than basic knowledge and technique. However, Mathematics and Computer Science applicants who are interviewed overseas will be given a written mathematics assessment. Music applicants will be asked to complete short tasks at interview, if called to interview.

Courses with a pre-interview written assessment

- Chemical Engineering: students studying Chemical Engineering via Engineering must sit the Engineering Admissions Assessment (ENGAA). Students studying Chemical Engineering via Natural Sciences must sit the Natural Sciences Admissions Assessment (NSAA). Some colleges may also ask you to take the STEP.
- Computer Science: Cambridge Test of Mathematics for University Admission (CTMUA).
- Economics: Economics Admissions Assessment (ECAA).
- Engineering: Engineering Admissions Assessment (ENGAA). Some colleges may also ask you to take the STEP.
- English: ELAT.
- Land Economy: TSA Section 1.
- Medicine: BMAT.
- Natural Sciences: Natural Sciences Admissions Assessment (NSAA).
- Veterinary Medicine: Natural Sciences Admissions Assessment (NSAA).

The pre-interview tests have two sections: a multiple-choice section (lasting around an hour) and longer-answer section (also lasting about an hour). For more details, visit www.admissionstesting.org/for-test-takers/cambridge-pre-interview-assessments.

Courses with an at-interview written assessment

- Archaeology
- Architecture
- Classics
- History and Modern Languages
- History of Art
- Law
- Linguistics
- Modern and Medieval Languages (MML)
- Philosophy
- Theology, Religion and Philosophy of Religion

Courses for which some colleges may set an at-interview assessment

- Anglo-Saxon, Norse and Celtic Studies
- Asian and Middle Eastern Studies
- Education
- Geography
- History
- History and Politics
- Human, Social and Political Sciences
- Mathematics
- Music
- Psychological and Behavioural Sciences

For details of what the tests involve, visit www.undergraduate.study.cam.ac.uk/applying/admissions-assessments/at-interview.

Some tips for taking specialist tests

- Remember that Oxford and Cambridge have designed these tests to try to give them another tool to differentiate between students. They are looking for those who are most academically suited to their courses. You should not need to spend hours preparing to take these tests; in fact, if you need to undertake an enormous amount of preparation, it is arguable that you may not be an appropriate candidate.
- The universities give a full description of what the specialist tests entail on their websites:
  - www.ox.ac.uk/admissions/undergraduate/applying-to-oxford/guide/tests
  - www.undergraduate.study.cam.ac.uk/applying/admission-assessments.
- Past papers or sample questions are available for all tests and it is vital that you practise some of these in mock exam conditions to familiarise yourself with the format of the tests and the time constraints on the test. Some sample questions are included below from a selection of admissions tests used by both universities.
- Do not be upset if you can't answer all the questions. The tests are devised to be stretching and it is important not to panic if you come across something unfamiliar. It is often how you approach a particular problem that will be considered rather than if you actually get a 'correct' answer.

Specimen papers for Oxbridge tests

Have a go at the following sample BMAT practice questions.

BMAT® Thinking Skills Practice Questions

DIRECTIONS (for full test):
Answer every question. Points are awarded for correct answers only. There are no penalties for incorrect answers. All questions are worth 1 mark.

1   You can only take the practical driving test after passing the theory test. You have failed the theory test, so you cannot take your practical test.

   Which one of the following most closely parallels the reasoning used in the above argument?

   A   You need to have lived in the UK for 5 years to become a citizen. You have lived in the UK for 5 years, so you will not be refused citizenship.

   B   People who are good at mathematics are likely to be good at music. You are good at mathematics, so you should learn to play a musical instrument.

   C   Pacifists refuse to fight in wars or join armies. You refuse to fight in wars or join an army, so you are a pacifist.

   D   To enter China you need a visa. You don't have a visa, so you cannot enter China.

   E   Smoking is bad for your health and can cause heart and lung problems. You smoke, so you will have heart and lung problems.

2   We have just installed a new boiler in our house. It has cost £4700 to install, but it will last for 9 years before it needs replacing. Nevertheless, the supplier assures us that it will cut our heating costs by 30%. This is good news as we currently pay, on average, £500 every quarter year. The supplier insists that it will pay for itself (i.e. save enough money to cover the cost of the purchase, before it needs replacing).

   How long will the boiler take to pay for itself?

   A   31 quarters

   B   32 quarters

   C   33 quarters

   D   34 quarters

   E   35 quarters

BMAT® Scientific Knowledge and Applications Practice Questions

DIRECTIONS (for full test):

Answer every question. Points are awarded for correct answers only. There are no penalties for incorrect answers. All questions are worth 1 mark. Some questions have more than 1 correct answer. Read carefully to ensure that you select the appropriate number of answers. Calculators are not permitted during any portion of the test.

3. A supermarket has a large open-topped deep freezer to keep products frozen but still visible to customers.

Which statement about the air in this freezer explains why the products remain frozen, even though it is open-topped?

A The temperature difference between the air inside and outside the freezer is too large for heat to enter the freezer.

B The temperature difference between the air inside and outside the freezer is too small for heat to enter the freezer.

C The warm air above the freezer is denser than cold air inside the freezer.

D The cold air inside the freezer is denser than the hot air above the freezer.

E The products inside the freezer trap the cold air so it cannot escape.

4. Which one of the following is a simplification of:

$$2 - \frac{2x+1}{4x^2 + 4x + 1}$$

A $\dfrac{4x+1}{2x+1}$

B $\dfrac{4x+3}{2x+1}$

C $\dfrac{4x+9}{2x+5}$

D $\dfrac{8x^2 + 4x + 1}{4x^2 + 2x + 1}$

E $\dfrac{8x^2 + 4x + 1}{4x^2 + 2x + 2}$

BMAT® Writing Practice Questions

DIRECTIONS (for full test):

YOU MUST COMPLETE ONLY ONE OF THE FOLLOWING TASKS
Please indicate which task (1, 2 or 3) you have chosen in the 'Task Chosen' box on the answer sheet.

Each of the tasks consists of a statement in bold followed by three prompts. It is important that you address all three parts of your chosen task.

1 **'Power tends to corrupt, and absolute power corrupts absolutely.' (John Dalberg-Acton)**

   Explain the reasoning behind this statement. Argue that power does not necessarily degrade or weaken the morals of those who hold it. To what extent is it possible for someone to hold power without using it for their own personal gain?

2 **Science and art once collaborated as equals to further human knowledge about the world. Today, science is far too advanced and specialised to work together with the arts for this purpose.**

   Explain what you think is meant by the statement. Argue that science and the arts can still work together to further understanding of the world. To what extent do you agree with the statement?

3 **There are now many different kinds of internet sites and apps offering medical advice, but they all share one thing in common: they do more harm than good.**

   Why might online sources of medical advice be said to 'do more harm than good'? Present a counter-argument. To what extent do you agree with the statement?

BMAT Thinking Skills Answers

1. D

2. B

BMAT Scientific Knowledge and Applications Answers

3. D

4. A

Source: www.admissionstesting.org/for-test-takers/bmat/
preparing-for-bmat/practice-papers/

TSA Oxford Section 1 sample questions and answers

1 The 21st century is witnessing a significant rise in the proportion of people being diagnosed by medical professionals as having a mental illness. For example, at the turn of the century, the number of Canadians being treated for depression increased by over 30% in just one year. A recent study in the US found that nearly twice the number of young people there were diagnosed with a mental disorder in 2018 as compared to 2003. The World Health Organization estimates that by 2028, depression will be the second leading type of disability worldwide. It is clear that aspects of the modern world make it more difficult for people to maintain good mental health.

Which one of the following is the best statement of the flaw in the above argument?

A Changes in health care and a decrease in stigma attached to mental illness may be responsible for higher diagnosis rates.

B Many people with a mental health diagnosis may be able to function well in society.

C Significant numbers of people may be hesitant to seek help for mental health concerns from doctors or other medical professionals.

D Some physical and behavioural factors may make mental health diagnoses more difficult.

E In some cultures people may prefer to seek help for mental health concerns from religious leaders as opposed to doctors.

2 In the game of tigball, two teams compete against each other to try to score points.

Points are scored as follows:

A 'penalty' scores 5 points.
A 'tigdown' scores 8 points.
A 'transformation' scores 3 points, but teams only have the opportunity to achieve a transformation after scoring a tigdown.

There are no other ways of scoring points.

Which of the following is the only one that is a possible scoreline in the game of tigball?

A 9–23

B 11–21

C 12–20

D 13–14

E 15–17

Answers

1. A

2. B

TSA Oxford Section 2 sample questions

YOU MUST ANSWER ONLY ONE OF THE FOLLOWING QUESTIONS.

1 Loss of schooling has a serious impact on children's lives; attending school during a pandemic may risk the health of other people through encouraging virus spread. Is there a rational method of balancing these concerns?

2 What is the best way to handle those aspects of the legacy of history which we deeply regret?

3 Are there moral questions that science can help us to answer?

4 Does the response to the COVID-19 pandemic make serious political action on climate and environmental issues any more or any less likely?

TSA sample questions are reproduced with kind permission of Cambridge Assessment: Admissions Testing, a non-teaching department of the University of Cambridge.

Source: www.admissionstestingservice.org/for-test-takers/ thinking-skills-assessment/tsa-oxford/preparing-for-tsa-oxford.

10| Surviving the interview

About four to eight weeks after you have submitted your application, a letter will drop through your door and you will usually be sent an email from the college you have applied to. However, do bear in mind that due to the pooling system you could be receiving a letter or email from a different college, so do read all correspondence carefully. At this stage you will find out whether you have been called for interview.

If you haven't, don't despair. There's always next year or another university. It's really not the end of the world.

If you have been called for interview – congratulations! Now make the most of the opportunity presented to you and do your preparation to make the experience a positive one.

Prepare properly: the practicalities

If you live a long distance from the universities or have an exam to take, the college may ask you to stay over the night before the interview. Being in college for a night or even a few days will give you an opportunity to meet some of the current students and other candidates and, while you may find it hard to get a good night's sleep in a strange bed, you should try to make the most of the experience. Some interviews may also be spread over the course of an entire day, especially if they entail some form of assessment test in addition to the actual interview, so give yourself plenty of time to get there and be prepared. Although it may be a stressful situation for you, try to relax and have fun. Not many people will get to sit these interviews at world leading universities, so congratulate yourself for being in that position and try to make the most of the experience.

Leave plenty of time to get to your first appointment

Arrive at least half an hour earlier than you planned to. You do not want to turn up stressed and sweating. Transport links to both universities are excellent and generally reliable but it's always worth assuming the worst-case scenario and arriving with plenty of time to spare.

Print off a map

Double check that you know your college's location and make sure you have enough money to get a taxi in case you arrive late or get lost.

Have the phone number of the admissions office

Save it on your mobile and write it down (in case your battery runs out) so you can let them know if you're delayed. It is also worth having the number of the Porters' Lodge as you will normally be required to report to them upon arrival for your interview. Each individual college will have its own Porters' Lodge so make sure you know the number for the college you have applied to before your arrival.

Know where your interview is taking place

When you arrive and are given the location of your interview room, go and find out exactly where it is. Oxbridge colleges can be confusing to navigate and many a candidate has arrived 10 minutes late to a 20-minute interview because they couldn't locate the right staircase. Be warned and be prepared. You can often find very good instructions online as to how to get around the colleges usually from students who have been for interviews before.

Dress as if you've made an effort

You don't have to wear a suit but you should look clean and not scruffy. Oxbridge colleges can be cold in December (or overheated). It's best to err on the safe side and bring clothes to cover both eventualities.

Make sure you have a book, some money for food, and a charged phone (plus your phone charger)

You may spend a lot of time waiting around. As already mentioned, some of the interviews and assessments can be spread over an entire day. For Oxford interviews, you may be seen by several different colleges over a number of days. The cities are expensive and you really don't want to run out of money.

Don't relax too much!

If you meet up with friends, please don't go out and party. You will not do well at your interview the next morning and tutors will be predictably unsympathetic if you turn up the worse for wear.

Prepare properly: the interview

There's no real mystery about what you are likely to be asked at the interview. The tutors are looking for the best-qualified candidates; people whom they will enjoy teaching and who will make a contribution to their academic department. The interview is a means of assessing your intellectual potential. It is not a test of knowledge but a chance for them to see how well you think on your feet. The tutorial system is not for everyone and it is important for you and the tutors to see whether you will feel comfortable discussing ideas in a small group on a regular basis.

When did you last read your personal statement?

You may not remember all the books that you said you had devoured but the tutor interviewing you will. You are **very** likely to be asked questions about your personal statement, so take a copy with you and be sure you know what you wrote in it. The same applies to any written work and any supplementary answers that you submitted. Make sure you have copies with you and re-read them before the interview.

Do you really know your subject?

Have you read the 'Introduction to ...' on the university and college's website? Have you read around your subject beyond the obvious choices? What else have you done that proves your interest in your subject? Once again your personal statement should reflect your motivation to study on the course that you have applied for and also tell the university what you have done to move a few steps closer to realising that ambition.

Is your body language right?

During mock interviews, practise walking into a room, looking your interviewer in the eyes, smiling and saying hello and shaking their hand. When you are called in to the interview room for real, try to greet your interviewers confidently even if you're feeling very nervous. Sit forward in your seat and look interested. You will score no extra points for slouching or seeming bored. Some candidates will even go as far as to try a technique called 'mirroring' where you copy the body language of the person interviewing you and this helps to build a rapport. Many interviewers will be wise to this technique, and please don't do it every single time, but they may be impressed that you've made the effort to impress them. These techniques are secondary so please don't try them at the expense of forgetting about your personal statement or giving an honest portrayal of yourself.

Do you know the sort of questions you may be asked?

First of all, don't worry about the apocryphal bizarre Oxbridge questions. Some of the strange questions you hear about will have occurred in the context of a particular discussion and may have made perfect sense at the time! Most of the questions asked will be about your A level subjects, any super-curricular activities in which you have engaged and other topics that should give you an opportunity to show your abilities. There is a list of questions below that have been asked by tutors over the past few years. It's useful to look at them to give you an idea of the type of questions that might come up, but that's all. You are much more likely to be asked a straightforward question about your subject than any of the ones on this list.

It's also important to read a decent newspaper and keep up to date with current affairs. You may be asked your opinion on something in the news, so it's definitely worth brushing up your knowledge of current affairs in preparation by reading newspapers or journals, or by listening to appropriate podcasts.

What happens if I can't answer their question?

Don't panic. There will often be no 'right' answer to whatever question you've been given. It's perfectly okay to ask for a few seconds to think about what you're going to say; something along the lines of 'That's an interesting question. Can I have a few moments to consider my answer?' makes you seem thoughtful, not desperate. In most cases the interviewer may not be looking for a particular answer to a question. It is often more about how you approach and think about the question rather than whether you can get a correct answer or not. The admissions tutors will be looking to pursue an intellectual conversation with you and so will look to see how you strike a balance between defending your answer in the face of their objections and adjusting your position when you recognise it is no longer sensibly defensible.

This, of course, is not so for the more obvious questions, so really think through and rehearse the answers to these questions as even strong candidates can fail to give convincing answers.

- Why do you want to read your subject?
- What is it about the course that interests you? (Do you know the structure of the course – not just the plan for the first year but for the later years too?)
- Why bother studying the subject at university? (This is a question it is very tempting to ask medical students who talk of their love of caring and modern language students who talk of their love of being able to switch into a different language. If caring interests you, then why not choose one of the many other related and valuable professions, such as nursing? If speaking a different language every day thrills you, why not simply move overseas and get a job?)

- What are the last three novels you have read?
- What are the last three books on your subject that you have read?
- What makes you more deserving of a place than the other five candidates applying for your place?

Remember, no tutor will be trying to make you feel small, trick you or humiliate you. A good interviewer will allow you to demonstrate your interest in your subject and your academic potential. They are most interested in your ability to think logically and express your ideas orally. If you can show how you are thinking and that you can think 'on your feet', that is more important than always getting the right answer. Remember that in certain subjects, there may not necessarily be a 'right answer' anyway. In mathematical and science subjects, how you are attempting to work out problems or how you are working out the answer while you are attempting to solve a problem could be equally important.

The big day

So the moment's finally arrived. What exactly will happen at the interview? Every experience can be different. Some colleges use a panel of interviewers, sometimes you will have consecutive interviews conducted by one individual (often the college admissions tutor, followed by one with a subject specialist) and sometimes interviewers do them in tandem.

In most cases two interviews is the standard but extra interviews may be given, or you may be sent to another college. Again, it varies.

The format will vary widely depending on subject. For some subjects (e.g. English) you may be given some prose or poetry to read before you go into your interview. You will then be asked questions on this by the tutors, who may then want to discuss the content of your personal statement – such as books you've mentioned reading or poetry you've enjoyed. For science subjects this is less common, and it is more likely that you will be given problems to solve or questions to answer. Generally these are designed to require no specific prior knowledge.

You may also be asked to attend a 'general' or 'college' interview. This is conducted by interviewers who don't teach your subject. It is possible that one of the purposes of this interview will be to see how you'll fit in with the college atmosphere and whether you are a well-rounded person who will be an asset to the college. You may be asked questions on your personal statement, about a topic of interest in the news or about your enthusiasm for your chosen subject.

Below are some examples of the sort of questions you may be asked and some students' experiences at their interviews. The case studies presented earlier in this book also cover some of the interview questions asked and how students responded to them. The University of Oxford also provides sample questions by course and these should be checked for updates when you apply at www.ox.ac.uk/admissions/undergraduate/applying-to-oxford/guide/interviews. Although the University of Cambridge does not have a list of sample questions in the same way, it does give more general advice on how you should prepare for your interview here: www.undergraduate.study.cam.ac.uk/applying/interviews/how-should-i-prepare.

General interview questions

- What made you want to study this subject?
- Excluding your A level reading, what were the last three books you read?
- What do you regard as your strengths and weaknesses?
- What extra-curricular activities would you like to take part in at this college?
- Why did you make an 'open application'?
- Give us three reasons why we should offer you a place.
- What will you do if we don't offer you a place?
- Why did you choose your A level subjects?
- How will this degree help in your chosen career?
- What are you intending to do in your gap year?
- Where do you see yourself in five years' time?
- How would your friends describe you?
- Tell us why we should accept you.
- Why have you chosen Cambridge and not Oxford (and vice versa)?

Subject-specific interview questions

Archaeology

- Why do civilisations erect monuments?
- What does Stonehenge mean to you?
- Being given an object and being told where it was found, then being asked what you could deduce from the object.
- Discussing an archaeological find.

Archaeology and Anthropology

- Name the six major world religions.
- What are the problems regarding objectivity in anthropological studies?
- Why should we approach all subjects from a holistic, anthropological perspective?

See also the Archaeology questions and the HSPS questions.

Architecture

A large part of the interview is likely to be dedicated to discussing your portfolio. Be prepared to discuss the ideas, purposes and motivations behind your work. Your work should also illustrate a well-developed ability to relate two- and three-dimensional experience through drawing and 3D models. Be aware that portfolio requirements can vary from college to college and it is advisable that you check the relevant college's website at www.undergraduate.study.cam.ac.uk/colleges/college-contacts. You should also be prepared to discuss your work experience. Below are some other questions that might be asked.

- Is architecture in decline?
- Could you describe a building that you recently found interesting?
- Do you have an architect whom you particularly admire? What is it about their work that you find attractive?
- If you could design a building anywhere in the world, and if money, space and time were unlimited, what would you design?

Biochemistry

For most questions related to biochemistry it is again not a final answer that interviewers are looking for and they will often understand if students say that they don't know the answer to a question. Once again it is how the candidate approaches the problem that will be assessed. The interviewers would expect a hypothesis to be built which can then be tested using the student's own knowledge. This will form the basis of a more detailed discussion that will test the student to see if they can come to a plausible answer. This approach is generally true of all of the science subjects.

- How do catalysts work?
- Describe the work of enzymes.
- Discuss the chemistry of the formation of proteins.
- Questions on oxidation, equilibria and interatomic forces.
- Questions on X-ray crystallography.
- Why do you wish to read biochemistry rather than chemistry?
- What scientific journals have you read lately? Is there a recent development in the field that particularly interests you?
- Why does most biochemistry take place away from equilibrium? (Or, how important is equilibrium to biochemical processes?)

Biology/Biomedical Sciences

- How does the immune system recognise invading pathogens as foreign cells?
- How does a cell stop itself from exploding due to osmosis?
- Why is carbon of such importance in living systems?
- How would you transfer a gene to a plant?
- Explain the mechanism of capillary action.

- What are the advantages of the human genome project?
- How would you locate a gene for a given characteristic in the nucleus of a cell?
- What is the major problem with heart transplants in the receiver?
- Should we be concerned about GMOs? Why or why not?
- Do cellular processes take place at equilibrium?
- How important are primary electrogenic pumps for transmembrane ion transport of organic molecules? Why are these important?
- Why do plants, fungi and bacteria utilise H+ gradients to energise their membranes whereas animals utilise Na+ gradients?
- Discuss a given picture of an abnormal chromosome sequence.
- Discuss a given graph showing the amount of a particular virus and the changes in T cells in the body over 12 years.

Chemistry

- Questions on carboxylic acids.
- Questions on mechanisms in reactions of electrophiles and nucleophiles.
- Questions on organic mechanisms.
- Questions on structure, bonding and energetics.
- Questions on acids and bases.
- Questions on isomerisation.
- Questions on practical chemical analysis.
- Describe the properties of solvents and mechanisms of solvation.

See also Biochemistry questions (page 152).

Classics

Interviewers would generally not ask questions on texts unless the student has specifically said that they have read them first either in the interview or in their personal statement. The interviewer may instead ask the candidate to talk about a piece of classical literature they have enjoyed and develop their questioning on the basis of that piece so it is important that you have some texts in mind and have something pertinent to say about them as your interviewer is going to be an expert in anything that you may have read and more.

- What are the defining characteristics of Latin and Ancient Greek?
- Which language do you prefer and why?
- Is ancient history simply 'the biographies of great men'?
- What, if anything, can the politics of the Late Republic tell us about politics in modern Britain?
- Defend the view that Plato was an embittered fascist.
- 'Virgil's Aeneid supports the regime of a fascist dictator.' Discuss.
- To what extent would you blame the Senate for the downfall of the Roman Republic in the 1st century BC?
- Was fifth-century Athenian democracy parasitic on slavery? Or on empire?

- To what extent do you agree with the view that Cicero was a self-serving hypocrite?
- Why did (virtually) no one oppose slavery in the ancient world?
- Select two or three similes from Homer that you particularly like and explain why.
- Discuss the view that Homer's use of direct speech in his epics makes Attic tragedy possible.
- How do you account for the forceful heroines of Greek tragedy, given the vigorous suppression of women in fifth-century Athens?
- What is the point of studying Latin/Ancient Greek/Ancient History/Classics?
- Do you have a hero or heroine from the ancient world, literature included?
- Discuss an instance of an intertextual reference, an allusion or parallel from a modern text to an ancient text and explain how the Classical text informs the modern one.
- Questions on classical civilisations and literature.
- How civilised was the Roman world?
- Apart from your A level texts, what have you read in the original or in translation?

Computer Science

Oxford has published some very useful sample problems here: www.cs.ox.ac.uk/admissions/undergraduate/how_to_apply/sample_interview_problems.html.

Earth Sciences (Geology)

It may be worth noting that Geology interview questions will frequently use a rock as a specimen, after which the interviewer will ask candidates to make interpretations of unfamiliar rock types and their formation. A working knowledge of the main types of igneous/sedimentary/metamorphic rocks (their appearances and formation) would be a good preparation for this style of question.

- Where would you place this rock sample in geological time?
- How would you determine a rock's age?
- Can you integrate this decay curve, and why would the result be useful?
- When do you think oil will run out?
- a) Calculate the mass of salt in the Earth's oceans. b) How did the Earth's oceans become saline?
- The Pacific plate is currently being subducted beneath the Eurasian plate. How long will it take for the Pacific plate to be completely destroyed?
- Why do we have mountains?
- How did Earth provide conditions necessary for life?
- How will the age of the ice change with distance walked up a glacier?

Economics

After one or two general questions such as 'what have you enjoyed most about economics' or 'what are you hoping to gain by studying at degree level', interviewers may then move on to more puzzle-based questions. Economics is highly mathematical, so don't be surprised to get some challenging puzzles to test your numeracy and logical thinking skills. It is a good idea to remember that no matter how mathematical the puzzle may be, they would be expecting you to link the ideas back to economic theory. Think about how you can use the ideas of utility or return or the allocation of resources to help explain your answers.

- Do oligopolists really play games?
- Outline the externalities of a Van Gogh painting.
- If we had everything we needed, we wouldn't need economics. Do you agree?
- Is anything really free?
- Police forces should be privatised. Do you agree?
- Motorists pay to use the roads; shouldn't pedestrians pay to use footpaths?
- Given the damage they cause, why aren't cigarettes £300 per packet?
- You're an economist. Give me a policy that would help solve the current knife crime epidemic.
- Explain how the Phillips curve arises.
- Would it be feasible to have an economy that was entirely based on the service sector?
- What do you know about the interaction between fiscal and monetary policy?
- I notice that you study mathematics. Can you see how you might derive the profit maximisation formula from first principles?
- If you were the Chancellor of the Exchequer, how would you maximise tax revenue?
- What would happen to employment and wage rates if the pound depreciated?
- How does the housing market affect inflation?
- How has social mobility changed in recent times?

Engineering

- Questions on mathematics and physics, particularly calculus and mechanics.
- Questions on mathematical derivations, for example on laws of motion.
- Look at this mechanical system sitting on my desk – how does it work?
- How do aeroplanes fly?
- What is impedance matching and how can it be achieved?
- How do bicycle spokes work?

- How would you divide a tetrahedron into two identical parts?
- What is the total resistance of the tetrahedron if there are resistors of 1 ohm on each edge?
- How would you design a gravity dam for holding back water?

English

It won't just be classical literature that the interviewer will expect you to have knowledge of but the impact of literature in general. Don't be surprised therefore to be asked questions on the Harry Potter books or the recent popularity of urban fantasy as a sub-genre. Of course, more specific questions will be related to works that you say you have enjoyed or learnt something from, so again make sure that you are confident of what you have written about in your personal statement as the chances are you will be asked questions on those works mentioned.

- What do you understand by 'realism' in the novel?
- Why does reading and studying literature in a digital age matter?
- 'No one shows us better than Shakespeare the stuff of human nature of which we are made.' What insights into human nature has Shakespeare's work enabled you to have?
- What literary work has excited you most and why?
- 'Poetry is language in excess of the functions of language' (Bruns). Is this your experience of poetry?
- 'A Fool sees not the same Tree a Wise Man sees' (Blake). What in your opinion makes one interpretation of a literary work better than another?
- Which works of literature have you particularly disliked and why?
- 'A poem must resist the intelligence almost successfully.' What do you think this statement means and is it helpful in tackling poems that you have found difficult to understand?
- What do you consider to be the most important work of literature of the 20th century?

Geography

- Why should geography be studied in its own right?
- Is geography just a combination of other disciplines?
- How can cities be made sustainable?
- If I were to visit the area where you live, what would I find interesting?
- Would anything remain of geography if we took the notion of place off the syllabus?
- How important is the history of towns when studying settlement patterns?
- Why is climate so unpredictable?
- What is the importance of space in global warming?
- Why do you think people care about human geography more than physical geography?

- What is more important, mapping or computer models?
- If you went to an isolated island to do research on the beach, how would you use the local community?
- Analyse a graph about a river. Why are there peaks and troughs?
- Look at a world map showing quality of life indicators. Explain the pattern in terms of two of the indicators.

See also Land Economy questions.

History

Candidates may be asked to discuss general concepts in history such as the role of the state, nationhood and the role of monarchy and parliament. Interviewers may also expect candidates to draw links between various related disciplines, for example politics and religion, and be asked to evaluate the relative impact of these ideas in a historical context. As history is so broad, the interviewer won't expect you to have detailed knowledge of many historical events but again if you have referred to something specifically in your personal statement, make sure you have done your research beforehand, as they are likely to ask you about it. Don't be surprised by a more light-hearted line of questioning, such as: 'if you were going to throw one of these historical figures out of a hot air balloon who would it be and why?'

- Are there any occasions where the lessons of history have been learned?
- Do you think that sometimes too much knowledge of history can be the problem?
- Should British history be a compulsory subject?
- 'The task of the historian is to understand the people of the past better than they understood themselves.' – H. Butterfield. Do you agree?
- Why does the classical world continue to exert such fascination?
- How far is today's world influenced by the ancient world?
- Discuss a historical movement that you find particularly interesting.
- How can one define revolution?
- Why did imperialism happen?
- Would history be worth studying if it didn't repeat itself?
- What is the difference between modern history and modern politics?
- What is the position of the individual in history?
- Would you abolish the monarchy for ideological or practical reasons?
- Why do historians differ in their views on Hitler?
- What skills should a historian have?
- Why is it important to visit historical sites relevant to the period you are studying?

History of Art

- What do we look for when we study art? What are we trying to reveal?
- Comment on this painting on the wall.

- Compare and contrast these three images.
- What exhibitions have you been to recently?
- How do you determine the value of art?
- Who should own art?
- What is art?
- Why is art important?
- What role do art galleries and museums play in society today?
- Are humans inherently creative?
- Apart from your studies, how else might you pursue your interest in art history while at university?
- What are some key themes in the history of art?
- How has the depiction of the human form developed through the centuries?
- Who invented linear perspective – artists or architects?
- When was the discipline of art history brought to England and by whom?

HSPS

- What is the value of the study of social anthropology?
- Do people need tabloids?
- How would you define terrorism?
- Do you believe in selective education? Are we participating in selective education here?
- Is it possible to pose a sociological problem without sociological bias?
- Does prison work?
- Are MPs only in it for the power?
- How has the study of race and racism changed over the past 20 years?

See also questions on Politics and Anthropology.

Human Sciences

- Talk about bovine spongiform encephalopathy and its implications, and the role of prions in Creutzfeldt–Jakob disease.
- What causes altitude sickness and how do humans adapt physiologically to high altitudes?
- Tell me about the exploitation of indigenous populations by Westerners.
- Why is statistics a useful subject for human scientists?
- Why are humans so difficult to experiment with?
- How would you design an experiment to determine whether genetics or upbringing is more important?
- What are the scientific implications of globalisation on the world?

Land Economy

- Will the information technology revolution gradually result in the death of inner cities?

- What has been the effect of the Channel tunnel on surrounding land use?

Law

Interviewers won't be expecting candidates to have detailed knowledge of modern law but will be expecting them to be able to discuss general concepts in law. From many questions candidates will be expected to formulate initial definitions from ideas such as 'steal' or 'duty of care' and use those to respond to hypothetical situations posed by the interviewers.

- Draft a piece of simple legislation, e.g. to stop eating (or drinking) in public.
- What types of promise should the law be prepared to enforce?
- What is the relationship between the law and morality?
- What makes something a law?
- What does it mean to 'take' another's car?
- Could you define 'theft'?
- A cyclist rides the wrong way down a one-way street and a chimney falls on him. What legal proceedings should he take? What if he is riding down a private drive signed 'no trespassing'?
- X intends to poison his wife but accidentally gives the lethal draught to her identical twin. Would you consider this a murder?
- Questions on legal issues, particularly current ones. Brexit (separation of powers); the rule of law (role of the judiciary); access to justice (legal aid); euthanasia.
- Define 'stalking'.
- Should judges have a legislative role?
- Do you think that anyone should be able to serve on a jury? (Relate this to the 'rule of law' and 'separation of powers'.)
- Should judges be elected?
- Do judges have political bias?
- To what extent do you think the press should be able to release information concerning allegations against someone?
- Who do you think has the right to decide about euthanasia?
- How does the definition of intent distinguish murder from manslaughter?
- Can you give definitions of murder and manslaughter?
- What is the role of intention in criminal liability?
- What is the difference between 'recklessness' and 'intention'?
- Should foresight of consequences be considered as intending such consequences?

Linguistics

- Is language a uniquely human phenomenon?
- Does it matter if a language becomes extinct?
- Are some languages easier to learn than others?

- Why do natural languages have irregular verbs?
- What can we learn about language by studying the brain?
- 'I have many pens and much ink.' What determines whether we use 'many' or 'much'?
- If you ask me whether I have two children and I have three, do I lie if I answer you with 'yes'?
- 'What you have not lost you still have. You have not lost a Ferrari. Therefore, you still have one.' Where does this reasoning go wrong?

Materials Science

- Questions on physics, particularly solid materials.
- Questions on mathematics, particularly forces.
- Investigations of sample materials, particularly structure and fractures.

Mathematics

- Pure mathematics questions on integration.
- Applied mathematics questions on forces.
- Computation questions on iterations, series and computer arithmetic.

Mathematics and Statistics

- What is linear regression?
- Where are chi-squared tests used?
- When is a Poisson distribution useful?
- What is selection bias?
- Derive Bayes' Theorem.
- What is the sharpshooter fallacy?
- Questions on probability.

Medicine

An intellectual curiosity about the field, strong academic achievement and a realistic view of modern medicine and all that it entails are the most vital pre-requisites for medicine. So expect questions that test your interest and commitment to medicine as well as your understanding of the less glamorous side of the profession. Medicine is tough and interviewers will be looking to weed out candidates who they don't think can stick the course. Expect work experience or volunteer placements to be assessed in terms of what you have learnt from those experiences. Some indication of your ability to work with others will be a big part of what they expect from you at interview.

- What did your work experience teach you about life as a doctor?
- What did you learn about asthma in your work experience on asthma research?
- How have doctors' lives changed in the past 30 years?
- Explain the logic behind the most recent NHS reforms.
- What are the mechanisms underlying diabetes?

- Why is it that cancer cells are more susceptible to destruction by radiation than normal cells?
- How would you determine whether leukaemia patients have contracted the disease because of a nearby nuclear power station?
- What does isometric exercise mean in the context of muscle function?
- What can you tell me about the mechanisms underlying sensory adaptation?
- What is an ECG?
- Why might a general practitioner not prescribe antibiotics to a toddler?
- Why are people anxious before surgery? Is it justifiable?
- How do you deal with stress?
- Why does your heart rate increase when you exercise?
- Questions on gene therapy.
- Questions on the ethics of foetal transplantation.
- Questions on biochemistry and human biology.

Modern Languages

Prepare for comprehension and translations and to answer questions on a text given immediately prior to the interview. Also be prepared to have a short conversation in the pre-studied language that you have chosen to study further at university.

Questions relative to a text:

- What are the elements making the book you have read interesting? (The plot, the characters, the descriptions of the social background, the humour ...)
- How important is the plot? Did you read this book mainly to find out what happens at the end or for other reasons?
- Were you struck by the beginning of the text?
- Are the characters realistic? What makes them realistic/not realistic?
- Can the characters be considered heroic? Why/why not?
- What is the name of the main character and how important is it?
- How important is the social/historical/cultural background? Does it have an influence on the characters and/or the plot?
- Could the book be set in a different place and/or time?
- Which is the main theme of the book you have read? Do you know other books on the same theme? Can you compare them?
- Does the language used in the book you have read differ from everyday language/newspapers' language? How so?
- Do you think that the book changes, perhaps losing something, in translation? If so, could you give a specific example?
- What genre does the book you have read belong to? What are the key characteristics defining this genre? I.e. what makes this book funny, tragic, moving, etc.?

- Do you know any other books, in the same language or in another, belonging to this genre? Can you compare them?
- Do you think people belonging to different cultures can understand the book you have read? E.g. If you have read a French book, do you think other Europeans can understand it?
- If the book you have read was written in a previous century, do you think it is still relevant nowadays?
- Do you think the book you have read will remain relevant in future?
- Would you read this book again? Why/why not?

Other questions:

- What are the similarities and differences between French and Spanish?
- What is a symbol?
- How can you explain the different variations of Spanish in Latin America?
- Why do you want to study this language and not another?
- Why is it important to study literature?
- What is the difference between literature and philosophy?
- How important is analysis of narrative in the study of literature?
- How important is knowledge of the biography of the author in the study of their literature?
- What is language?

Natural Sciences

See the questions for Biology, Chemistry, Computer Science, Earth Sciences (Geology), Materials Science and Physics.

Oriental Studies

- What do you know about the Chinese language and its structure?
- What are the differences between English and any oriental language with which you are familiar?
- Does language have an effect on identity?
- Compare and contrast any ambiguities in the following sentences:
  'Only suitable magazines are sold here.'
  'Many species inhabit a small space.'
  'He is looking for the man who crashed his car.'
- Comment on the following sentences:
  'He did wrong.'
  'He was wrong.'
  'He was about to do wrong.'

Philosophy

As well as discussing classical philosophical ideas, be prepared to be asked questions drawing links between different disciplines such as politics, economics and even mathematics. The quest of most of philosophy is to 'seek the truth' and candidates must be prepared to be able to break down questions into their constituent parts and use evidence and logical reasoning to present an argument. Listening to podcasts such as Philosophy Bites can be a very good way to get an overview of the main ideas in a very wide range of philosophical debates and arguments in a short, easy to digest format.

- Can killing the innocent ever be morally justifiable?
- What, if any, is the difference between knowing a proposition and believing a proposition?
- Could a computer ever be conscious?
- Can fish feel pain? How could we tell?
- Is tragedy in the eye of the beholder?
- Is it a matter of fact or logic that time travels in one direction only?
- What is required for me to choose to do something freely?
- Is our faith in the scientific method itself based on the scientific method? If so, does it matter?
- In virtue of what am I the same person as I was yesterday?
- Are words names for things?
- Do we perceive the world as it really is?
- What makes a joke funny?
- Could there be a society in which everyone lies all the time?
- How, if at all, can the word 'beautiful' be applied to such different things as a face and a landscape?
- Could translation be fully automated?

See also the questions for Theology (page 165).

Physics

Be prepared to answer any questions relating to the A level syllabus including the following.

- How does glass transmit light?
- How does depressing a piano key make a sound?
- How does the voltage on a capacitor vary if the dielectric gas is ionised?
- How has physics influenced political thinking during the past century?
- Questions on applied mathematics.
- Questions on mathematical derivations.
- What is an elastic collision?
- What happens when two particles collide – one moving and one stationary?
- What is friction?
- What is kinetic energy? How does it relate to heat?

Politics

- Can you define 'government'? Why do we need governments?
- Can you differentiate between power and authority?

- What makes power legitimate?
- What would be the result of a 'state of nature'?
- How can you distinguish between a society, a state and an economy?
- Will Old Labour ever be revived? If so, under what circumstances?
- What would you say to someone who claims that women already have equal opportunities?
- What would you do tomorrow if you were the leader of the former Soviet Union?
- How does a democracy work?
- What elements constitute the ideologies of the extreme right?
- What do you think of discrimination in favour of female parliamentarians?
- How would you improve the comprehensive system of education?
- Does the UN still have a meaningful role in world affairs?
- Is further EU enlargement sustainable?
- How important is national identity?
- Should medics pay more for their degrees?

Psychology

Expect to be asked questions covering a wide range of aspects in psychology. Questions on whether psychology is a science or not and hence its usefulness are not uncommon. Questions on the ethics or morality of some psychological research methods can also be asked. A scientific basis and evidence-driven approach to presenting arguments is expected so you may be given the outcome of some kind of research and asked to comment on it. Don't forget that it will be important for you to say you are making assumptions based upon the reliability of the initial data and perhaps question its validity but be prepared to make an argument based upon the evidence as presented to you.

- Is neuropsychology an exact science? If not, is it useful?
- Give some examples of why an understanding of chemistry might be important in psychology.
- A new treatment is tested on a group of people with depression, who are markedly better in six weeks. Does this show that the treatment was effective?
- There are records of violent crimes that exactly mimic scenes of violence on television. Does this indicate that television causes real violence?
- Can a robot ever think like a human?
- Why might one be able to remember items at the beginning and end of an aurally presented list better than items in the middle?
- Could a computer ever feel emotion?
- Is it ethically justifiable to kill animals for the purpose of research?
- What is emotional intelligence?
- Being given data from an experiment and being asked to analyse it.
- Should interviews be used for selection?

- Why do you want to study psychology?
- What aspects of psychology are you particularly interested in?
- Are humans the most intelligent species?
- What do you want to do after your psychology degree?
- What books have you read about psychology?
- What have you learned about psychology through your other A level subjects?
- Do you know what a psychology experiment is? Have you ever carried one out?
- Design a psychology experiment concerning colour blindness. How could you design an experiment to see if animals see in black and white?
- What is perception?

Theology

- Could an omnipotent being do anything?
- Can belief in God be grounded by reason?
- Is worship an essential part of a religion?
- What explains the 'new atheism' movement of the early 21st century?
- Does the rightness of an act consist in the kind of act it is or the kind of consequences it leads to?
- What, if anything, is wrong with voluntary euthanasia?
- What is the best reason that you can think of for believing in the existence of God?
- What relevance does theology have for art history?
- What relevance does archaeology have for theology?
- Can you comment on the portrayal of Jesus in John versus the other gospels?

See also questions for Philosophy (page 163).

Veterinary medicine

- Has your work experience influenced your future career aspirations?
- Can you discuss an aspect of animal physiology that has struck you as contrasting with what you know of human physiology?
- Would our knowledge of BSE have been of value in controlling foot and mouth disease?
- Tell me about the biochemistry of DNA.
- What animal did this skull belong to?

See also questions on Biological Sciences, Chemistry and Medicine.

Any questions?

At the end of the interview you may be asked if you have any questions to ask the interviewer(s). It is always a good idea to have a few questions up your sleeve. One or two is a good number; more than three questions is usually too many. Write them down on a notepad and bring it with you. You will appear professional and keen. You may be able to bring up one of your favourite topics that was not discussed during the main part of the interview.

You probably shouldn't ask about anything that you should know already or about information easily available on the website or prospectus as this will seem a bit desperate, rather dull and certainly not well prepared. Questions such as the following are not likely to impress.

- What will my first year course entail?
- Can I change courses once I'm up at university if I don't like the course I've enrolled on?
- What's special about this college?
- Do I have to live in college?
- Can I choose my room?

If, after all your research, you still have questions about your course or college, this is the time to ask. If there was a topic covered during the interview that you didn't understand, you could enquire about where you can read more about it, or get further clarification from the interviewers themselves. You might also ask for clarification on how you choose course options in your second, third or fourth year or where last year's graduates have ended up; for example, are they undertaking further academic studies, are they working in the City, or have they gone on to business school.

The most important things to remember for your interview are to be on time, relax, be yourself and try to have fun!

Case studies

Case study: Flora, Geography, Oxford

'At Oxford, I had separate human geography and physical geography interviews. At Cambridge, as a graduate applicant I had multiple-mini interviews; normal sixth-form undergraduate applicants will have longer interviews with college tutors.

'My advice would be: practise, practise, practise! The more familiar you are with the setting of an interview and the process, the more comfortable and at ease you will be on the day! Ask friends/family/teachers to help you. Become used to the idea of being pushed out of your comfort zone. A good interview should leave you feeling like you were being challenged and stretched. Read around your subject and think about how you can incorporate this into your interview. Be comfortable with talking about data (tables/graphs/compound structures/pictures of cells) that they might show you. Know your personal statement inside out.

'Make sure you go through what you have done in A level so far and that you understand everything – the questions they will ask you will build on that knowledge so you need to know the basics! Research who will be interviewing you. Many tutors will ask you about things that are relevant to their field of research (although this is not always the case!).

'Stay calm and THINK. Don't rush into giving an answer. Take a moment, think about what they have asked you and structure your answer in a clear way. If you don't understand the question, then don't be afraid to ask them for help. They aren't trying to catch you out; they are interested in how you approach a problem.

'It is a stressful time and you will most likely meet many of those competing for a place on your course. Don't be put off by them! Remember, Oxbridge attracts highly competitive people who like to show off but nine times out of ten they won't gain a place. Just be yourself. Although it's a pressured and stressful time, try to enjoy it! You are being given the opportunity to discuss your chosen subject with people who are at the top of the field!'

Case study: Toby, Natural Sciences, Cambridge

'It is difficult to say what a typical interview is like with Cambridge as every college does it differently and it depends on the subject. The first time I applied, when I didn't have A level Chemistry, Sidney Sussex gave me an interview focused on biology and one on biochemistry (it would have been straight chemistry but I hadn't studied it). Queens', on the other hand, asked for three topics I was good at beforehand and gave me a biology interview and a maths/chemistry/biochemistry interview. The maths part went very, very badly but I still managed to get in, so it's important to realise that they look at all your different academic attributes and it doesn't all rest on the interview. So the more outstanding your grades, the more you can afford to mess up the interview, basically.

'One thing I have found that differed from practice interviews is that Cambridge never quizzed me on my personal statement. They asked questions that assumed the knowledge of what was mentioned in the personal statement but they never said, "Tell me about this thing you've mentioned". I should also say, apart from the maths one which was a struggle, I really enjoyed my interviews and came out buzzing afterwards.'

Case study: Kathy, Engineering Science, Oxford

'Mine was an unusual situation, in that I only finally made up my mind to apply for Engineering at Oxford about a week before I completed my application. It was not that I was not interested in the subject; in fact, I was passionate about it and I had done related work experience and immersed myself in the subject through wider reading. My A level subjects were also compatible with studying Engineering at degree level. However, my family had really wanted me to apply for economics. I toyed with the idea of reading Economics and Engineering, a new course at the time, but I decided in the end to follow my heart and to aim for engineering.

'Once the decision was made, I continued to read widely and to engage in discussing related topics with my teachers. I also had some very useful mock interview practice with my college tutors who were also subject specialists. When I went for the interview, I tried to remain calm and I think this helped a lot.

'Although I had been prepared to answer lots of questions, I did not have to say very much during the interview itself. This was because the interviewers mainly gave me problems to do with mathematics and physics; my task was to find solutions to these problems. I think this style of interview was ideal for me. I really felt that I was working with the tutors to achieve a common goal.

'I am now in my second year at Oxford. Although it is very hard work, I am very pleased that I decided to apply for engineering.'

Case study: Liz, Classics, Cambridge

'Around a year ago I had my interview at Cambridge. I remember the horror stories I'd heard and how on the day of actual interview someone was throwing up in a College toilet. Yet, in retrospect, my interview day was not as terrible as I had thought it would be.

It is very difficult to describe Cambridge interviews in general terms as different departments and Colleges have their own ways of running them. Also, as an Open Applicant, I was not a typical case – I was picked by Colleges randomly for interviews. I had my first interview at Homerton college in the morning and my second at Jesus College in the afternoon.

'My general advice for interviews is: read. Read as much as you can before interviews. Read on any topics that fascinate you. Read outside of the school curriculums. At the end of the day, whether you are a gifted speaker or not is not as fatal as whether you have something clearly focused and interesting to discuss. Some interviewers will ask questions related to your personal statement, but there will definitely be others asking topics outside of it. One can never be sure what kind of questions will come up and you can only expect that you will be challenged and pushed to the point of confusion. Constant name-dropping is never a good tactic but expressing relevant ideas and concepts beyond the A level curriculum proves your genuine interest in the subject. You may not think extra reading can really help, but when your readings are accumulated and evaluated, they nicely permeate through your arguments during the interviews.

'Secondly, keep calm. A lot of people say they failed interviews due to nervous breakdown or mind blank. Practice may prevent this, but be aware that the actual interviews will never go as you have practised. I had one mock interview before the actual one and I think that was sufficient. In the interviews, don't rush to give answers immediately. You can always ask for a minute to consider the question. Showing your thinking process while answering is recommended. For me, I tried to define how I viewed any qualifiers in the question, what approaches I was taking and why. Do not give up even if you have absolutely no idea. Carry on thinking, experimenting and hypothesising. Anything is better than an awkward long silence. Not knowing the answer is not the end of the world, so do not panic. Quizzed on the adverbial use of a Latin word in an unseen Roman poem, I was hopelessly lost but kept trying out thoughts. If possible, try to enjoy the interview – however unrealistic it sounds! Oxbridge interviews are highly rare occasions during which the globally leading academics in your subject areas are carefully listening to what you say, and are interested in you as a person. Whether the interview goes successfully or not, it will be a memorable day. So keep calm, and carry on.'

The 'post-mortem'

Try not to dwell on how the interview went. Admissions tutors often say that students who think they have done badly in fact have acquitted themselves very well … and vice versa. Sometimes a lengthy interview and a good grilling will mean that they've given you a fighting chance to show your true colours.

I like to tell students the story of a candidate who came out of her interview and phoned her school teacher to report back on how her interview had gone. She told him that she had been given a poem to read and analyse and when she went into her interview she announced that she wasn't sure who had written it but she knew by the style of the writing that it had to be a woman. She then spent half her interview justifying her position. The teacher was silent on the other end of the line until he finally confessed that he knew the poem very well and in fact it was written by a man. Cue many tears of frustration and embarrassment.

Three weeks later, this student was offered a place to read English at Oxford. Remember, they are not looking at how much you know now but your potential. Tutors want students who display enthusiasm for their subject, along with a natural flair and ability. They want people who aren't afraid of putting forward their point of view, as long as they can justify it. Ultimately, they want students who will be fun and challenging to teach.

11 | Getting the letter

Once you've had your interview you will probably have mixed emotions about how well you have done. The majority of students have no strong feeling for whether they are likely to be successful. This is perfectly normal! It's worth remembering that admissions tutors have reported to us that often candidates feel they performed badly at interview when in fact they did very well.

Don't forget, too, that your interview is just one part of your 'package'; before the tutors make a final decision they will consider your application as a whole: your UCAS application and any supplementary question-naires, school reference, written work and specialist tests, as well as your performance at the interview. One tutor told me that at Cambridge they spend about 90 minutes considering every application in order to pick the best candidates and make the whole process as fair as possible.

Oxford decisions are usually sent by the end of January, and conditional offers are nearly always A*A*A–AAA depending on the subject. Cambridge decisions are usually received at the beginning of January, although officially they will be posted by the end of January 2023 for those interviewed in 2022. Conditional offers are nearly always A*A*A–A*AA depending on the subject. Cambridge applicants who submitted an extenuating circumstances form (ECF) may be made an offer that will take into account their special circumstances.

If you have applied to study Mathematics or a course involving mathe-matics, such as Mathematics with Physics, your offers will almost certainly be dependent on your grades in STEP papers. Some colleges may also ask for STEP for other courses. For example, Peterhouse typically asks for STEP for applications to read Engineering. Check the Cambridge website for details here: www.undergraduate.study.cam.ac.uk/applying/entrance-requirements/step.

The pooling system

The pooling system exists to ensure that all strong candidates get a good chance of being accepted to an Oxbridge college, but it means something slightly different at Cambridge and Oxford. Above all else, it is worth noting that the pool is not a secondary route in for an odd minority of students.

The Oxford pool

At Oxford, you may be 'pooled' after you have had an interview or interviews at your chosen college. This is the reason Oxford keeps applicants for several days during the interview process. You may be seen by other members of the faculty at different colleges during your stay. If you are a particularly strong candidate, academics at several colleges might ask you to interview, even if they are not at the college of your first choice and even if the academics at your preferred college already know they want to offer you a place. More often, being pooled indicates that, although you are a good candidate, your chosen college does not want to offer you a place but another college may. You will then be called for interview at the college that is considering offering you a place.

In the 2021 cycle at Oxford, around 26% of applicants received an offer at a college they did not apply to (see www.ox.ac.uk/admissions/undergraduate/colleges/do-you-choose-a-college).

The Cambridge pool

Some students who applied to Cambridge may find that they have been pooled. Pooling happens after the first interview process. If you are a strong candidate but there has been particularly high competition for places at your college, your interviewers may feel that they cannot offer you a place with them but that you deserve a place at Cambridge. They will then place you in the 'pool': a database that can be accessed by members of their faculty at different colleges. In a typical year, around 3,500 applicants are made offers by their preference/original college, and around 850–900 applicants are made an offer by another college through the pool.

Applicants are pooled for a variety of reasons, and are categorised by the pooling college as A (strongly recommended), B (probably worth an offer), P (outstanding on paper but less impressive at interview) or S (applicant in need of reassessment).

Sometimes a college wishes to see other applicants from the pool before it fills all of its places with direct applicants – this sometimes results in several applicants being pooled and subsequently being awarded places at their original college of choice. Some are subsequently invited for interview at other colleges; if this happens the college concerned will contact you to ask you to come for an interview early in January. If another college wishes to offer you a place following the pool, you should hear from it at the start or middle of January. Otherwise, your original college will write back to you by the end of January informing you that you have been unsuccessful.

In the 2021 cycle, 4,764 applications were pooled, of which 874 applicants received offers; only 15 of these were required to attend a second interview in January, and 194 of the pooled applicants received offers from the College that pooled them (see www.undergraduate.study.cam. ac.uk/files/publications/guide_to_the_winter_pool.pdf).

Rejection

If you are unsuccessful at either university, you will receive a rejection letter in the post between December and mid-January. If this is the case for you, do not despair. Remember that there is incredible competition to get a place at Oxbridge. Although on average one in five students who apply are accepted, for some subjects there are close to ten applicants per place. Many of the thousands of unsuccessful applicants per year will have been predicted three As or higher at A level, and are clearly intelligent and successful students.

If you are rejected, despite having a set of perfect grades and impeccable references, and you want to know why, ring the admissions tutor at your chosen college and ask for feedback. If your grades are good and you are really set on claiming a place at Oxbridge, think about why you did not succeed the first time and consider trying again. Neither Cambridge nor Oxford looks badly on students who apply twice. You may have been too young the first time or too focused on school exams to dedicate enough time to the application process. Alternatively, you may not have made an appropriate subject choice and were not passionate enough about your field. If once was enough, however, focus on your other university choices and draw on your Oxbridge experiences to help you in your preparation for future interviews.

Case study: Julia, Cambridge

'I have always been fascinated by the interaction of people, politics and cultures and enjoy the logic of subjects like languages and mathematics. This curiosity and interdisciplinary interest led me to choose my slightly unusual A level combination of History, French and Maths. It also led me to choose an unusual course, ASNC (a BA in Anglo-Saxon, Norse and Celtic), for my Cambridge application.

'I found the mock interview practice my college provided extremely helpful in identifying my strengths and weaknesses. While I had completed a lot of extra reading around my subjects, I found that I needed to interrogate these texts more to be able to adapt and apply them to the questions an interviewer might pose. This feedback helped me prepare both for my Cambridge interview and for those at my other university choices.

'I was very nervous at the interview itself but when it was over I realised I had enjoyed it. I also came away feeling that I had learnt more not only about the course but about different ways of thinking. When the decision came and I had not been successful, naturally I was disappointed but I focused on my other university options and took a place at KCL to read International Relations. In hindsight, I am sure that the interview experience itself was an excellent life experience – I do not believe that I will be as nervous as some other applicants when it comes to job interviews!

'Ultimately, there are so many other wonderful universities out there that it is important not to get stuck believing that "Oxbridge is the best". I truly feel that King's suits my personality, so it turns out that the Cambridge admissions office knows what it is doing.'

If you don't get the grades required

If you did not get the grades required by Oxbridge (for example you got an AAB rather than A*AA), your conditional offer will be withdrawn. You may wish to contact the admissions tutor at your college at this point, but you should be prepared for the fact that it is unlikely you will be accepted.

If there is a real and significant reason why you did not fulfil your potential in the exams (for example, illness or a bereavement in the family), you should ensure that the admissions tutor is aware of this (ideally this information will be corroborated with evidence and by your referee) as it may affect their decision.

UCAS has an 'Adjustment' system where students who get above their predicted grades can go back to universities which rejected them and try for a place, and a 'Clearing' system where unfilled places across a wide range of universities are opened up to students who did not originally apply for those courses at those institutions. Neither Oxford nor Cambridge participates in Clearing; and Oxford does not participate in Adjustment either, but Cambridge now does. However, only those students who were interviewed and were flagged as meeting at least three of Cambridge's five widening participation criteria are eligible. To meet these criteria, students will be from under-represented backgrounds at Cambridge. For example, a student will satisfy the first criterion if his or her home postcode is in the bottom 30% of locations indexed by various governmental measures of multiple deprivation.

The window for Adjustment applications is extremely short. In 2021, the process opened at 8.30am on results day, Tuesday 10 August, and closed less than five hours later at 1pm, with applications considered that afternoon and with applicants hearing that evening. For more information, visit www.undergraduate.study.cam.ac.uk/adjustment.

If you are unsuccessful, there is always the option of reapplying. Traditionally, students have been discouraged from retaking exams to try and secure a place at Oxford or Cambridge, but there are examples of students who have done so successfully at both institutions. Oxford and Cambridge will treat your application as a new application and so your previous application will have no bearing on your fresh one. Every year, plenty of reapplicants are admitted. Such successful candidates will almost certainly have applied with better grades and a personal statement that draws attention to everything else they have done with their extra year by way of enrichment. If you do not secure your offer, it is worth asking the admissions tutor whether you would be considered next year if you were to retake and/or reapply.

As a final word, though, remember that Oxford and Cambridge aren't everything. If you are a motivated and focused student, then you will excel at whichever university you go to; and if you love your subject, then your interest will flourish wherever you are. There is always the option of applying as a postgraduate if your undergraduate degree isn't enough for you!

Case study: Charlie, Oxford

'I initially applied to a college in Oxford to read History. I performed well in the interview, but did not get an offer, although the rejection letter still reassured me that I had been a strong candidate; it was simply that I was out-performed by the other applicants. I went on to get excellent A level grades.

'The rejection gave me a chance to reflect on what I really wanted to study at university. I had always been interested in English literature, but had not studied it at A level. Poetry has always been my favourite genre and I have been writing poetry in earnest since my early teens. In fact, I had a volume of poetry published during my enforced gap year. This led to a series of visits to schools and even prisons, where I gave readings from my book and discussed my work. Clearly, this augmented my confidence; it also crystallised my desire to study English Language and Literature at university and to reapply to Oxford in order to achieve this aim.

'The following year I enrolled on a one-year intensive A level course in English Literature. I thoroughly enjoyed the inspiring lessons given by my teacher and got on really well with my classmates. I finished the year with the top grade. Before reapplying to Oxford in the autumn term, I rang around the various colleges to see how they would view me as a candidate applying the second time around. Having heard about my profile, a surprising number said they would view my application favourably. I got my place; I am so glad I persevered.'

PART IV

College Profiles

The following information is intended to provide a brief overview of the undergraduate colleges at Oxford and Cambridge to give an idea of what each one offers and help you to narrow down your options. However, for the most detailed and up-to-date information, you should also consult individual college websites as part of your research.

For a full list of which courses are offered at each college, please see Table 9 (page 210) and Table 11 (page 243).

OXFORD

BALLIOL COLLEGE (founded 1263)

Number of students: 366 UGs (undergraduates).

Size and location: Medium-sized and very central college; the Bodleian Library, Weston Library, Radcliffe Camera, Modern Languages faculty, Oriental Institute Library and Sackler Library are all close by.

Accommodation:
- **Access**: Several specially adapted rooms and showers available for students with disabilities, both on the main site and in the College annexes. Wheelchair access available on the main site, and two lifts in the Jowett Walk annexe. Restricted access at the Holywell Manor site.
- **Main site**: Undergraduates are guaranteed accommodation for all three years, either at the main site or off site. Students not living in College either live in Jowett Walk annexe or rent privately.
- **Off site**: Jowett Walk and Master's Field are about 10 minutes' walk from the main site. They are made up of self-contained flats, including bedrooms with en-suite facilities; students can live there either individually or with a group of friends. The Master's Field is the home of Balliol's sports fields, squash courts and outdoor tennis pitches.
- **Rent**: The rent varies for each room between approximately £1,000 and £2,300 per term.

Food:
- **Hall**: Food served in College Hall seven days a week. Students charged a termly fixed living-in charge; this is reduced if students live out. Optional pre-payment schemes available for Hall food. Formal Hall served once a week and on guest nights.
- **Other**: JCR Pantry serving breakfast, lunch and dinner; Buttery serving drinks and light refreshments. No self-catering on main site; shared kitchens in Jowett Walk and Master's Field.

Facilities on site: Gym; studio theatre; music room; chapel; Balliol Day Nursery (in North Oxford).

Financial aid: Junior Maintenance Grant; Balliol short-term loans; College loans and grants for unexpected hardship; undergraduate project grants; miscellaneous grants (e.g. for travel, materials, etc.); Nettleship Instrumental Exhibition; Cadle Fund for sports expenditure; Georgina Horlick Childcare Bursaries; academic scholarships and exhibitions; other subject, essay and project prizes available.

Societies: Arnold and Brackenbury Society (comedy debating society); Balliol Literary Society; Left Caucus (left-wing issues); Balliol Music Society; Balliol Drama Society; Scrawl (creative writing magazine); Choir (non-auditioned); Mathematics Skoliasts (Classics); STEM-Sisters (female science and maths students).

Miscellaneous:
- Exchange scheme with the Maximilianeum (college attached to the University of Munich) for undergraduate and graduate students in any subject.

- Pathfinders Programme supports eight students to travel to America and Canada for six to eight weeks and stay with College alumni; two students to travel to Asia for six to eight weeks; and two students to Mexico for four weeks.

Alumni: Robert Browning; Yvette Cooper; Richard Dawkins; Graham Greene; Edward Heath; Gerard Manley Hopkins; Boris Johnson; Harold Macmillan; Lord Patten; Robert Peston; Dan Snow; Peter Snow; Simon Stevens.

Did you know ...?

Richard Dawkins studied at Balliol, as did 10 other members of his family. While at Balliol, Richard Dawkins read Zoology.

BLACKFRIARS HALL (permanent private hall — PPH)
(founded 1921; Priory founded 1221)

NB Accepts postgraduates only.

Number of students: 26 PGs.

Size and location: Very small and central college; located near Modern Languages, Classics and Linguistics faculties and the Oriental Institute.

Accommodation:
- **Access**: Wheelchair access for all principal spaces on site.
- **Main site**: No accommodation available.
- **Off site**: Small number of rooms available in two adjacent houses with shared kitchens.
- **Rent**: Fixed rate.

Food: Meals are not provided on the main site.

Facilities on site: Specialist Theology and Philosophy library.

Financial aid: Gym grant; cycle safety scheme.

Societies: Companions of Malta (charity that works with local Catholic and Anglican churches for the marginalised); Schola Magna (choir); Women's Group.

Miscellaneous: Note that you do not need to be Catholic to apply to study at the Hall.

Did you know ...?

Blackfriars is home to the Las Casas Institute, which organises lectures on issues relating to human dignity through Catholic social teaching, with Dr Rowan Williams recently invited to speak, and the Aquinas Institute, which holds seminars, conferences and summer schools on the study of St Thomas Aquinas.

BRASENOSE COLLEGE (founded 1509)

Number of students: 364 UGs.

Size and location: Medium college and very central; situated next to the Bodleian Library and Radcliffe Camera.

Accommodation: Provided for the duration of the course.
- **Access**: Adapted rooms available for students with disabilities.
- **Main site**: Provided for all first years and some third and fourth years.
- **Off site**: Frewin Hall complex houses second, some third and fourth years.
- **Rent**: Banded room prices.

Food:
- **Hall**: Breakfast, lunch and dinner, and brunch at the weekend. Pay-as-you-go system. Formal Hall served twice a week.
- **Other**: Bar and café (Gertie's) serving lunch and breakfast. Shared kitchens on Frewin site.

Facilities on site: Three libraries: main library; separate Law library; library with modern history, politics and geography books; practice rooms; chapel; boat-house; theatre/performance space.

Financial aid: Annual fund for academic or extra-curricular activities (non-means tested and means-tested); Harold Parr Fund (preference for Law/Mathematics); Undergraduate Freshers' Allowance; travel grants; vacation grants.

Societies: Choir (non-auditioning); Jazz Band; Debating Club (Addington Society); Ashmole (organises history talks); Creative Writing Society; Film Club; College Magazine.

Miscellaneous: Kathleen Lavidge Bursary to support three weeks' study at Stanford University.

Alumni: David Cameron; William Golding; Michael Palin.

Did you know ...?

The most likely explanation for the name 'Brasenose' is that it refers to a brass door-knocker in the shape of a nose.

CHRIST CHURCH (founded 1546)

Number of students: 448 UGs.

Size and location: Near the river (good for rowers) and Music and History of Art faculties.

Accommodation: Provided for the duration of the course, and is balloted after first year.
- **Access**: Two single rooms for disabled students on main site; specially equipped flat for up to three students available in Liddell Building.
- **Main site**: Houses all first years, some second and final years.

- **Off site**: Liddell Building, which has self-catering flats, each with three or four bedrooms.
- **Rent**: Fixed rate.

Food:
- **Hall**: Breakfast, lunch and dinner served Monday–Friday; brunch and dinner Saturday–Sunday. Breakfast, lunch and brunch: pay-as-you-go; dinner charged on termly basis. Formal Hall served every evening after first Hall.
- **Other**: No self-catering facilities; shared kitchens in Liddell Building.

Facilities on site: Separate Law library: picture gallery; art room and art tutor; music room; Cathedral of Oxford; boathouse; theatre/performance space.

Financial aid: Book grants; student support loans and grants; vacation grants; academic scholarships and exhibitions.

Societies: Cathedral Choir; College Choir; Orchestra; Music Society; Dramatic Society.

Miscellaneous:
- Site of the Cathedral of Oxford and Christ Church Meadow.
- Annual music festival run by the Music Society.
- Home Learning Scheme connects Christ Church students with local families.
- Accredited Fairtrade college.

Alumni: W.H. Auden; Lewis Carroll; Richard Curtis; David Dimbleby; William Ewart Gladstone; Howard Goodall; Robert Peel; Rowan Williams.

Did you know ...?

The author Lewis Carroll read Mathematics at Christ Church, and while there he met Alice Liddell, daughter of the Dean at Christ Church; Alice would later become Carroll's inspiration for the titular character in *Alice's Adventures in Wonderland* and *Through the Looking-Glass, and What Alice Found There*.

CORPUS CHRISTI COLLEGE (founded 1517)

Number of students: 268 UGs.

Size and location: One of the smallest colleges in Oxford; central college, near University Libraries, which looks out over Christ Church Meadow.

Accommodation: Provided for the duration of the course.
- **Access**: Accommodation available for disabled students.
- **Main site**: For all first years, some second, third and fourth years.
- **Off site**: Nine College houses and Liddell Building (three- or four-person flats) for some second, third and fourth years.
- **Rent**: Fixed rate.

Food:
- **Hall**: Breakfast, lunch and dinner served. Pay-as-you-go system. Formal Hall served twice a week.

- **Other**: Shared kitchens in off-site accommodation.

Facilities on site: Library; computer suite; auditorium; chapel; bar.

Financial aid: College offers both ongoing and emergency support for mainte-nance costs; moving-out loans for students living out of College accommodation (mainly for graduates); financial assistance towards the cost of books/scientific equipment; academic scholarships and exhibitions; vacation grants; travel grants.

Societies: Symposium (think tank); Owlets (drama); Choir; Corpus Cinema (film club); String Orchestra; Jazz Ensemble; Christian Union (CU).

Miscellaneous: Presidents' seminars: termly talks from visiting speakers.

Alumni: Robert Bridges; David Miliband; Ed Miliband; John Ruskin; C.P. Scott.

Did you know ...?

Corpus Christi keeps at least one tortoise as a college mascot and has an annual tortoise race to raise funds for charity.

EXETER COLLEGE (founded 1314; fourth-oldest college)

Number of students: 351 UGs.

Size and location: Medium-sized college. Central; near University Libraries.

Accommodation: Currently provided for three years.
- **Access**: Adapted facilities available at main and Iffley Road (East Oxford) sites, including accessible rooms.
- **Main site**: Houses first years.
- **Off site**: In later years, other accommodation provided across the road from the main site in Turl Street; East Oxford (self-catered); or Cohen Quad in Jericho (North Oxford).

Food:
- **Hall**: Breakfast, lunch and dinner served Monday–Saturday; brunch and dinner served on Sunday. Pay-as-you-go system. Formal Hall served three times a week.
- **Other:** Baguette bar and pizza bar on main site; café at Cohen Quad.

Facilities on site: Chapel; weights room; computer rooms; Fellows' Garden; cafe; music room; boathouse.
- **Cohen Quad:** lecture theatre and café; library; bar.

Financial aid: Exonian Bursaries; academic scholarships; travel grants; sports grants; choral awards; organ scholarships.

Societies: Choir; Music; John Ford Society (drama); Fortescue Society (Law); PPE Society; Feminist Magazine; ExVAC (student-run scheme that organises trips for children from disadvantaged backgrounds).

Miscellaneous:
- The College library is particularly good for History students.

- Exeter is the only college with a dedicated Careers Officer – it runs its own careers and internships office, separate from the University Careers Service.
- Rectors' seminars – recent speakers have included Philip Pullman, J.K. Rowling and Sir Peter Jackson.
- Runs subject-family events for students, where they are invited to learn about research in their academic field and beyond.

Alumni: Martin Amis; Alan Bennett; Reeta Chakrabarti; William Morris; Philip Pullman; J.R.R. Tolkien.

Did you know ...?

Exeter College forms the basis for the fictional Jordan College in Philip Pullman's trilogy *His Dark Materials*.

HARRIS MANCHESTER COLLEGE
(founded 1996; originally founded in Manchester in 1786)
NB Accepts mature UGs only.

Number of students: 102 UGs.

Size and location: Very small college, close to Science Area, English and Law faculties and History Library.

Accommodation:
- **Main site**: All College accommodation is situated on the main site and provided for first and final year students.
- **Rent**: Fixed rate, which includes food charge; see below.

Food:
- **Hall**: Fixed-rate accommodation charge includes a fee for 17 meals per week: breakfast, lunch and dinner Monday–Friday; and brunch on Saturday and Sunday. Formal Hall served twice a week.
- **Other**: Small kitchens on site. While self-catering is not possible, students may sign out of a few meals each term in exchange for credits.

Facilities on site: Computing room; library; bar.

Financial aid: College Hardship Fund; bursaries for outstanding first-year work; second undergraduate degree scholarships (based on academic merit); book bursaries; conference and travel grants.

Societies: Harris Manchester Chorale; Law Society; Drama Society; Film Club; Leftist Society; LGBTQ Society; Afro-Caribbean Society.

Did you know ...?

Harris Manchester is the only full college of the University to accept mature students only (students aged 21 or above, with no upper age limit). The others that accept only mature students are all permanent private halls.

HERTFORD COLLEGE (founded 1282)

Number of students: 399 UGs.

Size and location: Small and central college; next to Radcliffe Camera and the Bodleian.

Accommodation: Provided for the duration of the course.
- **Main site**: Houses first years.
- **Off site**: Other years are balloted and most live in Warnock or Abingdon House (near Christ Church Meadow) or in houses in North and South Oxford.
- **Rent**: Fixed charge (room rent and College facilities charge). Uniform rent structure, but College facilities charge varies depending on which College accommodation you live in.

Food:
- **Hall**: Pay-as-you-go system. Dinner is not provided on Saturdays. Formal Hall served twice a week.
- **Other**: All student rooms have access to shared kitchens. Cafeteria service at Warnock House available for breakfast and dinner.

Facilities on site: Chapel; gym; computing rooms; music room; library; bar.

Financial aid: Hertford Undergraduate Bursary for students from low-income families; Student Support Fund for unexpected financial hardship; travel and research grants; academic scholarships for first-year exam results; vacation grants.

Societies: Choir (non-auditioned); Orchestra; Jazz Band; Wind Band; Hertford College Music Society; Business and Economics; College Newspaper/Magazine.

Miscellaneous:
- Hertford debates at Formal Hall, featuring visiting speakers.
- Accredited Fairtrade college.

Alumni: Fiona Bruce; John Donne; Krishnan Guru Murthy; Natasha Kaplinsky; Evelyn Waugh.

Did you know ...?

Hertford has its own Undergraduate Bursary, guaranteeing up to £1,000 to students whose household income is below the specified threshold.

JESUS COLLEGE (founded 1571)

Number of students: 378 UGs.

Size and location: Very small, central, Turl Street college; near University Libraries.

Accommodation: Provided for the duration of the course.
- **First year**: Students live on Turl Street site or in an annexe close by.
  - **Rent**: Fixed nightly charge, inclusive of utilities and cleaning.
- **Other years**: Students are balloted and live in flats in North and East Oxford. Flats available for couples at the East Oxford site.

- ○ **Rent**: Weekly charges, which includes water but not other utilities. 40-week lease (though a 48-week lease is offered for couples).

Food: Pay-as-you-go system. Additional termly Hall charge payable, which is reduced for those living in College flats/private accommodation.
- **Hall**: Breakfast, lunch and dinner served Monday–Friday; breakfast and lunch on Saturday; lunch and dinner on Sunday. Formal Hall served five times a week.
- **Other**: Shared kitchens in some College accommodation.

Facilities on site: Chapel; computer suite; conservatory; music room; dark room; library; bar.

Financial aid: Access Bursaries (grants to assist with course-related costs); book grants; subject prizes; cultural, sporting and travel grants.

Societies: Non-auditioned Choir; Orchestra; English Society; History Society; College Newspaper/Magazine.

Miscellaneous: Jointly runs the Turl Street Arts Festival with Lincoln and Exeter Colleges.

Alumni: William Boyd; T.E. Lawrence; Harold Wilson.

Did you know ...?

The College was founded by Queen Elizabeth I.

KEBLE COLLEGE (founded 1870)

Number of students: 412 UGs.

Size and location: Medium-sized college; near to Radcliffe Science Library and Science Area, and adjacent to University Parks.

Accommodation: Provided for all first and second years, and most third years. Fourth years tend to live out (except for Modern Languages students).
- **Access**: Main areas are wheelchair accessible. The College has several ground-floor bedrooms and one bedroom with specially adapted en-suite facilities.
- **Main site**: All student accommodation is located within College grounds.
- **Rent**: Banded accommodation; 37-week lease for third years living in the ARCO Building. Rent equalisation subsidy available to third-year students who are not allocated College accommodation.

Food:
- **Hall**: Breakfast, lunch and dinner served Monday–Friday; brunch and dinner Saturday–Sunday. Pay-as-you-go system; charged on bill at the end of each term. Formal Hall served every evening.
- **Other**: College café (Café Keble) open all day during term time and pizza bar is open daily.

Facilities on site: Library; bar; O'Reilly Theatre (performance space for drama/musicals); Advanced Studies Centre (hosts talks with visiting speakers and is used for inter-disciplinary research); chapel.

Financial aid: Bursaries; College Student Support Fund for unexpected hardship; travel and research grants; vacation and internship bursaries; organ and choral scholarships.

Societies: Music Society; Harris Law Society; CU; Choir.

Miscellaneous: Hosts an annual arts festival.

Alumni: Ed Balls; Frank Cottrell-Boyce; Giles Coren; Tony Hall; Paula Hawkins.

Did you know ...?

Keble is home to the O'Reilly Theatre, which is a hugely popular venue for student musicals and plays; each term four or five plays are selected by a committee, and theatre groups must bid for a chance to perform their piece at the O'Reilly.

LADY MARGARET HALL (LMH) (founded 1878)

Number of students: 417 UGs.

Size and location: Large; 10 acres of gardens. Situated by University Parks, near to the Science Area.

Accommodation: Three years' worth of accommodation provided on site; balloted after second year.
- **Access**: Purpose-built accommodation available for students with disabilities.
- **Rent**: Fixed termly rate, regardless of size/location.

Food:
- **Hall**: Pay-as-you-go system. Three meals a day, Monday–Friday; brunch only on Saturday; dinner only on Sunday. Students are entitled to two free Formals (which are weekly) a year.
- **Other**: All bedrooms have shared kitchen access.

Facilities on site: Boathouse and punts; playing fields; tennis courts; netball court; gym; theatre; computer room; music practice rooms; chapel; library; bar.

Financial aid: Hardship Fund; Academic Development Fund; academic scholarships and exhibitions; organ scholarship; subject prizes.

Societies: Beaufort Society (literary group); Brading Biomedical Society; Chapel Choir (non-auditioned); CU; Cine-club; Daisy Circle (debating); Drama Society; Fashion Society; Film Society; History; Law; LGBTQ; LMH and Wadham Orchestra; Music Society.

Miscellaneous:
- Initially founded in 1878 as a women's college to allow women to study at Oxford for the first time; men weren't admitted until 1979 (first college in Oxford to go mixed).

- Accredited Fairtrade college.

Alumni: Danny Cohen; Michael Gove; Eglantyne Jebb; Nigella Lawson; Baroness Manningham-Buller; Ann Widdecombe.

Did you know ...?

LMH built its own library resources to cater for its first female students, as women weren't permitted to use the Bodleian or Oxford Union Libraries until the 1920s. The College received numerous gifts for its new library from advocates of women's education; notable book donors include John Ruskin and Lewis Carroll.

LINCOLN COLLEGE (founded 1427)

Number of students: 305 UGs.

Size and location: Very small Turl Street college; near University Libraries.

Accommodation: Provided for the duration of the course.
- **Access**: Adapted accommodation available on main site and in North Oxford.
- **Rent**: Three 'plans', each with its own fixed pricing structure: in-College plan for freshers; in-College plans for second and third years; out-of-College plan for second and third years.
  - Students living in off-site College residences are on a 37-week plan; students living in College are on a 25-week plan.
  - First and second years live in College or above the Mitre pub on the High Street.
  - Third and fourth years live in College properties, either in North Oxford (by Science Area), or opposite the College on the High Street.

Food:
- **Hall**: Breakfast, lunch and dinner provided every day. Pay-as-you-go system, which is billed at the end of each term. Formal Hall served six nights a week.
- **Other**: Bar that serves meals and light snacks (Deep Hall), which is open during term time. Third- and fourth-year accommodation has access to kitchens.

Facilities on site: Chapel; multi-faith room; computer room; library; bar.

Financial aid: Bursaries and hardship funds; book grant scheme; academic scholarships and exhibitions; academic and subject prizes; travel grants; organ scholarships; choral scholarships and exhibitions.

Societies: Chapel Choir; Lincoln Players (drama); Publications Committee; CU.

Miscellaneous:
- Co-hosts the Turl Street Arts Festival with Exeter and Jesus Colleges.
- VacProj: College charity, taking children from underprivileged backgrounds on holiday.

Alumni: John le Carré; Lord Florey; Dr John Radcliffe; Dr Seuss; John Wesley.

> **Did you know ...?**
>
> Lincoln was the first Oxford college to introduce a Middle Common Room (MCR) for graduate students to use.

MAGDALEN COLLEGE (founded 1458)

Number of students: 403 UGs (*c.* 118 admitted each year).

Size and location: Very large: 100-acre grounds, including a deer park and riverside walk. Located near English and Law faculties and the Examination Schools.

Accommodation: Provided for the duration of the course, either in College, in nearby annexes or in College properties.
- **Access**: Limited number of accessible ground-floor rooms available on main site, and two rooms with accessible en-suite facilities in Longwall Street, although access to the buildings on this street may not be suitable for some wheelchair users. Lift to the main Hall.
- **Rent**: Flat daily rate for all undergraduate rooms (59 nights per term).

Food: Pay-as-you-go system. In addition, there is a supplementary termly catering charge (reduced for students not living in College accommodation).
- **Hall**: Serves breakfast, lunch and dinner. Formal Hall served three times a week.
- **Other**: Old Kitchen Bar serves lunch options; JCR shop sells snacks. Self-catering facilities available across College accommodation.

Facilities on site: Chapel; library; bar; auditorium; music practice rooms; Modern Languages room; hard and grass tennis courts; squash courts; all-weather pitch; boat house with punts; private dining space and kitchen.

Financial aid: Student Support Fund to help with cost of living and studying; Hardship Fund (one-off financial hardship); academic scholarships, awards and prizes; travel grants; research grants; vacation grants.

Societies: Florio Society (poetry); Atkin Society (Law); Sherrington Society (Medicine); Choir; Orchestra; Magdalen Singers; Music Society; Magdalen College Swing Band; Magdalen Players (drama); Film Society; Raising Consciousness; Stokesley (debating); CU.

Alumni: Julian Barnes; King Edward VII; William Hague; Robert Hardy; Seamus Heaney; Ian Hislop; C.S. Lewis; George Osborne; Louis Theroux; Oscar Wilde.

> **Did you know ...?**
>
> The choir sings from the top of the Great Tower at 6am on May Morning (1 May) to celebrate the beginning of spring.

MANSFIELD COLLEGE (founded 1886)

Number of students: 255 UGs.

Size and location: Very small; located near the University Parks and Science Area.

Accommodation: Provided for all first, second and third years on site or in College-owned/College-run accommodation off site. New undergraduate accommodation has been provided for in a new building which also houses the Bonavero Institute of Human Rights.
- **Access**: Wheelchair access to all ground-floor facilities on the main site. The graduate accommodation block has one room suitable for a wheelchair user.
- **Main site**: Houses all first- and some second- and third-year students.
- **Off site**: Some second and third years live in the Ablethorpe Building (College annexe). College-owned houses are provided for second, third and fourth years.
- **Rent**: Fixed termly charge, which is subdivided into rent and utilities.

Food:
- **Hall**: Pay-as-you-go; charged termly. Breakfast, lunch and dinner served. Formal Hall served twice a week.
- **Other**: Student café, bar and terrace. Kitchens available on site for self-catering.

Facilities on site: Four libraries (including separate libraries for Theology, Law and PPE); chapel; student café, bar and terrace.

Financial aid: Hardship Fund; academic scholarships and prizes; travel grants.

Societies: Drama Society; Chapel Choir; Film Club; 1887 (Geography); 1963 (History); Poetry; CU; Nonconformist (College newspaper); Gender Equality; Music Society.

Miscellaneous: Many of the sports teams are combined with Merton College (Mansfield shares Merton's sports grounds).

Alumni: Chris Bryant; Adam Curtis; Justin Rowlatt.

Did you know ...?

As part of a joint initiative between Mansfield's Principal, Baroness Helena Kennedy, QC and the faculty of Law, as of October 2017, Mansfield is home to the Bonavero Institute of Human Rights, which is a significant addition to the faculty of Law.

MERTON COLLEGE (founded 1264)

Number of students: 306 UGs.

Size and location: Medium-sized college; main site close to University Libraries; Holywell Street annexe near Science Area.

Accommodation: Provided for the duration of the course.
- **Access**: Two rooms available for disabled students, including a suite with an adjacent room for a carer.

- **Main site**: First years live in houses on Merton Street or in Rose Lane, which are adjacent to the main site. Third years live in main College complex.
- **Off site**: Most second and fourth years live in College-owned houses in Holywell Street, which is a short walk from the College.
- **Rent**: Flat-rate charges, although there is a higher flat-rate charge for en-suite bedrooms.

Food:
- **Hall**: Pay-as-you-go meals. Breakfast, lunch and dinner provided Monday–Saturday, with brunch and dinner on Sunday. Formal Hall served six days a week.
- **Other**: Kitchen on main site and shared facilities in some Holywell Street accommodation.

Facilities on site: Gym; chapel; music practice room; lecture theatre; games room; library; bar.

Financial aid: Student Financial Support Fund for unexpected financial hardship; academic scholarships and prizes; choral and organ scholarships; annual book grant; travel grant; research grant.

Societies: Bodley (organises visiting talks); Merton Floats (drama); Music Society; Neave Society (politics and current affairs); Art Club; Signs and Wonderings (Theology); Chalcenterics (Classics); CU; Choir (auditioned); Orchestra.

Miscellaneous: Merton organises its own Arts Festival annually.

Alumni: T.S. Eliot; Mark Haddon.

Did you know ...?

J.R.R. Tolkien was Merton's Professor of English Language and Literature, having studied at Exeter College as an undergraduate. While a don, Tolkien met regularly with other academics as a member of the Inklings, an informal literary society. Another notable member of the group was C.S. Lewis, who was a Tutorial Fellow at Magdalen and later Professor of Medieval and Renaissance Literature at Cambridge, having first studied at University College in Oxford.

NEW COLLEGE (founded 1379)

Number of students: 413 UGs (c. 120 admitted each year).

Size and location: Large college, near University Libraries, English and Law faculties.

Accommodation: Provided for first, second and fourth years in College or near to College. Some third-year accommodation available.
- **Rent for majority of undergraduate accommodation**: Fixed rent, which includes utilities, internet and evening meals.
- **Sacher Building and Savile House**: Fixed rent at second-highest rate, which includes the cost of services. 39-week lease available.

- **New College Lane and Bodicote House**: Fixed rent at highest rate, to include the cost of services and term-time evening meals. 38-week lease in New College Lane, and option of a 38-week lease in Bodicote House.

Food:
- **Hall**: Breakfast, lunch and dinner Monday–Friday; brunch and dinner Saturday–Sunday. Termly pre-payment for food; supplementary meals charged to subsequent termly bill, and any remaining credit is credited back to the student's account. Formal Hall served three times a week.
- **Other**: Some self-catering facilities available.

Facilities on site: Chapel; practice rooms; band room; computer room; library; bar.

Financial aid: Choral scholarships (men only); organ scholarship; instrumental scholarships; academic scholarships and prizes; travel grants; Sporting and Cultural Award.

Societies: Choir (auditioned); Wykeham Singers (non-auditioned); Orchestra.

Miscellaneous:
- New College Chalet on Mont Blanc is used for reading parties and walking holidays, and is shared with Balliol and University Colleges.
- JCR Art Store has artwork available for students to put up in their rooms.

Alumni: Kate Beckinsale; Tony Benn; Richard Dawkins; Hugh Grant.

Did you know ...?

As well as being an alumnus of the College, Hugh Grant was also made an Honorary Fellow in 2012.

ORIEL COLLEGE (founded 1326)

Number of students: 324 UGs.

Size and location: Medium-sized college, located by the University Libraries.

Accommodation: Provided for the duration of the course. All first years live on site.
- **Access**: Several adapted rooms available.
- **Rent**: Banded accommodation; each band has its own fixed termly charge and is banded according to size, location, facilities and condition.

Food:
- **Hall**: Pay-as-you-go system. Breakfast, lunch and dinner served Monday to Saturday. Brunch and dinner served on Sunday. Formal Hall served six days a week.
- **Other**: Some self-catering available, depending on the area of the College where the accommodation is located. There is also a JCR Tuck Shop.

Facilities on site: Undergraduate shop; annexe for meetings/gatherings; music practice room; two gyms; squash court; chapel; multi-faith room.

Financial aid: Oriel College Bursaries for students in financial need; Hardship grants for unexpected financial hardship; choral scholarships; organ scholarships; academic scholarships and prizes; travel grants; vacation grants.

Societies: Chapel Choir; Oriel Lions (drama); Music Society; Pantin Society (History); Whately Society (politics, philosophy, current affairs and arts); CU; Acaporiel (a cappella choir); The Poor Print (College newspaper).

Miscellaneous: The College holds termly Joint Academic Forums, featuring discussion of interdisciplinary research topics/questions.

Alumni: Jim Cooper; Sir Walter Raleigh; Rachel Riley.

Did you know ...?

Each year, the College plays host to a Visiting Musician, who holds master-classes with the students and gives concerts; past visitors include mezzo-soprano Sarah Connolly and pianist Joanna MacGregor.

PEMBROKE COLLEGE (founded 1624)

Number of students: 378 UGs.

Size and location: Medium-sized college, located near the Music and History of Arts faculties and the river.

Accommodation: Provided for three years.
- **Access**: Five rooms for wheelchair users and adapted rooms for hard of hearing students. Wheelchair access available to all areas of the main site.
- **Main site**: Houses for first years, and some second and third years.
  - **Rent**: Banded accommodation on site.
- **Off site**: Sir Geoffrey Arthur Building (GAB) by the river for some second and third years.
  - **Rent**: Fixed rate, nine-month contract for those living in the GAB.

Food: Hall serves lunches and dinner Monday–Friday, and dinner on Sunday. The Farthings Café is open Monday–Saturday, serving breakfast, sandwiches and snacks. The College runs two meal plans, which apply to students living on the main site.
- **Plan 1**: Pre-paid termly evening meal plan, which covers six nights a week during term (Monday–Friday and Sunday). Lunch is served in Hall on a pay-as-you-go basis on weekdays. Formal Hall is compulsory for three nights a week. This plan is automatically taken out by first years.
- **Plan 2**: After first year, students can purchase a flexible meal plan (slightly more expensive than the standard meal plan), and can divide the allowance between brunches, lunches and dinners in Hall or the Farthings Café.
- **Students living in annexe**: Students living here do not take out a meal plan; they use a pay-as-you-go system if they choose to eat in Hall or Farthings.
- **Other**: The GAB annexe is self-catering, and there are some shared kitchens on the main site.

Facilities on site: Auditorium; art gallery; chapel; library; bar.

Financial aid: College Hardship Fund; JCR Art Fund (unexpected hardship); travel grants; vacation grants; academic scholarships and prizes (including rent reductions for scholars and exhibitioners); choral scholarships; organ scholarships; vocal scholarships; Sir Roger Bannister Scholarships for all-round excellence.

Societies: Pembroke Writers Guild; The Pink Times (student publication); Social Sciences Society; Feminist Discussion Group; Pembroke College Choir; Pembroke College Music Society; Pembroke Chamber Singers; CU.

Miscellaneous:
- Pembroke was the first Oxford college to have a JCR-owned art collection. The collection is housed in the College's art gallery, where public exhibitions and speaker events are held throughout the year.
- The College puts on a Film Masterclass series.

Alumni: Senator J. William Fulbright; Samuel Johnson.

Did you know ...?

Pembroke contains the first building to be built by Sir Christopher Wren: the college's chapel.

REGENT'S PARK COLLEGE
(founded 1810, moved to Oxford in 1927 and became a PPH in 1957)

Number of students: 114 UGs.

Size and location: Very small; located near to Modern Languages faculty, Oriental Institute, Classics (Sackler Building); Mathematical Institute; and Linguistics, Philology and Phonetics faculty.

Accommodation: Provided for first and third years (and some second years).
- **Main site**: All first years live on site.
- **Off site**: Third years live in College flats nearby, and there is also College-owned accommodation on Banbury Road, North Oxford.
- **Rent**: Fixed termly charge.

Food:
- **Hall**: Breakfast, lunch and dinner served Monday–Friday. Term-time charges for students living on site normally include lunch and dinner; however, students can opt out of a certain number of these. Students living out charged for a small number of meals per week, but can take more meals in college for an additional charge. Formal Hall served once a week.
- **Other**: Student accommodation has access to communal kitchens.

Facilities on site: Library, with a strong Theology section; chapel; bar.

Financial aid: Please see Oxford's fees and funding pages (www.ox.ac.uk/students/fees-funding) for details of financial support available, or contact the College for further information on its funding arrangements.

Societies: Advent Choir; Gospel Choir; CU; Rowing.

Miscellaneous:
- JCR 'brew', where students come together for tea and biscuits in the JCR, is a regular feature of College life.
- The College has its own tortoise.
- Recently ranked number 1 mixed college for student satisfaction.

Did you know ...?

Regent's Park specialises in the arts, humanities and social science subjects.

SOMERVILLE COLLEGE (founded 1879)

Number of students: 417 UGs.

Size and location: Medium-sized college, next to Language Centre, Mathematics, Engineering and Philosophy departments (Radcliffe Observatory Quarter) and near to the Science Area.

Accommodation: Provided on site for first and final years, and some second years. Second-year accommodation is allocated via ballot.
- **Access**: Lift access to Hall and Terrace Bar. Library, function room and chapel wheelchair accessible.
- **Rent**: Termly charge; 10% premium for en-suite rooms.

Food:
- **Hall**: Breakfast, lunch and dinner served Monday–Friday; brunch and dinner served Saturday–Sunday. Students pay for food in cash or on a pre-paid card, which allows students to purchase food at a discount. Formal Hall served approximately once a week.
- **Other**: Terrace café bar open during term time. Shared kitchens throughout College.

Facilities on site: Library; bar; chapel; fitness suite; music rooms; computer rooms; dark room; St Paul's Nursery (open Monday–Friday).

Financial aid: College bursary; academic scholarships and prizes; book grant for second-year students; travel grants; choral exhibitions.

Societies: Drama Society; Music Society; College Choir; Somerville Writing Group; Somerville Album Club; History Society; Somerville Gender Equality Group.

Miscellaneous:
- The College was founded for women when they were barred from the University; male students were first admitted in 1994.
- Recently voted best college for food.

Alumnae: Vera Brittain; A.S. Byatt; Susie Dent; Indira Gandhi; Dame Iris Murdoch; Lucy Powell; Esther Rantzen; Dorothy L. Sayers; Margaret Thatcher.

Did you know ...?

Somerville was the first non-denominational Oxford college and it continues to be non-denominational in the present day. Along with St Hilda's, St Hugh's and St Edmund Hall, it typically has one of the highest levels of imports (applicants who applied to other colleges or who did not state a preference on their application).

ST ANNE'S COLLEGE (founded 1879)

Number of students: 429 UGs.

Size and location: Large college located near University Parks, opposite Radcliffe Observatory Quarter and near Science Area.

Accommodation: Provided for three years on site; students on four-year courses (with the exception of Modern Languages) are required to live out in their second, third or fourth year.
- **Access**: Adapted accommodation available.
- **Rent**: Fixed annual rate, which includes utilities.

Food:
- **Hall**: Breakfast, lunch and dinner Monday–Friday; brunch Saturday–Sunday. Pay-as-you-go system. Formal Hall served once every fortnight.
- **Other**: St Anne's Coffee Shop. Self-catering shared kitchenettes in all accommodation.

Facilities on site: Library; bar; gym facilities; rowing room; art gallery; dark room; chapel; lecture theatres; music practice rooms; College nursery.

Financial aid: Unexpected hardship grants; travel grants; music bursaries to help meet the cost of music lessons.

Societies: Music Society; Classics Society; Geology Society; Choir; Ensemble ANNIE; STACappella; Orchestra (with St John's); Life Drawing; CU; Feminist Discussion Group; Book Club.

Miscellaneous:
- Vacation Laboratory studentships for science students.
- A Year in Japan offers the opportunity to study in Japan, receive Japanese-language tuition and teach English.
- The College runs its own Careers Week.

Alumni: Danny Alexander; Edwina Currie; Helen Fielding; Diana Wynne Jones; Sir Simon Rattle; Polly Toynbee.

Did you know ...?

The Danson Foundation at St Anne's supports St Anne's students in growing start-up businesses on a nine-week project; students are given working capital and money for legal/administrative costs as part of the Incubator

Projects. Danson internships offer paid placements, mostly in London and in a range of sectors. St Anne's has a high student intake and accepts one of the largest numbers of students per year.

ST BENET'S HALL (PPH; founded 1897)

Number of students: 79 UGs.

Size and location: Small college, near Modern Languages, Classics and Oriental faculties, Radcliffe Observatory Quarter and Mathematical Institute.

Accommodation: Provided for first and final years on site and in Norham Gardens (North Oxford), which also has teaching rooms and common areas.
- **Access**: As the Hall is a listed building, the main site is not very suitable for wheelchairs; however, the Hall welcomes applications from students with disabilities.
- **Rent**: Flat-rate daily charge. See under 'Food' for additional Hall charges.

Food:
- **Hall**: Flat-rate daily Meals & Facilities charge, which is reduced for students living out. This charge includes breakfast, lunch, tea and dinner, two Formals, a served Sunday lunch, one Formal guest night, and use of laundry and Hall facilities. Formal Hall served three times a week.

Facilities on site: IT centre; croquet lawn; chapel; library.

Financial aid: See Oxford's fees and funding pages (www.ox.ac.uk/students/fees-funding) for details of financial support available, or contact the College for further information on its funding arrangements.

Societies: Drama.

Miscellaneous:
- As of 2016, the Hall now admits female undergraduates.
- The Hall is involved in the OxDev Project, during which students intern in developing countries.

Did you know ...?

As a small college, St Benet's is known for its familial atmosphere; there is no high table, as everyone in the Hall sits at a common table.

ST CATHERINE'S COLLEGE (Catz)
(founded 1962 – newest college; very modern buildings)

Number of students: 496 UGs.

Size and location: Large; extensive grounds, including a water garden. Near Social Sciences (Politics, International Relations, Economics, Sociology), English and Law faculties and Science Area.

Accommodation: Most students live on site for three years.
- **Access**: Adapted accommodation available for students with disabilities.
- **Rent**: Fixed rate.

Food:
- **Hall**: Serves breakfast, lunch and dinner. Pay-as-you-go system. Formal Hall served every day.
- **Other**: Buttery open on weekdays, serving snacks. Kitchens and pantries in each staircase.

Facilities on site: Library; bar; music house; theatre; punt house; squash courts; tennis courts; sports pitches; gym; games room.

Financial aid: Travel awards; College prizes; Répétiteur Scholarship for pianists, working between Catz and New Chamber Opera; Nick Young Award (grant to gain television experience working with Director's Cut Productions in London).

Societies: Arts; Biomedical; Catzapella; CU; Femsoc; Geography; International Students Society; Law; Mathematics; Music.

Miscellaneous: The College was originally part of a society that was formed to encourage students from less-privileged backgrounds to study at Oxford.

Alumni: Emilia Fox; Joseph Heller; Peter Mandelson; James Marsh; Jeanette Winterson.

Did you know ...?

St Catz has a strong reputation for drama. Its Cameron Mackintosh Chair of Contemporary Theatre is a Visiting Professorship to promote the study of contemporary theatre and give lectures and workshops. Past holders include Simon Russell Beale, Stephen Fry, Sir Trevor Nunn, Kevin Spacey, Sir Patrick Stewart, Sir Tim Rice, Stephen Daldry, Lord Attenborough, Arthur Miller, Sir Ian McKellen and Stephen Sondheim.

ST EDMUND HALL (Teddy Hall) (founded 1278)

Number of students: 379 UGs.

Size and location: Small college, located just off the High Street, near to Examination Schools and English and Law faculties.

Accommodation: Provided for first and third years.
- **Access**: Most principal areas of the main College site are accessible.
- **Main site**: All first years live on site.
- **Off site**: Three annexes in North and East Oxford with shared kitchens.

Food:
- **Hall**: Breakfast, lunch and dinner served Monday–Friday; brunch and dinner Saturday–Sunday. Students living on site pay for a minimum number of breakfasts and dinners each term; some meals can be refunded if not used by the end of term. Formal Hall served twice a week.
- **Other**: All sites have self-catering facilities.

Facilities on site: Music room; games room; chapel; library; bar.

Financial aid: Undergraduate College grants to meet academic costs; College Hardship Fund; organ scholarships; choral scholarships; travel awards; subject-specific prizes; academic scholarships and exhibitions.

Societies: Chapel Choir (non-auditioning); Alternative Choir; Jazz Band; Music Society; Arts Society; CU; John Oldham Society (drama); PPE; Hall Writers' Forum; Venus Society (organises fundraising events for Macmillan Cancer Support).

Miscellaneous:
- Full college of the University of Oxford, but has retained its title of 'Hall'.
- The College runs a Masterclass scheme, which offers a grant for students to receive advanced coaching in extra-curricular areas such as music, sport, art, drama and writing. In addition, the Frank di Renzio Masterclass Award offers a grant for coaching in drama and theatre.
- The College organises a Bridge to Business programme, offering an insight into writing CVs, interview and presentation preparation and career planning.

Alumni: Nicholas Evans; Terry Jones; Stewart Lee; Al Murray.

Did you know ...?

The College has a strong writing tradition across a range of genres, and hosts weekly creative-writing workshops for students during term and regular writing events.

ST HILDA'S COLLEGE (founded 1893)

Number of students: 404 UGs.

Size and location: Large grounds. Located at the very end of the High Street, right by the river and near to the Iffley Road sports complex.

Accommodation: Provided for all first years and most final years in College. Currently building a new accommodation block to provide additional undergraduate accommodation.
- **Access**: Two adapted rooms for students with disabilities and disabled toilet facilities in the principal College building. The Hall, JCR, chapel and library all have wheelchair access.
- **Main site**: First years and some finalists.
  - **Rent**: Fixed rate; higher charge for en-suite rooms, which are allocated to final years.
- **Off site**: Off-site College properties for some second-year and final-year students. 40-week lease.

Food:
- **Hall**: Breakfast, lunch and dinner served Monday–Friday; brunch served on Saturday. Pay-as-you-go meals and takeaway options. The Hall has round tables; only college to have this. Formal Hall served once a week.
- **Other**: The Buttery (student-run snack bar). Student kitchenettes/kitchens in College; size/kitchen facilities varies depending on the accommodation block.

Facilities on site: Jacqueline du Pré Music Building; netball court; tennis court; College punts; chapel; library; bar. Current building work will provide new accommodation, social and teaching spaces, including a new MCR, Porters' Lodge and entrance.

Financial aid: JCR Hardship Fund; academic scholarships; book grants; travel fund; D.D. White Fund to meet costs of sports equipment.

Societies: Choir; Orchestra; Running Club; Hildabeats (jazz and blues band); Drama; CU.

Miscellaneous: Originally a women's college, but now admits both male and female undergraduates.

Alumnae: Wendy Cope; Adèle Geras; Val McDermid; Katherine Parkinson.

Did you know ...?

Nestled in picturesque riverside gardens, St Hilda's is one of Oxford's best-kept secrets; it often receives the lowest number of direct applications among the Oxford colleges, and among the highest number of imports. Other colleges receiving low numbers of direct applications include Mansfield, St Hugh's, Corpus Christi and St Peter's. Among its extensive list of on-site facilities, St Hilda's is home to the Jacqueline du Pré Music Building which, as well as including four practice rooms, an auditorium and recording studio, hosts regular concerts from renowned professional musicians.

ST HUGH'S COLLEGE (founded 1886)

Number of students: 428 UGs.

Size and location: Large; extensive grounds (14 acres). Near Radcliffe Observatory Quarter and Institute of Social and Cultural Anthropology.

Accommodation: Provided for the duration of the course on site; ballot after first year.
- **Access**: Limited number of rooms available with disabled access.
- **Rent**: Flat rate.

Food:
- **Hall**: Breakfast, lunch and dinner Monday–Friday; brunch Saturday and Sunday. Pay-as-you-go system. Formal Hall served once a week.
- **Other**: Elizabeth Wordsworth Tea Room serves snacks and drinks on weekdays, including lunch. All rooms in College have access to shared kitchens.

Facilities on site: Gym; chapel; music practice rooms; library; bar.

Financial aid: Academic scholarships and exhibitions; academic and subject-specific prizes; travel grants; Year Abroad Grant for Modern Languages students; Financial Hardship Fund; organ scholarships; choral awards.

Societies: Choir; Arts Society; Debating; St Hugh's Players (drama); Blue Pen (gender equality); Jazz Band Society; Poker; Real Ale Society; Swan Newspaper; SHCAS (film); CU.

Miscellaneous: The College has over 100 fellows, meaning that students are able to have many of their classes on site, especially in the first year.

Alumnae: Aung San Suu Kyi; Amal Clooney; Theresa May; Nicky Morgan.

Did you know ...?

St. Hugh's was founded in 1886 to offer an education to young women who were unable to afford the costs of the other halls and colleges.

ST JOHN'S COLLEGE (founded 1555)

Number of students: 401 UGs.

Size and location: Fairly large college; near to Languages, Oriental Studies, Classics and Linguistics faculties.

Accommodation: Provided for the duration of the course. Students balloted after first year. Accommodation available for couples and families.
- **Access**: Adapted accommodation available for students with disabilities, including en-suite facilities and adapted kitchens. One property on Museum Road has an adapted kitchen suitable for wheelchair users, blind and partially sighted students.
- **Main site**: Houses first years, some second and final years.
- **Off site**: College-owned houses behind Tommy White Quad, for groups of five to eight students in their second or final years.
- **Rent**: Banded, with an additional fixed charge per term to cover services.

Food:
- **Hall**: Serves breakfast, lunch and dinner; pay-as-you-go system. Formal Hall served six nights a week.
- **Other**: Kendrew Café serves food and coffee. All first years have access to a shared kitchen and the rooms in Kendrew Quad also have access to cooking facilities. The off-site properties have their own kitchens.

Facilities on site: Art gallery; two squash courts; two gyms; auditorium; music rooms; library; bar.

Financial aid: College hardship grants; academic grant for books, materials, etc.; special grants (e.g. for travel); vacation grants; Blues Squad Grants; choral scholarships; Mapleton Bee Prize for work in the Creative Arts.

Societies: Choir; St John's and St Anne's Orchestra (non-auditioning); Music Society; Mummers Drama Society; Poker Society.

Alumni: Tony Blair; Angela Eagle; Robert Graves; Philip Larkin; Victoria Coren Mitchell; Hugh Schofield.

> **Did you know ...?**
>
> One of the newest additions to the College buildings is the award-winning Kendrew Quadrangle, which features solar panels for hot water, geothermal heat pumps for underfloor heating and air conditioning, low-energy lighting and a biomass boiler.

ST PETER'S COLLEGE (founded 1929; became a college in 1961)

Number of students: 351 UGs.

Size and location: Very small college; near to History, Archaeology, Modern Languages and History of Art faculties.

Accommodation: Accommodation provided for first year and final year. Final-year rooms are decided via ballot.
- **Access**: Most of the main site is accessible for wheelchair users, apart from the library and music room. The Hall is accessible via a lift.
- **Main site**: All first years live on site and some final years.
- **Off site**: Three College annexes, each of which is en suite.
- **Rent**: Fixed rate; the lease length varies, depending on whether you live on or off site.

Food:
- **Hall**: Breakfast, lunch and dinner served Monday–Friday; brunch and dinner Saturday–Sunday. Pay-as-you-go system. Formal Hall served twice a week.
- **Other**: Limited cooking facilities on site; JCR has a kitchen and there are kitchens in some, but not all, staircases on site. Annexes have shared kitchens and en-suite rooms.

Facilities on site: Lecture theatre; large chapel, offering ample performance space; music room; library; separate Law library; bar; gym.

Financial aid: Hardship Fund for unexpected hardship; academic scholarships and exhibitions; subject prizes; choral scholarships; organ scholarships; instrumental awards; travel grants; vacation grants; Compulsory Fieldwork Grant.

Societies: Choir; Orchestra; Cross Keys Drama Society; Misc (photography, art and poetry publication); College Newspaper.

Miscellaneous:
- The College runs its own Arts Week.
- The College's Careers Society runs talks, mentorship schemes, CV clinics and other events to connect current students with St Peter's alumni.

Alumni: Rev Wilbert Awdry; Mark Carney; Hugh Dancy; Hugh Fearnley-Whittingstall; Libby Lane; Ken Loach; Dr Chris van Tulleken.

> **Did you know ...?**
>
> St Peter's alumna the Right Revd Dr Libby Lane, Bishop of Stockport, was the first female bishop in England.

ST STEPHEN'S HOUSE (PPH; founded 1876)

NB Accepts mature students only.

Number of students: 4 UGs.

Size and location: Very small college, located opposite Iffley Road sports complex.

Accommodation: Provided for the duration of the course; accommodation ranges from single occupancy to flats and properties, suitable for couples and families.
- **Rent**: Weekly average rate, which varies depending on the room.

Food:
- **Hall**: Breakfast, lunch and dinner served Monday–Friday, in addition to afternoon tea. Brunch served on Saturday and breakfast and lunch served on Sunday. Students living in are on half-board and pay a weekly charge, which entitles them to discounts on other meals and includes celebratory meals. Students living out are required to pay a small annual catering charge, which entitles them to discounted meals and includes celebratory meals.
- **Other**: Large student kitchen on site and kitchens in College houses.

Facilities on site: Chapel; Bodley Church; brick barbecue; computer room; library.

Financial aid: See Oxford's fees and funding pages (www.ox.ac.uk/students/fees-funding) for details of financial support available, or contact the College for further information on its funding arrangements.

Miscellaneous: Anglican foundation specialising in theological teaching and research.

Did you know ...?

St Stephen's House recently came top for student satisfaction in the Student Barometer of all the Oxford colleges and permanent private halls.

THE QUEEN'S COLLEGE (founded 1341)

Number of students: 346 UGs.

Size and location: Medium-sized college, near to Examination Schools, English and Law faculties and Science Area.

Accommodation: Provided for duration of the course.
- **Access**: Most areas of the main site are wheelchair accessible via permanent ramps.
- **Main site**: Some second and final years.
- **Off site**: First years live in two independent annexes for the first year, rather than on site as happens in most other colleges. Some second years live in the Cardo Building near the main site.
- **Rent**: Flat-rate termly fee, which includes kitchen overhead charge. Shared rooms and smaller rooms available for those who want to reduce their rent.

Food:
- **Hall**: Food served daily. Breakfast and lunch pay-as-you-go; dinner booked online for a fixed charge. Formal Hall served once a week.
- **Other**: Two first-year annexes serve breakfast. JCR tea served daily.

Facilities on site: Library; separate libraries for Law and Egyptology; auditorium; music practice rooms; chapel; bar. Cardo annexe (first-year annexe) has squash courts. Carrodus Quad annexe (second years and above) has an on-site gym.

Financial aid: Queen's Hardship Fund; book grants; academic support grants (travel, books, printing, etc.); choral, organ and instrumental awards; travel grants; sports fund to meet the cost of equipment/kit.

Societies: Choir; Eglesfield Musical Society (EGMS) Chorus; EGMS Orchestra; EGMS A Cappella; EGMS Jazz Band; String Quartet; Eglesfield Players (drama); Addison Society (dining society); CU.

Alumni: Rowan Atkinson; Sir Tim Berners-Lee; Edwin Hubble; Henry V.

Did you know ...?

As well as having a renowned choir, Queen's College is one of the best colleges in Oxford for music as an extra-curricular, with numerous student vocal and instrumental ensembles.

TRINITY COLLEGE (founded 1555)

Number of students: 297 UGs.

Size and location: Fairly large college, near University Libraries.

Accommodation: Provided for the duration of the course.
- **Access**: Several adapted rooms available for students with disabilities. Hall, chapel, library, toilets and some teaching rooms are wheelchair accessible.
- **Main site**: Students live on site for first two years.
  - **Rent**: Flat-rate fee; 180-day licence.
- **Off site**: Third and fourth years live in a self-catered College annexe in North Oxford.
  - **Rent**: Prices off site vary; 264-day licence.

Food:
- **Hall**: Breakfast, lunch and dinner served Monday–Friday; brunch and dinner Saturday–Sunday. Pay-as-you-go system. Gowns worn for dinner every night. Formal Hall served five nights a week.
- **Other**: JCR kitchen. Off-site College accommodation has shared kitchens.

Facilities on site: Gym; squash court; music practice room; chapel; library; bar.

Financial aid: Levine Bursary (for students not eligible for an Oxford Opportunity Bursary (OOB) or whose OOB entitlement doesn't cover financial needs); academic grants for subject-related projects; book grants; travel grants; Year Abroad Fund for Modern Languages.

Societies: Chapel Choir (non-auditioned); Swing Band; Chamber Orchestra; Music Society; Trinity Players (drama); The Broadsheet (student newspaper); The Gryphon (debating); World Music Group; Trinity Singers; CU; Law Society.

Alumni: Sir Richard Burton; Constantine Louloudis; Sir Terence Rattigan; Jacob Rees-Mogg; David Yates.

Did you know ...?

Trinity holds an annual Richard Hillary Memorial Lecture with notable guest speakers; recent lecturers include Philip Pullman, Carol Ann Duffy, Sir Tom Stoppard and Sir Andrew Motion.

UNIVERSITY COLLEGE (Univ) (founded 1249)

Number of students: 414 UGs.

Size and location: Medium-sized college on the High Street, next to the Examination Schools, and near to the English and Law faculties.

Accommodation: Provided for three years on site and in annexes in North and East Oxford.
- **Access**: Three fully accessible rooms and several other adapted rooms for students with disabilities.
- **Rent**: Flat-rate termly fee, which includes facilities charge.

Food:
- **Hall**: Breakfast, lunch and dinner served Monday–Friday; brunch and dinner Saturday–Sunday. Pay-as-you-go system. Formal Hall served three times a week.
- **Other**: Some shared kitchens on Stavertonia site (North Oxford) and on site.

Facilities on site: Squash court; library; separate Law library; chapel; bar.

Financial aid: Old Members' Trust Bursary (needs-based); Univ Support Fund for unexpected financial hardship; academic scholarships and exhibitions; travel grants; vacation grants.

Societies: Choir (non-auditioned); College Orchestra; Music Society; Univ Players (drama); Debating Society; Eldon Society (Law); Univ Mooting; CU; Sikh Society; Ambassador Scheme (see 'Did you know ...?' below).

Miscellaneous:
- The College co-owns a French chalet with Balliol and New Colleges.
- The College offers a pre-term Maths Week for Biochemistry, Biomedical Sciences, Chemistry, Computer Science, Earth Sciences, Engineering, Mathematics, Medicine and Physics students.
- Staircase12 (www.univ.ox.ac.uk/applying-to-univ/staircase12) is a College-run website for school and sixth-form students.

Alumni: Bill Clinton; Stephen Hawking; C.S. Lewis; Sir Andrew Motion; Harold Wilson.

Did you know ...?

University College, or Univ, as it is more commonly known, has its own Ambassador Scheme, a volunteering programme where Univ students work as mentors for young people, providing advice and information about higher education and applying to Oxford, doing tours of the College, school visits and helping out on open days and at summer schools and taster days.

WADHAM COLLEGE (founded 1610)

Number of students: 472 UGs.

Size and location: Large college with six acres of grounds. Near Science Area and University Libraries.

Accommodation: Provided for first and final years.
- **Access**: Adapted accommodation available for students with disabilities.
- **Rent**: Flat-rate fee. For students living on site, board and lodging charge includes accommodation, evening meals Monday–Friday (in Hall or Refectory), utilities, internet and basic insurance cover.

Food:
- **Hall**: Serves dinner Monday–Friday. No Formal Hall.
- **New Refectory**: Serves breakfast, lunch and dinner Monday–Friday and brunch on Saturdays. Breakfast, lunch and brunch pay-as-you-go. Dinner is included in board and lodging charge for students living on site; students living off site must pre-book dinner online.
- **Other**: JCR kitchen, and some staircases have kitchenettes.

Facilities on site: Library; bar; Holywell Music Room (concert hall); Sir Claus Moser Theatre (doubles as a badminton court); music practice rooms; gym; squash court; rowing machine room.

Financial aid: Student Support Grants for unforeseen financial hardship; students living out are given a grant to help with living costs; academic-related grants to meet academic costs; academic scholarships and subject prizes; vacation grants; travel grants.

Societies: Chapel Choir; Dot's Funk Odyssey (funk/soul band); Wadham Jazz Band; Orchestra (joint with Keble).

Miscellaneous:
- Accredited Fairtrade college.
- Only college to have a single students' union – the JCR and MCR are combined.
- Student Ambassador Scheme for outreach events.
- The College organises Wadstock (music festival) annually.

Alumni: Melvyn Bragg; Felicity Jones; Rosamund Pike; Michael Rosen; Rowan Williams; Sir Christopher Wren.

WORCESTER COLLEGE (founded 1714)

Number of students: 428 UGs.

Size and location: Very large – 26 acres of grounds, including lake, orchards and sports fields. Near Archaeology, Modern Languages, Linguistics and History faculties and Oriental Institute.

Accommodation: Three years' accommodation offered; all rooms on site or within a few hundred metres of the College.
- **Rent**: Banded accommodation. Length of contract varies from year to year: 176 nights for first years; 174 nights for second years; 258 nights for third and fourth years.

Food:
- **Hall**: Breakfast, lunch and dinner served Monday–Saturday; breakfast and Formal Hall on Sunday. Pay-as-you-go system. Formal Hall served three times a week.
- **Other**: Buttery serving drinks and snacks. Shared kitchens/diners in most student accommodation.

Facilities on site: Sports fields; gym; tennis courts; library; Law library; chapel; bar; theatre/performance space; multi-faith prayer room.

Financial aid: Financial Hardship Fund; academic scholarships and exhibitions; choral, organ and instrumental scholarships; travel grants; vacation study grants; book allowance.

Societies: Buskins Drama Society; two Chapel choirs; College Orchestra; Music Society; Woosta Source (College newspaper).

Alumni: Russell T Davies; Rupert Murdoch; Emma Watson.

Did you know ...?

Set in 26 acres, including a lake, Worcester is the only Oxford college to have its sporting fields on site, catering for rugby, football, hockey, lawn and hard tennis, cricket, rounders and croquet. In addition, there is also an on-site gym and a tennis court.

WYCLIFFE HALL (PPH; founded 1877)

NB Accepts mature students only.

Number of students: 22 UGs.

Size and location: Small college near Science Area and University Parks.

Accommodation: Priority given to ordinands. Independent students eligible for Hall accommodation on a first-come, first-served basis, and only after all ordinands in that year have been allocated a room. Family accommodation available; again, priority is given to ordinands.

- **Access**: Some of the buildings on the main site are accessible to wheelchair users.
- **Rent**: Fixed annual cost. Around half of the rooms on site are on an all-year lease (38-weeks); the other half are for term time only.

Food: Breakfast, lunch and dinner served seven days a week. Rent for a Hall room includes the cost of 180 meals (60 per term).

Facilities on site: Specialist theological library; chapel.

Financial aid: See Oxford's fees and funding pages (www.ox.ac.uk/students/fees-funding) for details of financial support available, or contact the College for further information on its funding arrangements.

Miscellaneous:
- Evangelical theological college.
- Sports are joint with Queen's College.
- Also offers an Undergraduate Certificate in Theological Studies; and Undergraduate Diploma in Theological Studies (available to students with 'Senior Status', i.e. students who have already completed an undergraduate degree).

Did you know ...?

As an evangelical college, Wycliffe Hall has one of the best college libraries for Theology in Oxford.

Norrington table

Table 8 Norrington Table – Oxford 2019–2020

Rank	College	Score
1	New College	83.5%
2	St Catherine's	82.5%
3	Queen's	81.7%
4	St Peter's	81.5%
5	Merton	81%
6	Wadham	80.9%
7	Brasenose	80.4%
8	St John's	80.2%
9	Oriel	79.8%
10	Lincoln	79.5%
11	Hertford	79.2%
12	Trinity	79.1%
13	University	78.9%
14	Worcester	78.8%
15	St Hugh's	78.8%
16	Balliol	78.6%
17	St Hilda's	78.3%
18	Jesus	78%
19	Pembroke	78%
20	Magdalen	77.4%
21	Harris Manchester	77.4%
22	St Anne's	77%
23	Corpus Christi	77%
24	Keble	76.6%
25	St Edmund Hall	76.4%
26	Exeter	75.8%
27	Lady Margaret Hall	75.7%
28	Christ Church	75.6%
29	Mansfield	75.5%
30	Somerville	72.8%
31	St Stephen's House (PPH)	80%
32	Regent's Park (PPH)	74.3%
33	St Benet's Hall (PPH)	69.5%
34	Wycliffe Hall (PPH)	63.6%

Oxford map

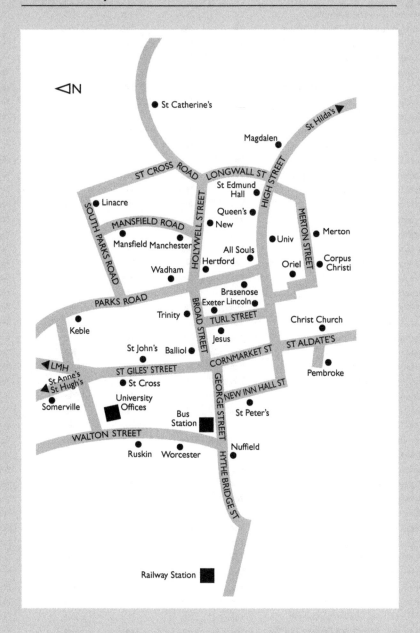

Table 9 Undergraduate courses available at Oxford colleges (continues on pages 212–214)

Course	Balliol	Blackfriars Hall	Brasenose	Christ Church	Corpus Christi
Archaeology and Anthropology	No	No	No	No	No
Biochemistry (Molecular and Cellular)	No	No	Yes	Yes	Yes
Biology	Yes	No	Yes	Yes	No
Biomedical Sciences	Yes	No	No	No	Yes
Chemistry	Yes	No	Yes	Yes	Yes
Classical Archaeology and Ancient History	Yes	No	Yes	Yes	Yes
Classics	Yes	No	Yes	Yes	Yes
Classics and English	No	No	Yes	No	Yes
Classics and Modern Languages	Yes	No	Yes	Yes	No
Classics and Oriental Studies	Yes	No	Yes	Yes	No
Computer Science	Yes	No	No	Yes	No
Computer Science and Philosophy	Yes	No	No	Yes	No
Earth Sciences (Geology)	No	No	No	No	No
Economics and Management	Yes	No	Yes	Yes	No
Engineering Science	Yes	No	Yes	Yes	No
English Language and Literature	Yes	No	Yes	Yes	Yes
English and Modern Languages	Yes	No	Yes	Yes	No
European and Middle Eastern Languages	No	No	Yes	Yes	No
Fine Art	No	No	Yes	Yes	No
Geography	No	No	Yes	Yes	No
History	Yes	No	Yes	Yes	Yes
History (Ancient and Modern)	Yes	No	Yes	Yes	Yes
History and Economics	Yes	No	Yes	No	No
History and English	Yes	No	No	No	Yes
History and Modern Languages	Yes	No	Yes	Yes	No
History and Politics	Yes	No	Yes	Yes	Yes
History of Art	No	No	No	Yes	No
Human Sciences	No	No	No	No	No
Law (Jurisprudence)	Yes	No	Yes	Yes	Yes
Law with Law Studies in Europe	Yes	No	Yes	Yes	Yes
Materials Science	No	No	No	No	Yes
Mathematics	Yes	No	Yes	Yes	Yes
Mathematics and Computer Science	Yes	No	No	Yes	Yes
Mathematics and Philosophy	Yes	No	Yes	Yes	Yes
Mathematics and Statistics	Yes	No	Yes	Yes	Yes
Medicine	Yes	No	Yes	Yes	Yes
Medicine (Graduate Entry)	No	No	No	No	No
Modern Languages	Yes	No	Yes	Yes	No
Modern Languages and Linguistics	Yes	No	Yes	Yes	No
Music	No	No	No	Yes	No
Oriental Studies	Yes	No	No	Yes	No
Philosophy and Modern Languages	Yes	No	Yes	Yes	No
Philosophy, Politics and Economics (PPE)	Yes	Yes	Yes	Yes	Yes
Philosophy and Theology	No	Yes	No	Yes	No
Physics	Yes	No	Yes	Yes	Yes
Physics and Philosophy	Yes	No	Yes	No	No
Psychology (Experimental)	No	No	Yes	Yes	Yes
Psychology, Philosophy and Linguistics (PPL)	No	No	Yes	Yes	Yes
Religion and Oriental Studies	No	Yes	No	Yes	No
Theology and Religion	No	Yes	No	Yes	No

Exeter	Harris Manchester	Hertford	Jesus	Keble	Lady Margaret Hall	Lincoln	Magdalen	Mansfield	Merton
No	Yes	Yes	No	Yes	No	No	Yes	No	No
Yes	No	Yes	No	No	Yes	Yes	Yes	No	Yes
No	No	Yes	Yes	Yes	Yes	No	Yes	No	Yes
Yes	No	No	No	Yes	No	Yes	Yes	No	No
Yes	No	Yes	Yes	Yes	Yes	Yes	Yes	No	Yes
Yes	No	No	No	Yes	Yes	Yes	Yes	No	Yes
Yes	No	No	Yes	No	Yes	No	Yes	No	Yes
Yes	Yes	No	Yes	No	Yes	No	Yes	No	No
Yes	No	No	Yes	No	Yes	No	Yes	No	Yes
Yes	Yes	No	No	No	No	No	Yes	No	No
No	No	Yes	Yes	Yes	Yes	No	Yes	No	Yes
No	No	Yes	Yes	No	Yes	No	No	No	Yes
Yes	No	No	No	No	No	No	No	No	No
Yes	Yes	Yes	Yes	Yes	Yes	No	No	No	Yes
Yes	Yes	Yes	Yes	Yes	Yes	Yes	Yes	Yes	No
Yes	Yes	Yes	Yes	Yes	Yes	Yes	Yes	Yes	Yes
Yes	No	Yes	Yes	Yes	Yes	No	Yes	No	Yes
No	No	No	Yes	No	No	No	Yes	No	No
Yes	No	No	No	No	Yes	No	Yes	No	No
No	No	Yes	Yes	Yes	No	No	No	Yes	No
Yes	Yes	Yes	Yes	Yes	Yes	Yes	Yes	Yes	Yes
Yes	No	No	No	Yes	Yes	Yes	Yes	No	Yes
No	Yes	No	Yes	No	No	No	No	No	No
Yes	No	No	Yes	No	No	No	No	No	Yes
Yes	No	Yes	Yes	Yes	Yes	Yes	Yes	No	Yes
No	Yes	Yes	Yes	Yes	Yes	Yes	Yes	No	Yes
No	Yes	No	No	No	No	Yes	No	No	No
No	Yes	Yes	No	Yes	No	No	Yes	Yes	No
Yes	Yes	Yes	Yes	Yes	Yes	Yes	Yes	Yes	Yes
Yes	Yes	Yes	Yes	Yes	Yes	Yes	Yes	Yes	Yes
No	No	No	No	No	No	No	No	Yes	No
Yes	No	Yes	Yes	Yes	Yes	Yes	Yes	Yes	Yes
Yes	No	No	Yes	Yes	Yes	No	Yes	No	Yes
Yes	No	No	Yes	No	Yes	No	Yes	No	Yes
Yes	No	No	Yes	Yes	Yes	Yes	Yes	Yes	Yes
Yes	No	Yes	Yes	Yes	Yes	Yes	Yes	No	Yes
No	Yes	No	No	No	No	No	Yes	No	No
Yes	No	Yes	Yes	Yes	Yes	Yes	Yes	No	Yes
Yes	No	Yes	Yes	Yes	Yes	No	Merton	No	Merton
Yes	No	Yes	Yes	Yes	Yes	Yes	Yes	No	Yes
No	Yes	Yes	No	No	No	No	No	Yes	No
Yes	No	Yes	Yes	Yes	Yes	Yes	Yes	No	Yes
Yes	Yes	Yes	Yes	Yes	Yes	Yes	Yes	Yes	Yes
No	Yes	No	Yes	Yes	Yes	No	No	Yes	No
Yes	No	Yes	Yes	Yes	Yes	Yes	Yes	Yes	Yes
No	No	Yes	No	No	Yes	No	Yes	No	Yes
No	Yes	No	Yes	No	Yes	No	Yes	No	No
No	No	No	Yes	No	Yes	No	Yes	No	No
No	Yes	No	No	No	Yes	No	No	No	No
No	Yes	No	No	Yes	Yes	No	No	Yes	No

Course	New	Oriel	Pembroke	Queen's	Regent's Park	Somerville
Archaeology and Anthropology	No	No	No	No	No	No
Biochemistry (Mollecular and Cellular)	Yes	Yes	Yes	Yes	No	Yes
Biology	Yes	No	Yes	Yes	No	Yes
Biomedical Sciences	Yes	Yes	No	Yes	No	No
Chemistry	Yes	Yes	Yes	Yes	No	Yes
Classical Archaeology and Ancient History	No	Yes	No	No	Yes	Yes
Classics	Yes	Yes	No	Yes	Yes	Yes
Classics and English	No	Yes	No	Yes	Yes	No
Classics and Modern Languages	Yes	Yes	No	Yes	No	Yes
Classics and Oriental Studies	Yes	Yes	No	Yes	No	Yes
Computer Science	Yes	Yes	No	No	No	Yes
Computer Science and Philosophy	Yes	Yes	No	No	No	No
Earth Sciences (Geology)	No	No	No	No	No	No
Economics and Management	Yes	No	Yes	No	No	No
Engineering Science	Yes	Yes	Yes	No	No	Yes
English Language and Literature	Yes	Yes	Yes	Yes	Yes	Yes
English and Modern Languages	Yes	Yes	Yes	Yes	No	Yes
European and Middle Eastern Languages	Yes	No	Yes	Yes	No	Yes
Fine Art	Yes	No	No	Yes	No	No
Geography	No	No	No	No	Yes	No
History	Yes	Yes	Yes	Yes	Yes	Yes
History (Ancient and Modern)	Yes	Yes	No	Yes	Yes	Yes
History and Economics	Yes	Yes	Yes	No	Yes	Yes
History and English	No	No	Yes	Yes	Yes	Yes
History and Modern Languages	Yes	Yes	Yes	Yes	No	Yes
History and Politics	Yes	Yes	Yes	Yes	Yes	No
History of Art	No	No	No	No	No	No
Human Sciences	No	No	No	No	No	No
Law (Jurisprudence)	Yes	Yes	Yes	Yes	Yes	Yes
Law with Law Studies in Europe	Yes	Yes	Yes	Yes	No	Yes
Materials Science	No	No	No	Yes	No	No
Mathematics	Yes	Yes	Yes	Yes	No	Yes
Mathematics and Computer Science	Yes	Yes	No	No	No	Yes
Mathematics and Philosophy	Yes	Yes	Yes	Yes	No	No
Mathematics and Statistics	Yes	Yes	No	Yes	No	Yes
Medicine	Yes	Yes	Yes	Yes	No	Yes
Medicine (Graduate Entry)	No	No	Yes	No	No	Yes
Modern Languages	Yes	Yes	Yes	Yes	No	Yes
Modern Languages and Linguistics	Yes	Yes	Yes	Yes	No	Yes
Music	Yes	Yes	Yes	Yes	No	Yes
Oriental Studies	No	No	Yes	Yes	No	No
Philosophy and Modern Languages	Yes	Yes	Yes	Yes	No	No
Philosophy, Politics and Economics (PPE)	Yes	Yes	Yes	Yes	Yes	Yes
Philosophy and Theology	No	Yes	Yes	No	Yes	No
Physics	Yes	Yes	Yes	Yes	No	Yes
Physics and Philosophy	No	Yes	Yes	Yes	No	Yes
Psychology (Experimental)	Yes	No	Yes	Yes	No	No
Psychology, Philosophy and Linguistics (PPL)	Yes	No	Yes	Yes	No	No
Religion and Oriental Studies	No	No	Yes	No	Yes	Yes
Theology and Religion	No	Yes	Yes	No	Yes	Yes

St Anne's	St Benet's Hall	St Catherine's	St Edmund Hall	St Hilda's	St Hugh's	St John's	St Peter's	St Stephen's House
No	No	No	No	No	Yes	Yes	Yes	No
Yes	No	Yes	Yes	Yes	Yes	Yes	Yes	No
Yes	No	Yes	No	Yes	Yes	Yes	Yes	No
Yes	No	Yes	Yes	Yes	Yes	Yes	No	No
Yes	No	Yes	Yes	Yes	Yes	Yes	Yes	No
Yes	No	No	No	Yes	No	Yes	No	No
Yes	Yes	No	No	Yes	Yes	Yes	No	No
Yes	No	No	No	No	Yes	No	No	No
Yes	No	No	No	No	Yes	Yes	No	No
Yes	Yes	No	No	Yes	Yes	Yes	No	No
Yes	No	Yes	No	No	Yes	Yes	No	No
Yes	No	Yes	No	No	No	Yes	No	No
Yes	No	No	Yes	No	Yes	No	Yes	No
No	No	Yes	Yes	Yes	Yes	No	Yes	No
Yes	No	Yes	Yes	Yes	Yes	Yes	Yes	No
Yes	No	Yes	Yes	Yes	Yes	Yes	Yes	No
Yes	No	Yes	Yes	Yes	Yes	Yes	Yes	No
Yes	No	No	No	Yes	Yes	Yes	No	No
Yes	No	Yes	Yes	No	Yes	Yes	No	No
Yes	No	Yes	Yes	Yes	No	Yes	Yes	No
Yes	Yes	Yes	Yes	Yes	Yes	Yes	Yes	No
Yes	No	No	No	Yes	Yes	Yes	No	No
Yes	No	Yes	No	Yes	No	Yes	Yes	No
No	No	Yes	No	Yes	Yes	No	Yes	No
Yes	No	Yes	Yes	Yes	Yes	Yes	Yes	No
Yes	No	Yes	Yes	Yes	Yes	Yes	Yes	No
No	No	Yes	No	No	No	Yes	Yes	No
No	Yes	Yes	No	No	Yes	Yes	No	No
Yes	No	Yes	Yes	Yes	Yes	Yes	Yes	No
Yes	No	Yes	Yes	Yes	Yes	Yes	Yes	No
Yes	No	Yes	Yes	No	No	No	No	No
Yes	No	Yes	Yes	Yes	Yes	Yes	Yes	No
Yes	No	Yes	No	No	Yes	Yes	No	No
Yes	No	Yes	Yes	Yes	Yes	Yes	Yes	No
Yes	No	Yes	Yes	Yes	Yes	Yes	Yes	No
Yes	No	Yes	Yes	Yes	Yes	Yes	Yes	No
Yes	No	Yes	No	No	Yes	No	Yes	No
Yes	No	Yes	Yes	Yes	Yes	Yes	Yes	No
Yes	No	Yes	Yes	Yes	Yes	Yes	Yes	House
Yes	No	Yes	No	Yes	Yes	Yes	Yes	No
Yes	Yes	No	No	No	No	Yes	No	No
Yes	No	Yes	Yes	Yes	Yes	Yes	Yes	No
Yes	Yes	Yes	Yes	Yes	Yes	Yes	Yes	No
No	Yes	No	No	No	No	Yes	Yes	No
Yes	No	Yes	Yes	Yes	Yes	Yes	Yes	No
No	No	Yes	Yes	Yes	No	No	Yes	No
Yes	No	Yes	Yes	Yes	Yes	Yes	No	No
Yes	No	Yes	Yes	Yes	Yes	Yes	No	No
No	Yes	No	No	No	No	Yes	Yes	No
No	Yes	No	No	No	No	Yes	Yes	Yes

Course	Trinity	University	Wadham	Worcester	Wycliffe Hall
Archaeology and Anthropology	No	No	No	No	No
Biochemistry	Yes	Yes	Yes	Yes	No
Biology (Mollecular and Cellular)	No	No	Yes	Yes	No
Biomedical Sciences	Yes	Yes	No	No	No
Chemistry	Yes	Yes	Yes	Yes	No
Classical Archaeology and Ancient History	No	Yes	Yes	Yes	No
Classics	Yes	Yes	Yes	Yes	No
Classics and English	Yes	Yes	Yes	Yes	No
Classics and Modern Language	Yes	Yes	Yes	Yes	No
Classics and Oriental Studies	No	Yes	Yes	Yes	No
Computer Science	Yes	Yes	No	Yes	No
Computer Science and Philosophy	No	Yes	No	No	No
Earth Sciences (Geology)	No	Yes	No	Yes	No
Economics and Management	Yes	No	Yes	Yes	No
Engineering Science	Yes	Yes	Yes	Yes	No
English Language and Literature	Yes	Yes	Yes	Yes	No
English and Modern Languages	Yes	Yes	Yes	Yes	No
European and Middle Eastern Languages	No	Yes	Yes	Yes	No
Fine Art	No	No	No	Yes	No
Geography	No	No	No	Yes	No
History	Yes	Yes	Yes	Yes	No
History (Ancient and Modern)	Yes	Yes	Yes	Yes	No
History and Economics	No	No	Yes	Yes	No
History and English	No	No	Yes	No	No
History and Modern Languages	Yes	Yes	Yes	Yes	No
History and Politics	Yes	Yes	Yes	Yes	No
History of Art	No	No	Yes	No	No
Human Sciences	No	No	Yes	No	No
Law (Jurisprudence)	Yes	Yes	Yes	Yes	No
Law with Law Studies in Europe	Yes	Yes	Yes	Yes	No
Materials Science	Yes	No	No	No	No
Mathematics	Yes	Yes	Yes	Yes	No
Mathematics and Computer Science	No	Yes	Yes	Yes	No
Mathematics and Philosophy	No	Yes	Yes	Yes	No
Mathematics and Statistics	Yes	Yes	Yes	Yes	No
Medicine	Yes	Yes	Yes	Yes	No
Medicine (Graduate Entry)	No	No	No	Yes	No
Modern Languages	Yes	Yes	Yes	Yes	No
Modern Languages and Linguistics	Yes	Yes	Yes	Yes	No
Music	Yes	Yes	No	Yes	No
Oriental Studies	No	Yes	Yes	No	No
Philosophy and Modern Languages	Yes	Yes	Yes	Yes	No
Philosophy, Politics and Economics (PPE)	Yes	Yes	Yes	Yes	No
Philosophy and Theology	Yes	No	No	Yes	Yes
Physics	Yes	Yes	Yes	Yes	No
Physics and Philosophy	No	Yes	Yes	Yes	No
Psychology (Experimental)	No	Yes	Yes	Yes	No
Psychology, Philosophy and Linguistics (PPL)	No	Yes	No	Yes	No
Religion and Oriental Studies	No	No	No	No	No
Theology and Religion	Yes	No	No	Yes	Yes

CAMBRIDGE

CHRIST'S COLLEGE (founded 1505)

Number of students: 420 UGs.

Size and location: Medium-sized college, close to New Museums site (African Studies, Anthropology, Chemical Engineering, History and Philosophy of Science, Materials Science, Social and Political Sciences and Zoology) and Downing site (Archaeology, Anthropology, Biochemistry, Earth Sciences, Experimental Psychology, Genetics, Geography, Neuroscience, Pathology, Plant Science and Veterinary Anatomy).

Accommodation: Three years' accommodation provided, either on site or in College-owned houses in adjacent streets.
- **Access**: Three adapted rooms for students with disabilities. Upper Hall, library, practice rooms and toilets accessible via lift. JCR and TV room have ramped access.
- **Rent**: Banded room prices.

Food:
- **Hall**: Termly Kitchen Standing Charge. Upper Hall serves breakfast, lunch and dinner; Hall serves Formal Hall and occasion dinners.
- **Other**: Buttery café, including Costa Coffee, offering a discount on high-street prices. Kitchen facilities available across Christ's accommodation.

Facilities on site: Theatre; gym; squash court; outdoor swimming pool; music practice rooms; Visual Arts Centre; chapel; library; bar.

Financial aid: Organ and choral scholarships; instrumental awards; travel grants; vacation grants; book grants for first years; sporting awards.

Societies: Choir (auditioned); Christ's Film Society; Christ's Amateur Dramatic Society (CADS); Christ's Amnesty (Amnesty International); Christ's College Board Games Society; Christ's College Music Society; COGLES (Geography); Chess; CU; Darwin Society (science); RAG (Raising & Giving); Fair Trade; Film Production; Law; MEDSOC; Milton Society (debating); Politics; Seeley Society (History); Marguerites (men's sporting society); Hippolytans (women's sporting society); Visual Arts Society.

Alumni: Sacha Baron Cohen; Lady Margaret Beaufort; Charles Darwin; John Milton; John Oliver; Andy Parsons; Simon Schama; Richard Whiteley.

Did you know ...?

Christ's is well known for its promotion of the visual arts and has its own Visual Arts Centre with a gallery and resident artists' studios, where weekly life-drawing classes are also held, and the Yusuf Hamied Centre, which is a performance and exhibition space.

CHURCHILL COLLEGE (founded 1958 by Sir Winston Churchill)

Number of students: 485 UGs.

Size and location: One of the largest college campuses in Cambridge (40 acres). Near to West Cambridge site.

Accommodation: Provided for three years; all undergraduate rooms on site. Staircases shared by students from different year groups and subjects, and one fellow.
- **Access**: Adapted rooms available for wheelchair users and students with hearing difficulties, and there is a disabled toilet on the main site. Lift in the main building, providing access to Hall, JCR, TV room and bar. Wolfson Theatre and Archives Centre also have lift access.
- **Rent**: Banded room prices on a 30-week contract. Every student has to pay an advance deposit, which pays for a term and a half's credit; students living out get the deposit returned minus a few College charges (e.g. for meals).

Food:
- **Hall**: Lunch and dinner served Monday–Friday; breakfast, lunch and dinner served Saturday–Sunday. Pay-as-you-go system (billed termly). Formal Hall served six nights a week.
- **Buttery**: All-day bar/coffee shop serving breakfast Monday–Friday and snacks and drinks for the rest of the day.
- **Other**: All rooms have access to shared kitchen facilities.

Facilities on site: Library; bar; pitches; squash courts; tennis courts; gym; 300-seat theatre/cinema (Wolfson Theatre); music centre with performance and recording facilities; art studio; chapel; Archives Centre (houses papers of prominent political, military and scientific figures from Churchill to the modern day).

Financial aid: Winston Churchill Memorial Trust Bursaries; College hardship grants; emergency loans; choral scholarships; instrumental and vocal bursaries; organ scholarships; Accompanist Bursary; College Choir Directorship; Music Sizarship (responsible for overseeing, promoting and arranging musical activities in College); small grants for sport, music and drama tours; travel grants; vacation grants; academic scholarships and subject prizes.

Societies: Art Society; Chapel Choir; CU; GODS (drama); Music Society; Poker; Phoenix Society (visiting speakers).

Miscellaneous: When the College was founded, it was originally envisaged as a science-based college, but it also accepts arts students.

Alumni: Baroness Brinton; Francis Crick; Peter Fincham; James Watson.

Did you know ...?

Churchill College was founded by Sir Winston Churchill and has a statutory requirement in place stipulating that 70% of its students and teaching staff should study or teach in the areas of mathematics, science and technology.

CLARE COLLEGE (founded 1326; second-oldest college)

Number of students: 519 UGs.

Size and location: Medium-sized college on the river; near to the University Library and Sidgwick site (arts and humanities).

Accommodation: Provided for the duration of the course.
- **Access**: Six rooms accessible for wheelchair users. Lift for JCR, cafeteria, bar, Hall, chapel and library. One disabled toilet on main site.
- **Main site**: Accommodates first years and some final years.
- **Off site**: Second years live in Colony annexe (near Magdalene College), as do most third and fourth years.
- **Rent**: Banded accommodation. Students pay a Kitchen Fixed Charge, which pays for staffing, production, meal service and utilities.

Food:
- **Buttery**: Self-service, three meals a day; pay-as-you-go system.
- **Hall**: Salad bar Monday–Friday; pay-as-you-go system. Can be booked for society, subject and occasion dinners. Formal Hall served four times a week.
- **Other**: Most rooms have access to a 'gyp room' (kitchenette).

Facilities on site: Clare Cellars (College bar): venue for live music, stand-up, theatre, etc.; practice rooms; punts; chapel; Riley Auditorium; library.

Financial aid: Hardship grants; undergraduate bursaries; choral scholarships; organ scholarships; instrumental awards; book grants; travel and research grants; Sports Award (assistance with sporting costs); cycle helmet/lights subsidies; academic scholarships and subject-specific prizes.

Societies: Choir; Music Society; Amnesty; Chess; CU; Clare Actors; Clare College Music Society; Clare Comedy; Clare Jazz; Clare Voices; Clare Sound (sound and lighting); Clare Growers (allotment); Clare Vegans; Clare Live (music); Clare Canaries (vocal group); Fair Trade; LGBT+; Life Drawing; Dilettante Society (debating); VetMed Soc; Whiston Society (science); Clare College Student Investment Fund; QCOEF (fundraises for educational projects in developing countries); numerous sports clubs and politics societies.

Miscellaneous:
- The College has an on-site careers adviser. Summer placements (medical, veterinary and scientific research) and work experience are offered in the College archives and the library.
- The Mellon Fellowship Fund supports students wanting to study at Yale for part of their course.

Alumni: Sir David Attenborough; John Rutter; Siegfried Sassoon; James Watson.

Did you know ...?

The College was founded in 1326 as University Hall and is the second-oldest surviving college after Peterhouse.

CORPUS CHRISTI COLLEGE (founded 1352)

Number of students: 290 UGs.

Size and location: Small college. Main site near New Museum site and Downing site. Leckhampton (graduate site, but also used by undergraduates) is a 10-minute walk from Corpus site.

Accommodation: Provided for the duration of the course. First years are usually grouped on the main site or nearby.
- **Access**: One accessible flat on the main site, and one in Bene't Street hostel (the latter includes an adapted bathroom and kitchen). Bar, cafeteria, dining hall and library accessible via lift.
- **Rent**: Room prices are banded. The College offers two types of lease: 30-week (term time only), or 39-week (continual use of room from end of September to end of June).

Food:
- **Cafeteria**: Termly Kitchen Fixed Charge. Lunch and dinner served Monday–Friday; brunch served on Sunday. Pay-as-you-go system; billed termly.
- **Bar**: Serves breakfast every day.
- **Other**: Formal Hall served twice a week. Shared gyp rooms and more extensive self-catering facilities available throughout the College.

Facilities on site:
- **Main site**: Chapel; practice rooms; library; bar.
- **Leckhampton**: Playing fields (cricket and football); tennis and squash courts; gym; outdoor pool and gardens.

Financial aid: Travel awards; book awards for recipients of the Cambridge Bursary; hardship grants; academic scholarships and prizes; study grants for research, travel, materials, etc.; Frisby Sports Grants; organ scholarships; choral awards; instrumental awards.

Societies: Chapel Choir; Amnesty International; Corpus Films; Bene't Club (music); Green Society; Healthy Living Society; Pelican Poets and Writers; Natural Sciences Society; Finance and Investing; History; Nicholas Bacon Law Society; Northern Ireland Society; Lewis Society of Medicine; CU; Fletcher Players (drama).

Miscellaneous: The College owns a theatre, the Corpus Playroom, which is next to King's College.

Alumni: Hugh Bonneville; Christopher Isherwood; Christopher Marlowe; Kevin McCloud; Owen Paterson; Samuel Wesley.

Did you know ...?

Corpus Christi was founded by Cambridge residents, and is the only Cambridge college to have been founded in this way.

DOWNING COLLEGE (founded 1800)

Number of students: 425 UGs.

Size and location: Large; extensive grounds, including a paddock. Near Downing site and New Museums site.

Accommodation: Provided for three years on main site or adjacent to College; some accommodation available for fourth years. First years live on site; ballot thereafter.
- **Access**: Six adapted rooms available for students with disabilities; three are usually reserved for graduates. Lift access to library, Howard Building and Howard Theatre. Accessible toilets.
- **Rent**: Banded accommodation. All students required to pay a deposit at the start of their course.

Food:
- **Butterfield Café and Bar**: Serves breakfast and light snacks Monday–Saturday.
- **Servery**: Lunch and dinner Monday–Friday; brunch and dinner Saturday–Sunday. Pay-as-you-go; billed termly.
- **Other**: Formal Hall served three times a week. Shared kitchen facilities available for making light snacks in all accommodation areas.

Facilities on site: Howard Theatre (includes a Steinway piano and music practice room); gym; two courts (for tennis/basketball/netball); chapel; library; bar.

Financial aid: Downing Bursary for unexpected financial hardship; Downing Association Student Support (assistance with the cost of books, course materials, travel, vacation studies or conferences); travel fund grants; academic scholarships and prizes.

Societies: Amnesty International; Astronomical Society (the College owns a telescope); CU; Dance Society; Downing Dramatic Society; Chapel Choir; Jazz Band; Music Society; PPDO (Pembroke, Peterhouse and Downing Orchestra); Blake Society (Humanities); Brammer Geographical Society; Cranworth Law Society; Danby Society (Natural Sciences, Computer Science, Mathematics and Engineering); Maitland Historical Society; Mathias Society (Economics and Land Economy); Whitby Medical Society (Medicine and Veterinary Science).

Miscellaneous: Discover Downing (www.discoverdowning.com) is a separate site for schools and colleges with subject resources and student blogs.

Alumni: Quentin Blake; John Cleese; Andy Hamilton; Howard Jacobson; Thandie Newton; Trevor Nunn.

Did you know ...?

Downing's Blake Society holds lectures, discussions, poetry and sketching sessions throughout the year. Each year the society holds a black-tie dinner with its patron, alumnus Quentin Blake.

EMMANUEL COLLEGE (Emma) (founded 1584)

Number of students: 470 UGs.

Size and location: Large; extensive grounds, including paddock and ponds. Near New Museums site and Downing site.

Accommodation: Provided for the duration of the course.
- **Access**: Four rooms on the main site suitable for wheelchair users, with adapted bathroom and kitchen. One adapted room for a deaf student. Lift access to Hall, library and Queen's Building.
- **Rent**: Banded accommodation. Students pay for 10 weeks each term, and rent includes a Catering Fixed Charge.

Food:
- **Hall**: Breakfast, lunch and dinner Monday–Saturday; brunch and dinner on Sunday. Pay-as-you-go (charged termly). Formal Hall served most evenings.
- **Other**: Buttery shop sells snacks.

Facilities on site: Library; bar; tennis court; outdoor swimming pool; squash court; fitness suite; table tennis room; tennis courts and croquet lawn on the Paddock in Easter Term; chapel; free laundry service (only Cambridge college to offer this service).

Financial aid: Hardship and welfare support; funding for academic activities; choral and organ scholarships.

Societies: Amnesty International; Music; Revised Emmanuel Dramatic Society; Chess; CU; Mountaineering; Fair Trade; CinEmma; Photographic; Choir; Orchestra; Creative Writing; Jazz Band; Debating Society; Politics and Economics.

Alumni: Sebastian Faulks; Maggie O'Farrell; Griff Rhys Jones.

Did you know ...?

Sebastian Faulks won an open exhibition to read English at Emmanuel, and is also an Honorary Fellow.

FITZWILLIAM COLLEGE
(founded 1869 to widen access to Cambridge; became a college in 1966)

Number of students: 463 UGs.

Size and location: Fairly small college with a modern design. Near to the Mathematics faculty and West Cambridge site.

Accommodation: Provided for the duration of the course.
- **Access**: Two en-suite rooms suitable for wheelchair users. Buttery, coffee shop/bar, Gatehouse Court, auditorium, Central Building and library accessible via lift. Several disabled toilets on site.
- **First years**: Accommodated on site.
- **Other years**: Balloted; some students live in College-owned houses nearby. Students can pay for 29-week (term time) or 39-week leases.

- **Rent**: Banded accommodation. Students required to pay a deposit on the first bill.

Food: Minimum Meals Charge billed at the start of each term; can be used for any meals, including Formal Hall, but cannot be carried over to the next term. Kitchen Fixed Charge (lower for students not living on the main College site).
- **Coffee Shop**: Serves breakfast every day. Becomes a bar in the evening.
- **Hall (Buttery)**: Serves lunch and dinner every day. Pay-as-you-go system.
- **Other**: Formal Hall served twice a week. College has some gyp rooms; limited cooking facilities for first-year students. The Stretton Room can be hired out and has a fully equipped kitchen and dining room.

Facilities on site: Auditorium, including Steinway piano and practice rooms; allotment; arts studio; gym; squash courts; chapel; library; bar; University radio station.

Financial aid: Maintenance Bursary; Goldman Sachs Bursaries for students of promise; travel awards (for academic and non-academic purposes); assistance with music lessons; sports bursaries; support towards the cost of taking part in charitable and community projects; Sailbridge Special Project Award; vacation project accommodation allowances for undergraduates undertaking research projects/academic-related internships in the Cambridge area.

Societies: Music Society; Chapel Choir; Fitz Swing; Fitz Sirens (female a cappella); Fitz Barbershop; Fine Arts Society; Debating Society; Amnesty International; CU; Communal Gardens (allotments); Feminist Society; Medical and Veterinary Society; History Society; Economics and Finance Society; Law Society; The Mitchell Society of Industry and Technology for interest in the applied sciences, engineering and technology; Natural Sciences Society; Literary Society.

Miscellaneous:
- Fitzwilliam Chamber Opera (only permanent College-based opera company in Cambridge).
- The College was a joint winner in the FreeFrom Eating Out Award 2015 in the Schools, Colleges and Universities category for its Hall food.

Alumni: Andy Burnham; Vince Cable; James Norton.

Did you know ...?

The College supports charity and community work, and offers funding to students towards participation in charitable or community projects. In addition, the Sailbridge Special Project Award is open to students looking to undertake educationally, environmentally, charitably or entrepreneurially valuable projects.

GIRTON COLLEGE (founded 1869)

Number of students: 500 UGs.

Size and location: Very large; 50 acres of grounds. Two miles from city centre. Separate site nearer city centre (Wolfson), which is near the University Library and next to the Centre for Mathematical Sciences.

Accommodation: Provided for a minimum of three years. Most accommodation is mixed, but there is an all-female corridor that students can choose.
- **Access**:
  - **Main site**: One flat for wheelchair users, with adapted bathroom and kitchen, and an annexe for a carer. Two rooms adapted for students with hearing impairments. Six disabled toilets.
  - **Wolfson Court**: One purpose-built flat for wheelchair users, including adapted bathroom and kitchen.
- **First years**: Live in College.
- **Other years**: Second and third years choose between College, a College-owned house, or Wolfson Court through a ballot.
- **Rent**: Fixed annual charge for first three years, which includes Christmas and Easter vacations (37 or 38 weeks). Rent is inclusive of Kitchen Fixed Charge. Facilities charge levied for students living out of College accommodation.

Food:
- **Main site**: Cafeteria serves breakfast, lunch and dinner Monday–Friday; lunch on Saturday; and lunch and dinner on Sunday. Formal Hall served once a week.
- **Wolfson**: Cafeteria serves breakfast, lunch and dinner Monday–Friday; lunch on Saturday; and lunch and dinner on Sunday.
- **Other**: Communal kitchens on each corridor.

Facilities on site:
- **Main site**: Sports facilities (football, rugby, cricket, squash, volleyball, multi-gym, indoor heated swimming pool); self-service cafeteria; museum (Lawrence Room); library; bar.
- **Wolfson Court**: Cafeteria; library (including a Law library).

Financial aid: Emily Davies Bursaries and Rose Awards (for all subjects); subject-specific bursaries in Medicine, History, Classics, HSPS and Economics; College Tutorial Hardship Funds (small grants or larger loans); travel grants; academic scholarships and prizes; choral and organ awards; instrumental awards.

Societies: Chapel Choir; Music Society; Orchestra on the Hill (Girton, Magdalene, New Hall, Churchill and Fitzwilliam); Girton Banking Society; CU; Amateur Dramatics; Music; Law; History; Joan Robinson Society (Economics); Medical and Veterinary Society; Natural Sciences Society; Photographic; Poetry; LGBT; Allotment Society.

Miscellaneous: Originally a female college – became co-educational in 1976.

Alumnae: Margaret Mountford; Sandi Toksvig.

Did you know ...?

The College runs a Chamber Music scheme, offering musicians interested in performance advice on repertoire, coaching with professional musicians and performance opportunities.

GONVILLE & CAIUS COLLEGE (Caius) (founded 1348)

Number of students: 537 UGs.

Size and location: Medium-sized college. Very central; near New Museums site.

Accommodation: Provided for the duration of the course on West Road site (where all first years live), nearby Old Court site and in College-owned houses near the University's cricket ground.
- **Access**: All main buildings are wheelchair accessible and there are purpose-designed rooms for disabled students.
- **Rent**: Banded accommodation, which includes utilities and internet. Free laundry facilities on site. The College offers a continuation agreement for students from second year onwards; students living in certain College accommodation can leave their possessions there throughout the academic year (38 weeks) and pay reduced rent during the vacation.

Food: Students pay for 36 dinners a term up front (minimum dining requirement), and can choose which nights they want to eat in Hall.
- **Bar**: Serves breakfast and offers a lunchtime meal deal.
- **Hall**: Lunch and dinner served every day. Formal Hall served most nights.
- **Other**: All accommodation has access to shared cooking facilities.

Facilities on site: College bar open during day to serve coffee, and runs a loyalty card scheme; gym; library.

Financial aid: Tutor's Donation Fund for academic activities; book grants; examination prizes; scholarships and exhibitions; travel awards; instrumental awards; music awards for students studying Music in financial need; Bell-Wade Bursary for sporting and academic excellence.

Societies: Shadwell Society (drama); Choir; Orchestra; Poker; Film; Debating; Yoga; Amnesty; Music; Jazz; Board Games; Bridge; CU; Politics.

Alumni: Alastair Campbell; Jimmy Carr; Francis Crick; Alain de Botton; David Frost; Simon Russell Beale; John Venn.

Did you know ...?

The astrophysicist Stephen Hawking was a fellow of Gonville & Caius for over 50 years.

HOMERTON COLLEGE
(founded 1768; moved to Cambridge from London in 1894; became a college in 2010)

Number of students: 550 UGs.

Size and location: One of the largest colleges; extensive grounds. Near the train station.

Accommodation: Provided for the duration of the course on site.
- **Access**: 10 purpose-built rooms for wheelchair users. Lift access to library, Mary Allen and Cavendish Buildings, as well as accommodation blocks.

- **Rent**: Fixed rate, which varies depending on the accommodation block. Students pay a deposit on the first term's rent.

Food: Students pay a termly Minimum Meal Contribution, which enables them to purchase food in the Hall and Buttery at a discount.
- **Buttery (The Griffin)**: Serves breakfast daily.
- **Great Hall**: Serves lunch and dinner Monday–Friday; brunch on Saturday and dinner on Sunday. Pay-as-you-go system. Formal Hall served once a week.
- **Other**: All accommodation has access to shared kitchenettes.

Facilities on site: Auditorium; music practice rooms; dance studio; drama studio; sports grounds; tennis courts; croquet pitch; gym; library; bar.

Financial aid: College hardship grants; vacation study grants; internship bursaries; Year Abroad Grant; Dissertation Grant; grants for academic scholarships; travel awards; choral scholarships; organ scholarships; instrumental awards; accompanist scholarships.

Societies: Absolute Pandemonium (steel pan); Amateur Theatrical Society; Allotment Society; Charter Chapel Choir (auditioned); Homerton Singers (non-auditioned); Music Society; CU; Jazz Orchestra; G.O.D.S. (ballroom dancing).

Alumni: Olivia Colman; Sir Peter Maxwell Davies.

Did you know ...?

Homerton has the highest intake for the Education Tripos and provides teaching across the three tracks, including practical Drama. The College also co-sponsors the Cambridge/Homerton Research and Teaching Centre for Children's Literature and the College has strong library resources in this area.

HUGHES HALL (founded 1885 - oldest graduate college; majority of students are postgraduates)

NB Admits mature UGs and affiliate students (students who already have an honours degree from another university) only.

Number of students: 150 UGs.

Size and location: Small college, halfway between town and station, by Parker's Piece and Fenner's Cricket Ground.

Accommodation: Provided on site for the duration of the course. New accommodation block opened September 2016 with an additional 80 rooms on Gresham Road. Accommodation for couples available.
- **Access**: Five rooms suitable for wheelchair users. Full kitchens located near adapted accommodation.
- **Rent**: Banded. In addition to the Kitchen Fixed Charge (see below), students pay a yearly Computer Facilities Charge (reduced for students living in private accommodation).

Food: Annual Kitchen Fixed Charge (reduced for students living in private accommodation).

- **Hall**: Lunch and dinner served Monday–Friday; brunch served Saturday–Sunday. Pay-as-you-go system. Formal Hall served twice a week.
- **Other**: All accommodation has access to shared kitchen facilities.

Facilities on site: Gym; Pavilion Room (performance space); practice rooms; library; bar.

Financial aid: Subject awards; scholarships and bursaries for current or former students applying for a higher course.

Societies: Choir; Chess Club; Writing Club; Black & Minority Ethnic (BAME); Film Society; Photography; Law Society; Music; CU; LGBT+; Enterprise; Music.

Did you know ...?

Unlike most colleges at Cambridge, there is no high table at Hughes Hall, and students are also allowed to walk on the College lawns.

JESUS COLLEGE (founded 1495-1516)

Number of students: 500 UGs.

Size and location: Spacious grounds (24 acres). Situated near ADC Theatre and Cambridge Union.

Accommodation: Accommodation provided for the duration of the course. Most accommodation is on site (College-owned houses are across the road from the College).
- **Access**: Four rooms accessible to wheelchair users and two ground-floor rooms. Most areas on the main site are accessible.
- **Rent**: Banded.

Food: Students pay a Kitchen Fixed Charge each term.
- **Cafeteria**: College café serves lunch and dinner (and breakfast during Easter Term); pay-as-you-go system.
- **Other**: Formal Hall served five times a week. Each staircase shares kitchen/diner in the first year. College-owned houses have kitchens.

Facilities on site: Playing fields all on site (football, rugby, cricket, hockey); tennis courts; squash courts; gym; chapel; dark room; library; bar.

Financial aid: Grants and loans for student hardship; choral and organ scholarships; travel bursaries; academic scholarships and exhibitions; subject prizes.

Societies: Two College Choirs (men and women; men and boy choristers); Alcock Players (drama); Amnesty International; Art Collection; Big Band; CU; Debating; Eliot's Face (College arts magazine); Jesus Smoker (comedy); Music; Medicine; Natural Sciences; Scientific Society; Roosters; Comedy Debating Society; Short Story.

Miscellaneous: The College plays host to the University Visual Arts Society, which organises presentations and talks by artists and sculptors.

Alumni: Samuel Taylor Coleridge; Thomas Cranmer; Prince Edward, Earl of Wessex; Nick Hornby.

> **Did you know ...?**
>
> The college's chapel is the oldest university building in Cambridge still in use, predating the foundation of the college by 350 years and the university itself by half a century.

KING'S COLLEGE (founded 1441)

Number of students: 430 UGs.

Size and location: Large college; very central, on the river.

Accommodation: Provided for the duration of the course. Most accommodation is on the main site, and the rest is in hostels within easy reach of the College.
- **Access**: Wheelchair-accessible room and adapted en suite in New Garden Hostel. Another wheelchair-accessible room with adapted en suite available on main site. Access to most main buildings is limited, but there are level access and ramps to certain areas, including the cafeteria, Hall, library and chapel.
- **Rent**: Banded accommodation on 29- or 35-week contracts.

Food: Termly catering charge levied.
- **Servery**: Serves breakfast, lunch and dinner Monday–Friday; brunch and dinner Saturday–Sunday. Students billed at end of term, and charged on pay-as-you-go basis.
- **Other**: Formal Hall served once a week. King's Coffee Shop serves snacks and drinks. King's also has allotments for students to grow food. Most accommodation has access to gyp rooms.

Facilities on site: Library; Rowe Music Library; coffee bar; Student Bunker (music/drama venue); art room; gym; rowing machine room; croquet lawn; volleyball; water polo; canoeing; climbing; yoga; allotments; bar.

Financial aid: College Hardship Fund for unexpected difficulties; support for travel; academic and essay prizes; instrumental scholarships; choral and organ scholarships.

Societies: Choir; King's Voices; Musical Society; Photographic; Film.

Alumni: Lily Cole; E.M. Forster; John Eliot Gardiner; George the Poet; Hugh Johnson; Sir Salman Rushdie; Zadie Smith; Alan Turing.

> **Did you know ...?**
>
> Along with Trinity College, King's College typically receives the most direct applications. King's has a renowned choir and has been broadcasting the *Festival of Nine Lessons and Carols* to radio listeners across the world since 1928, having begun the tradition in 1918. Since 1919, the service has always opened with the hymn *Once in Royal David's City*.

LUCY CAVENDISH COLLEGE (founded 1965)

NB Accepts mature female UGs only.

Number of students: 350 UGs.

Size and location: Large college with spacious grounds. Near Applied Mathematics and Theoretical Physics faculties.

Accommodation: Provided for the first three years. Accommodation on the main site is for single occupancy; most undergraduates live on site. On the Histon Road complex, there are some one- and two-bedroom apartments, which would be suitable for couples and families.
- **Access**: Three en-suite adapted rooms for students with disabilities, which are near to adapted kitchens. Level access to College and lift access to computer facilities, Hall, library and cafeteria.
- **Rent**: Banded accommodation. All students are required to pay a deposit before they arrive. Students living in off-site accommodation can keep their rooms over the vacation.

Food: Students asked to pre-purchase a small amount of credit each term, which can be used for lunches, dinners, Formal Halls or takeaways.
- **Hall**: Breakfast, lunch and dinner served Monday–Friday. Al fresco dining area. Formal Hall served once a week.
- **Other**: Shared kitchen facilities available in all accommodation.

Facilities on site: Music and Meditation Pavilion; gym; library; bar.

Financial aid: Childcare grants; hardship funds; academic scholarships; sports prizes.

Societies: Lucy Cavendish/Hughes Hall combined Boat Club; Student Choir; College Newspaper; Running Club; Period Drama; Cavendish Chorale.

Miscellaneous: The College runs an annual national fiction prize for unpublished writers, as well as conferences and festivals dedicated to women in the arts.

Did you know ...?

Lucy Cavendish is the only women's college in Europe for mature students.

MAGDALENE COLLEGE (founded 1428)

Number of students: 360 UGs.

Size and location: Medium-sized college on the river. The College is split over three sites: one on each side of Magdalene Street, and Cripps Court on Chesterton Road.

Accommodation: Provided for the duration of the course in College-owned houses within easy reach of the College, or on the main site.
- **Access**: Two purpose-built rooms with adapted bathrooms and kitchens close by. Cripps Court is fully accessible, and the Magdalene Street sites have level access and ramps between courts.

- **Rent**: First years are allocated a room; afterwards it is banded and rooms are organised via ballot.

Food: All students pay a termly Kitchen Fixed Charge.
- **Ramsay Hall**: Serves breakfast, lunch and dinner Monday–Friday; brunch and dinner Saturday–Sunday. Pay-as-you-go system. Formal Hall served every night.
- **Other**: All rooms have access to a gyp room.

Facilities on site: Library; bar; gym, squash and fives courts on site; auditorium for lectures, drama and music.

Financial aid: Student Support Fund for unexpected financial difficulty; travel awards; academic prizes.

Societies: Choir; Arts Magna; CU; Drama; Law; Music; Vox Society.

Alumni: Katie Derham; Julian Fellowes; C.S. Lewis; Mike Newell; Samuel Pepys; Sir Michael Redgrave; John Simpson.

Did you know ...?

The College houses the Pepys Library. The College acquired some 3,000 books from Samuel Pepys' library, which are arranged from smallest to largest.

MURRAY EDWARDS COLLEGE
(founded 1954 as New Hall; renamed Murray Edwards in 2008)
NB Accepts female students only.

Number of students: 387 UGs.

Size and location: Extensive gardens. Near to the Centre for Mathematical Sciences.

Accommodation: Provided for the duration of the course on main site or in nearby College houses. First years live together in Pearl House.
- **Access**: Some adapted en-suite accommodation available in the newer blocks. Main building has a lift between all floors except in Old Block.
- **Rent**: Banded accommodation. Refundable 'Caution Money' payable at the start of the course.

Food: Students pay a termly overhead charge, which is reduced for students not living in College accommodation.
- **Hall (The Dome)**: Serves breakfast Monday–Friday; brunch on Saturday; lunch Monday–Friday and Sunday; dinner Monday, Wednesday, Thursday, Friday and Sunday. Dinner is served at Fitzwilliam College on Saturdays. Pay-as-you-go cashless system, which gives students a discount on meals. Formal Hall served once or twice a week.
- **Other**: All rooms have access to shared kitchen facilities.

Facilities on site: Library; bar; music practice rooms; craft room; dark room; gym; tennis courts.

Financial aid: Student Support Fund for financial hardship; travel awards; Gateway Challenges Funding for students participating in the Gateway Programme (see under 'Did you know …?' for further information); Gateway Gap Year Awards (awarded to those who might benefit from taking a gap year prior to starting at Cambridge and who would otherwise be unable to fund a gap year).

Societies: Consultancy; Climbing; Dog-walking; Femsoc; Film; Music; Madhouse (drama); Choir (regularly joins with Fitzwilliam).

Alumnae: Joanna MacGregor; Tilda Swinton; Claudia Winkleman.

Did you know …?

The College has an extensive College-based career development scheme, the Gateway Programme, which offers academic and career development through study workshops, CV clinics, mock interviews, networking sessions, internships, work-shadowing and funding for students who want to build their skills by pursuing their own interests. Murray Edwards often makes a high number of winter pool offers, as do Churchill, Homerton, Newnham and Girton.

NEWNHAM COLLEGE (founded 1871)
NB accepts female students only.

Number of students: 380 UGs.

Size and location: 17 acres of gardens. Located opposite the Sidgwick site.

Accommodation: All undergraduates housed on the main site for up to three years.
- **Access**: One adapted flat available in graduate accommodation block, which includes accessible bathroom, kitchen and living room. Lift access to bar and library. The Buttery has automatic doors and most of the main areas are at ground level.
- **Rent**: Rooms on a ballot system. Same rent paid within each year group. Termly and continuous contracts available. Rent is inclusive of utilities, internet, insurance and Kitchen Fixed Charge. Recipients of Cambridge or Newnham Bursary receive a rent subsidy. Deposit required at start of the course.

Food:
- **Buttery**: Serves breakfast, lunch and dinner Monday–Friday; lunch and dinner on Saturday; brunch and dinner on Sundays. During the exam season in Easter Term, breakfast is also served on Saturdays. Payment of food in Buttery is by cash or charged to termly bill.
- **Other**: Formal Hall served once or twice a week. Well-equipped self-catering kitchens throughout the site.

Facilities on site: Library; bar; sports field; tennis courts; netball courts; gym; The Old Labs (performing arts centre); practice rooms; art room; dark room.

Financial aid: Hardship bursaries; choral awards (available from Selwyn College); annual book grants; travel grants (including subject-specific grants); research expenses for dissertations or project work; academic equipment grants; music grants (e.g. for music lessons); Music Organisers; instrumental and vocal awards; sport funds; opportunity funds; academic scholarships and prizes; financial assistance to students with limited mobility; undergraduate bursary to travel in the USA over the summer vacation.

Societies: Raleigh Music Society; Choir; Voices of Newnham (a cappella choir); College Orchestra; Newnham Anonymous Players (drama); Arts and Photography; CU.

Miscellaneous: The College runs an Active Career Development Programme.
- Newnham Associates (group of alumnae) run termly careers workshops, help arrange work placements and offer advice.
- Alumnae network holds networking lunches.
- Sprint Programme (career development programme).
- Veronica Crichton Presentation Skills courses.
- Career support grants (for travel/placements).
- Lodge seminars offering career advice from successful women.

Alumnae: Diane Abbott; Clare Balding; Mary Beard; Germaine Greer; Miriam Margolyes; Dame Iris Murdoch; Sylvia Plath; Emma Thompson.

Did you know ...?

As well as accepting only female students, the College has an all-female fellowship, which includes the classicist Mary Beard.

PEMBROKE COLLEGE (founded 1347)

Number of students: 430 UGs.

Size and location: Large college, near Plant Sciences and Engineering faculties.

Accommodation: Provided for the duration of the course on site and in College-owned houses. First years live on site; ballot thereafter.
- **Access**: Two adapted rooms available for wheelchair users with en-suite facilities. Level access to College and all areas ramped. Library, computer facilities, laundry, sports facilities and music room have lift access.
- **Rent**: Banded accommodation. Rent covers between eight and 10 weeks during term.

Food: Supplementary termly overhead costs (reduced for students not living in College-owned accommodation).
- **Hall**: Serves breakfast, lunch and dinner Monday–Friday; breakfast, brunch and dinner on Saturday and brunch and dinner on Sunday. Pay-as-you-go system; students receive a discount on marked prices when they pay with their Pembroke student card. Formal Hall served every night.
- **Other**: Café Pembroke open Monday–Friday and serves hot food until 5pm. Basic gyp rooms in most College accommodation and shared kitchens in College-owned houses.

Facilities on site: Library; bar; gym and exercise room; table tennis room; dark room; art room; performance space; practice rooms; chapel.

Financial aid: Means-tested maintenance support; hardship grants for unforeseen hardship; Pembroke Merit Awards; support for study-related costs and course-related travel (book grants, vacation residence, music lessons, travel, exchange schemes with other universities; sports grants; and equipment support).

Societies: Pembroke Players (drama); Smokers (stand-up comedy); Music; Art and Photographic; Chapel Choir; Orchestra; Pembroke Street Publication; The Penn (poetry society); Stokes Society (weekly talks); Chess Club; Africa Society.

Miscellaneous: Pembroke runs Easter and Summer Schools for overseas university students, which Pembroke students can work on as programme assistants.

Alumni: Bunny Austin; Peter Bradshaw; Jo Cox; Naomie Harris; Tom Hiddleston; Ted Hughes; Clive James; Bill Oddie; Edmund Spenser.

Did you know ...?

Pembroke has a College Musician, currently pianist Joseph Middleton, and also hosts the Sir Arthur Bliss International Song Series, where professional musicians come to the College to work with students and give performances.

PETERHOUSE (founded 1284, oldest college in Cambridge)

Number of students: 260 UGs.

Size and location: Fairly spacious grounds, including a deer park. Near Engineering faculty.

Accommodation: Provided for the duration of the course on or adjacent to the main site.
- **Access**: One room suitable for wheelchair users, which includes en-suite facilities. Due to the College's age, access is difficult, but lift access is available to the library and Upper Hall.
- **Rent**: Banded accommodation on a 10-week lease. Electricity is charged as an extra as a proportion of use across the College. Caution money (deposit) is paid before arrival.

Food: Students pay a charge each term towards upkeep of the College kitchens. Students are required to eat a minimum of 35 Qualifying Meals (QM) in College (lunches and dinners that are worth a certain minimum amount are equivalent to one QM; Formal Hall is equivalent to two QMs). Students are charged at a daily rate for any shortfall in the number of QMs. Up to 10 QMs can be carried over from one term to the next.
- **Servery**: Serves breakfast, lunch and dinner Monday–Friday; brunch and dinner on Saturday; dinner on Sunday. Pay-as-you-go system.
- **Other**: Formal Hall served every night. Most rooms have access to gyp rooms.

Facilities on site: Theatre; practice rooms; deer park; squash court; gym; chapel; bar.

Financial aid: Choral scholarships/exhibitions; organ scholarships; travel grants; book grants; Donation Fund (for hardship, vacation residence and medical expenses); Cowling Fund (bursaries for historians); Edward Lipman Fund (Classics, English, History, Music and Politics); Bruckmann (language study and travel abroad for conferences and research); Friends of Peterhouse (hardship, medical, sporting and research); Stemson (University sport); Plevy Newman Fund (conferences and related costs for medical students); Kidd Bequest (vacation study grant).

Societies: Choir; Music Society; CU; Politics; Kelvin (science); Heywood (drama).

Alumni: Charles Babbage; Sam Mendes; David Mitchell; Michael Portillo.

Did you know ...?

Peterhouse is the oldest college in Cambridge and the Hall, dating back to 1290, is still in use today for Formal Hall, which is served by candlelight. The College has the smallest number of fellows and students in the University.

QUEENS' COLLEGE (founded 1448)

Number of students: 500 UGs.

Size and location: Medium-sized college on the river.

Accommodation: Students accommodated for three years on site; some off-site accommodation is available to third and fourth years. Flats for couples available in the city.
- **Access**: Two adapted rooms for wheelchair users with en-suite facilities. Access to older parts of the College is difficult, due to a number of listed buildings on site.
- **Rent**: Banded rooms. Separate charge for central heating in Michaelmas and Lent Terms. Caution money payable at the start of the course.

Food: No separate Kitchen Fixed Charge; Cover Charge is levied at 25% per item.
- **Buttery**: Breakfast, lunch and dinner served Monday–Friday; brunch and dinner Saturday–Sunday. Pay-as-you-go system.
- **Other**: Formal Hall served four times a week in the Cripps Dining Hall. Gyp rooms available in all buildings on site. In addition to the Buttery, food is available in the College bar and conservatory.

Facilities on site: Library; bar; gym; squash courts; Fitzpatrick Hall (lectures and film viewings).

Financial aid: Hardship grants; travel grants; sports grants; arts grants; academic scholarships and prizes; organ and choral scholarships.

Societies: Arts; Chess; Chapel Choir; CU; Contemporary Dance; Debating; Erasmus (History); Medical Society; Milner Society (Natural Sciences); Music at Queens'; Mooting Society; Queens' Bench Law Society; QEngineers; Jewish Society; Photographic; QFilms; T Society (Politics); BATS (drama); The Dial (new writing publication); Queens' Labour Club.

Miscellaneous: Queens' has a nursery at Owlstone Croft in Newnham, which is open daily from 8.30am to 4.30pm and can accommodate up to 25 children.

Alumni: Simon Bird; Erasmus; Stephen Fry.

Did you know ...?

The College has a Dance Artist in Residence, who offers contemporary dance technique classes, choreography workshops and performances.

ROBINSON COLLEGE (founded 1979)

Number of students: 386 UGs.

Size and location: Medium-sized college opposite the University Library and near the Sidgwick site.

Accommodation: Accommodation provided for the duration of the course on site or in College houses.
- **Access**: One fully adapted and one partially adapted room for wheelchair users. One adapted room for students with visual impairments. Two lifts and walkways give access to most of the College site.
- **Rent**: Banded accommodation. Deposit charged at the start of the course.

Food: No Kitchen Fixed Charge.
- **Garden Restaurant**: Serves breakfast, lunch and dinner Monday–Friday; and brunch Saturday–Sunday. Pay-as-you-go system.
- **Other**: Formal Hall served twice a week in the Dining Hall. Red Brick Café Bar open daily and serves light food during the day. Catering facilities in each staircase.

Facilities on site: Library; bar; Maria Björnson Theatre; auditorium; practice rooms; recital room; chapel.

Financial aid: College bursaries; J.P. Morgan Bursaries (for female UGs in their second year in any subject other than Architecture, Medicine or Veterinary Medicine); Book and Equipment Loan Fund; vacation accommodation awards; Student Activities Fund (sport, music, vacation work placement, conferences and other academic expenses); Sporting Achievement Fund; subject-specific funds for Architecture, Archaeology, Geography, Geology and Medieval and Modern Languages (MML); academic scholarships and subject prizes.

Societies: Brickhouse Theatre Company; Music Society; Chapel Choir; Art and Photography; Chess; CU; Film; Vocal Cords.

Alumni: Nick Clegg; Konnie Huq; Robert Webb.

Did you know ...?

As Cambridge's newest college, Robinson is one of the colleges to have been co-educational from the very beginning.

SELWYN COLLEGE (founded 1882)

Number of students: 440 UGs.

Size and location: Small college, adjacent to Sidgwick site and near to University Library.

Accommodation: Provided for the duration of the course on site. First years assigned rooms; other years balloted.
- **Access**: Several rooms for students with disabilities. Cafeteria, JCR, Hall and computer facilities have lift access. Level and ramped access available to all areas on main site.
- **Rent**: Banded. There is also a termly facilities and IT charge, which is reduced for students living out.

Food: Termly Kitchen Fixed Charge and Minimum Meals Charge; both are reduced for students living out.
- **Hall**: Breakfast, lunch and dinner served Monday–Saturday; brunch and dinner on Sunday. Formal Hall served twice a week.
- **Other**: Each corridor has gyp rooms for making light snacks.

Facilities on site: On-site gym; practice rooms; The Diamond (performance space); chapel; library; bar.

Financial aid: Selwyn Support Grants for unexpected financial hardship; travel funds; T.S. Cordiner Travel Bursary for study in the USA during the long vacation; sports grants; subject-related grants in Mathematics, Engineering and Architecture; academic scholarships and subject-specific prizes.

Societies: Chapel Choir (auditioned); Music; Drama.

Alumni: Tom Hollander; Simon Hughes; Hugh Laurie.

Did you know ...?

Selwyn is unique among Oxbridge colleges in that it holds an annual Winter Ball known as the Selwyn Snowball, which traditionally takes place on the night of the last Friday of Michaelmas term.

SIDNEY SUSSEX COLLEGE (founded 1596)

Number of students: 350 UGs.

Size and location: Medium-sized college, close to New Museums site.

Accommodation: Provided for the duration of the course.
- **Access**: One fully accessible flat, including bathroom and kitchen. Most areas accessible, apart from South Court. Lift access to most upper floors.
- **Rent**: Banded.

Food: Students are required to pay a termly Kitchen Fixed Charge.
- **Hall**: Breakfast, lunch and dinner served Monday–Friday; brunch and dinner on Saturday; dinner on Saturday. Pay-as-you-go system; billed termly.
- **Other**: Private dining events available to book for students. Most accommodation has basic self-catering facilities.

Facilities on site: Gym; squash court; practice rooms; chapel; library; bar.

Financial aid: College access bursaries and grants; Welfare Fund for unexpected hardship; academic prizes; travel awards; choral and organ scholarships; instrumental awards; sports awards for blues and half-blues.

Societies: Choir (auditioned); Music Society; Medical and Veterinary Society; Wilson Society (science); Confrat (History).

Miscellaneous:
- The College hosts the Sidney Greats lecture series.
- The catering department has won several university-wide catering awards.

Alumni: Alan Bennett; Oliver Cromwell; Chris Grayling; Carol Vorderman.

Did you know ...?

The College has a strong mathematical history; it played a key part in the codebreaking work at Bletchley Park during World War II. Mathematics fellow Gordon Welchman helped to enlist talented undergraduates such as John Herivel, who played a crucial role in breaking the Enigma code. In the 1960s the inventor of 'surreal numbers', John Conway, was a fellow.

ST CATHARINE'S COLLEGE (founded 1473)

Number of students: 440 UGs.

Size and location: Small college near New Museums site, Sidgwick site and Mill Lane lecture theatres.

Accommodation: Provided for the first three years.
- **Access**: Several en-suite rooms that can be adapted for wheelchair users. Level access to main site. Most entrances off Front Court have steps, but wheelchair access can be arranged in advance.
- **Main site**: First and third years.
- **Off site**: Second years accommodated in an annexe (St Chad's) 10 minutes away, which is composed of student flats.
- **Rent**: Banded.

Food: Students pay a termly Kitchen Fixed Charge.
- **Hall**: Breakfast, lunch and dinner served Monday–Saturday; brunch and dinner served on Sunday. Pay-as-you-go system. Formal Hall served once a week.
- **Other**: Gyp rooms on every corridor on site. Flats in the annexe have fully equipped kitchens.

Facilities on site: Library; bar; gym; auditorium; larger performance space; practice room; chapel.

Financial aid: College bursaries; Hardship Fund; assistance with course costs (e.g. for medical placements); travel grants; assistance with sports/music costs; help with unpaid internships; academic prizes and scholarships; choral and organ scholarships; instrumental scholarships.

Societies: Choir (auditioned); CU; John Ray (Natural Sciences, Computer Sciences and Chemical Engineering); MedSoc; Engineering; Music; Film; Amnesty International; Careers; SCATZ (singing); Orchestra.

Alumni: Richard Ayoade; Sir Ian McKellen; Ben Miller; Jeremy Paxman.

Did you know ...?

For recipients of the Cambridge Bursary who undertake unpaid internships during the vacation, St Catharine's offers grants to help meet this cost. Those students on unpaid internships who do not receive the Cambridge Bursary can apply to the Travel Grant Fund to help support their work.

ST EDMUND'S COLLEGE (Eddies) (founded 1896)
NB Accepts mature UGs only.

Number of students: 124 UGs.

Size and location: Fairly large site, covering six acres. Near to the Centre of Mathematical Sciences.

Accommodation: Undergraduate and graduate students are divided into three categories and accommodation is allocated accordingly. At undergraduate level, priority is given to students in their first or final years; affiliated undergraduates who haven't lived in previously; clinical veterinary medicine or medical students (three years out of five). Second years are in the middle priority group. The College has six maisonettes and seven apartments suitable for families and flats for couples.
- **Access**: Three purpose-built wheelchair-accessible rooms with en-suite facilities. Most areas of the College are accessible. Lift access to library and sports facilities.
- **Rent**: Both single rooms and family accommodation are banded. Caution money charged at the start of each year spent living in College accommodation. Family accommodation is charged monthly.

Food: Minimum termly kitchen charge (reduced for students living off site).
- **Hall**: Breakfast, lunch and dinner served Monday–Friday; brunch on Saturday; lunch on Sunday.
- **Other**: Kitchens in Norfolk Building, Benet House, Richard Laws Building and Brian Heap Building. Flats and maisonettes have their own kitchens.

Facilities on site: Library; bar; gym; practice room; chapel; one combination room (common room) for undergraduates, postgraduates and fellows.

Financial aid: Hardship awards; instrumental awards; Amenities Fund (for sport, music and art).

Societies: Music Society; Chapel Choir; Chapel Schola (smaller choir); Law.

Miscellaneous: The College offers workshops for instrumentalists, vocalists, conductors and composers.

Did you know ...?

St Edmund's College is the only college in Cambridge to have a Catholic chapel.

ST JOHN'S COLLEGE (founded 1516)

Number of students: 658 UGs.

Size and location: Very large college on the river.

Accommodation: Provided for the duration of the course. Students in second and third years are balloted.
- **Access**: Two adapted suites on site, and a room for a carer. One adapted room in College hostel. Level access to main site, and most areas are accessible. Library, computer facilities and practice rooms accessible via lift.
- **First years**: Live on site.
- **Second years**: Can share a set on site with another student or have a single room in an undergraduate hostel.
- **Third years**: Can share a set on site with another student or have a single en-suite room on site.
- **Other years**: Can choose from single rooms, shared sets or live with a group of students in College-owned houses.
- **Rent**: Banded accommodation. Students pay for September–June, which includes the vacations.

Food: Students are required to pay an annual Kitchen Fixed Charge.
- **Buttery**: Serves breakfast, lunch and dinner Monday–Saturday, and lunch and dinner on Sunday. Pay-as-you-go system.
- **Other**: Formal Hall served six times a week. Some College accommodation has access to shared kitchens.

Facilities on site: Library; bar; fitness centre; music rooms; chapel; art room; Old Divinity School (performance space); playing fields directly behind college.

Financial aid: College Studentships (students whose household income is less than the stated threshold can receive support towards their living costs); academic scholarships and prizes; Beard Fund (sport grants); College hardship grants; choral scholarships; organ scholarships; instrumental awards for chamber music.

Societies: Adams Society (Mathematics); Classics; Economics; Goody Society (Archaeology and Anthropology); History; Humanities; Larmor Society (Natural Sciences); Medical; Modern Languages; Palmerston (HSPS); Parsons (Engineering); Purchas (Geography and Land Economy); Theological; Veterinary; Wilkes (Computer Science); Winfield (Law); Amnesty International; Art; Caledonian; Chess; CU; Gentlemen of St John's; Jazz at John's; Lady Margaret Players; LGBT; Music; Photographic; Picturehouse; Choir (auditioned; men only).

Miscellaneous: St John's College coordinates Innovation internships at ROADmap Systems Limited and Archipelago Technology Group.

Alumni: Douglas Adams; Sir Cecil Beaton; Sir John Cockcroft; Sir Fred Hoyle; Derek Jacobi; William Wilberforce; William Wordsworth.

Did you know ...?

The College runs various exchanges with overseas institutions: Caltech (summer project); Collegio Ghislieri Pavia (academic year); China UK Development Centre Exchange Programme with universities in China (two weeks); Forbes College, Princeton University Exchange (one week); Heidelberg University Exchange (10 months); MIT Exchange (academic year); Nagoya University, Japan Exchange (two weeks); Shanghai Jiao Tong University (summer); and St Xavier's College, India (two weeks).

TRINITY COLLEGE (founded 1546)

Number of students: 720 UGs.

Size and location: Large college on the river.

Accommodation: Provided for the duration of the course. First years assigned rooms; ballot thereafter. Flats available for spouses and families.
- **Access**: One adapted room for a wheelchair user, and another room adapted for a student with limited mobility. Most areas are accessible, but listed buildings make putting in permanent ramps difficult. Lift access to Hall, Wolfson Building and Winstanley Lecture Theatre.
- **Rent**: Banded, and the College gives you the option to state the maximum weekly charge you are willing to pay.

Food: Students are required to pay a termly Kitchen Fixed Charge.
- **Hall**: Serves breakfast, lunch and dinner Monday–Saturday; brunch and dinner on Sunday.
- **Other**: Gyp rooms in College. Larger kitchens in Burrell's Field accommodation. Bar also serves food during the week.

Facilities on site: Library; bar; nine practice rooms; recording studio; chapel.

Financial aid: Gwalia Scholarships for outstanding students from Wales; hardship funds; essay prizes and academic scholarships; choral and organ scholarships; funds for travel, music, sports, books, summer projects and academic costs.

Societies: Choir (auditioned); Music; Dryden (drama); Travisty (College magazine); RAG; Trinema; CU; Economics; Engineering; Fine Art; French; Geography; History; Jewish; Law; Literary; Mathematics; Medical; Oriental; Philosophy; Photography; Politics; Science.

Alumni: Alexander Armstrong; Francis Bacon; Stanley Baldwin; Prince Charles; John Dryden; George VI; George Herbert; Andrew Marvell; A.A. Milne; Isaac Newton; Enoch Powell; Eddie Redmayne; Bertrand Russell; Alfred, Lord Tennyson; Ralph Vaughan Williams.

Did you know ...?

Trinity has 32 affiliated Nobel Laureates, the most of any of the Cambridge colleges.

TRINITY HALL (founded 1350)

Number of students: 387 UGs.

Size and location: Small college on the river.

Accommodation: Provided for three years and for some students in their fourth year.
* **Access**: One room on the main site suitable for a wheelchair user with a nearby adapted bathroom. Seven wheelchair-accessible rooms on the Wychfield site, each with an en-suite bathroom. Level access across main site, and most public areas are wheelchair accessible. Lift access to computer facilities, music and seminar rooms and stair-lift access to coffee shop and bar.
* **Main site**: All first years are allocated a room on site according to their price bands.
* **Off site**: Two College annexes. Wychfield is in West Cambridge, near Fitzwilliam College, while Thompson's Lane is near to the main site and the College boathouse.
* **Rent**: Banded accommodation.

Food:
* **Cafeteria**: Serves breakfast, lunch and dinner daily, charged to each student's account.
* **Other**: Formal Hall served twice a week. Coffee shop serves drinks and snacks. Each staircase has a gyp room.

Facilities on site:
* **Main site**: Music room; chapel; lecture theatre; coffee shop; library; bar.
* **Wychfield**: Sports facilities (gym; pavilion; squash courts; football; hockey; rugby; cricket; and tennis (clay and grass)).

Financial aid: Hardship bursaries; travel grants; organ scholarships.

Societies: Amnesty; CU; Jazz Band; Life In Colour (Film); MMA (Mixed Martial Arts); Music; Politics; History; Law; Student newspaper (the Titbit); Engineering; Choir (auditioned).

Alumni: Stephen Hawking; Tom James; Andrew Marr; J.B. Priestley; Rachel Weisz.

Did you know ...?

Often overshadowed by its neighbour, Trinity College, Trinity Hall is the fifth oldest remaining college in Cambridge and is set in riverside gardens; Henry James called the gardens the 'prettiest corner in the world'. Originally founded for the study of canon and civil law, the College continues to have a strong law tradition.

WOLFSON COLLEGE (founded 1965)

NB Accepts mature UGs and affiliate students only.

Number of students/fellows: 150 UGs.

Size and location: Medium-sized college in West Cambridge, near the Cambridge Rugby Football Club.

Accommodation: Provided for the duration of the course. Accommodation available for couples and families.
- **Access**: Two purpose-built rooms for wheelchair users; four rooms near a disabled toilet can be adapted. College grounds and public areas are accessible. Hall and library have lift access.
- **Rent**: Banded accommodation. Flexible letting periods, starting from 26 weeks.

Food: No Kitchen Fixed Charge, Minimum Meals Charge or catering-related charge.
- **Cafeteria**: Serves breakfast, lunch and dinner daily at a discounted price for students.
- **Other**: Formal Hall served twice a week. Some College accommodation has access to shared kitchens.

Facilities on site: Library; bar; basketball/tennis court; table tennis; gym.

Financial aid: Each student can apply for a small sum to help towards course-related costs; Hardship Fund; Instrumental Awards Scheme for Chamber Music; Brian Moore Accompanist Scholarship; choral scholarships.

Societies: Non-auditioning Choir; Chamber Singers; CU; Language and Culture Society; Humanities Society; Public Speaking; Wolfson Contemporary Reading Group; Tango; College Howler (comedy); Music; Science.

Miscellaneous: There are no high table and no separate common rooms for fellows, undergraduates or graduates.

Did you know ...?

From its outset, the college set out to be a cosmopolitan and egalitarian institution that differed from the older and more traditional Cambridge colleges: no Senior Combination Room, no 'High Table' reserved for Fellows at formal dinners in the college and no portraits in the Dining Hall.

Tompkins table

Table 10 Tompkins table – Cambridge (2019)

Position	College	Score	Percentage of Firsts
1	Christ's	75.7%	44.0%
2	Trinity	74.1%	42.5%
3	Pembroke	72.3%	36.8%
4	Peterhouse	71.2%	34.9%
5	Churchill	71.1%	34.1%
6	Queens'	70.6%	32.5%
7	Emmanuel	70.3%	33.3%
8	Selwyn	70.1%	32.1%
9	St Catharine's	69.9%	31.0%
10	Trinity Hall	69.7%	30.3%
11	Corpus Christi	69.4%	31.1%
12	King's	69.0%	31.3%
13	Sidney Sussex	68.8%	29.4%
14	Jesus	68.6%	29.9%
15	St John's	68.4%	28.6%
16	Gonville & Caius	68.3%	27.3%
17	Fitzwilliam	68.3%	27.9%
18	Magdalene	67.6%	24.4%
19	Murray Edwards	66.2%	24.6%
20	Girton	65.4%	22.3%
21	Robinson	65.1%	22.0%
22	Newnham	65.0%	22.8%
23	Downing	64.9%	21.7%
24	Clare	64.8%	22.1%
25	Hughes Hall	64.4%	21.9%
26	Homerton	63.2%	18.6%
27	Wolfson	61.2%	17.4%
28	St Edmund's	60.5%	18.2%
29	Lucy Cavendish	60.1%	16.3%

Source: www.varsity.co.uk/news/17736.
Reprinted with kind permission of Varsity.

Cambridge map

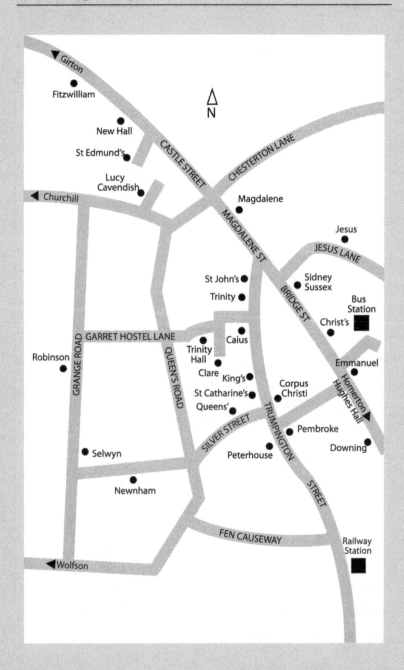

Table 11 Undergraduate courses available at Cambridge colleges

Course	Christ's	Churchill	Clare	Corpus Christi	Downing
Anglo-Saxon, Norse and Celtic	Yes	Yes	Yes	Yes	Yes
Archaeology	Yes	Yes	Yes	Yes	Yes
Architecture	Yes	Yes	Yes	Yes	Yes
Asian and Middle Eastern Studies	Yes	Yes	Yes	Yes	Yes
Chemical Engineering	Yes	Yes	Yes	Yes	Yes
Classics	Yes	Yes	Yes	Yes	Yes
Computer Science	Yes	Yes	Yes	Yes	Yes
Economics	Yes	Yes	Yes	Yes	Yes
Education	Yes	Yes	Yes	No	Yes
Engineering	Yes	Yes	Yes	Yes	Yes
English	Yes	Yes	Yes	Yes	Yes
Geography	Yes	Yes	Yes	Yes	Yes
History	Yes	Yes	Yes	Yes	Yes
History and Modern Languages	Yes	Yes	Yes	Yes	Yes
History and Politics	Yes	Yes	Yes	Yes	Yes
History of Art	Yes	Yes	Yes	Yes	Yes
Human, Social and Political Sciences	Yes	Yes	Yes	Yes	Yes
Land Economy	Yes	No	Yes	No	Yes
Law	Yes	Yes	Yes	Yes	Yes
Linguistics	Yes	Yes	Yes	Yes	Yes
Management Studies (Part II course)	Yes	Yes	Yes	Yes	Yes
Manufacturing Engineering (Part II course)	Yes	Yes	Yes	Yes	Yes
Mathematics	Yes	Yes	Yes	Yes	Yes
Medicine	Yes	Yes	Yes	Yes	Yes
Modern and Medieval Languages	Yes	Yes	Yes	Yes	Yes
Music	Yes	Yes	Yes	Yes	Yes
Natural Sciences	Yes	Yes	Yes	Yes	Yes
Philosophy	Yes	Yes	Yes	Yes	Yes
Psychological and Behavioural Sciences	Yes	Yes	Yes	Yes	Yes
Theology, Religion and Philosophy of Religion	Yes	No	Yes	Yes	Yes
Veterinary Medicine	No	Yes	Yes	No	Yes

Table 11 Undergraduate courses available at Cambridge colleges (continued)

Course	Emmanuel	Fitzwilliam	Girton	Gonville & Caius
Anglo-Saxon, Norse and Celtic	Yes	Yes	Yes	Yes
Archaeology	Yes	Yes	Yes	Yes
Architecture	Yes	Yes	Yes	Yes
Asian and Middle Eastern Studies	Yes	Yes	Yes	Yes
Chemical Engineering	Yes	Yes	Yes	Yes
Classics	Yes	Yes	Yes	Yes
Computer Science	Yes	Yes	Yes	Yes
Economics	Yes	Yes	Yes	Yes
Education	Yes	Yes	No	Yes
Engineering	Yes	Yes	Yes	Yes
English	Yes	Yes	Yes	Yes
Geography	Yes	Yes	Yes	Yes
History	Yes	Yes	Yes	Yes
History and Modern Languages	Yes	Yes	Yes	Yes
History and Politics	Yes	Yes	Yes	Yes
History of Art	Yes	Yes	No	Yes
Human, Social, and Political Sciences	Yes	Yes	Yes	Yes
Land Economy	No	Yes	Yes	Yes
Law	Yes	Yes	Yes	Yes
Linguistics	Yes	Yes	Yes	Yes
Management Studies (Part II course)	Yes	Yes	Yes	Yes
Manufacturing Engineering (Part II course)	Yes	Yes	Yes	Yes
Mathematics	Yes	Yes	Yes	Yes
Medicine	Yes	Yes	Yes	Yes
Modern and Medieval Languages	Yes	Yes	Yes	Yes
Music	Yes	Yes	Yes	Yes
Natural Sciences	Yes	Yes	Yes	Yes
Philosophy	Yes	Yes	Yes	Yes
Psychological and Behavioural Sciences	Yes	Yes	Yes	Yes
Theology, Religion, and Philosophy of Religion	Yes	Yes	Yes	Yes
Veterinary Medicine	Yes	Yes	Yes	Yes

Homerton	Hughes Hall	Jesus	King's	Lucy Cavendish	Magdalene	Murray Edwards	Newnham
Yes	Yes	Yes	Yes	Yes	Yes	Yes	Yes
Yes	Yes	Yes	Yes	Yes	Yes	Yes	Yes
Yes	No	Yes	Yes	Yes	Yes	Yes	Yes
Yes	Yes	Yes	Yes	Yes	Yes	Yes	Yes
Yes	Yes	Yes	Yes	Yes	Yes	Yes	Yes
Yes	Yes	Yes	Yes	Yes	Yes	Yes	Yes
Yes	Yes	Yes	Yes	Yes	Yes	Yes	Yes
Yes	Yes	Yes	Yes	Yes	Yes	Yes	No
Yes	Yes	Yes	No	Yes	Yes	No	No
Yes	Yes	Yes	Yes	Yes	Yes	Yes	Yes
Yes	Yes	Yes	Yes	Yes	Yes	Yes	Yes
Yes	Yes	Yes	Yes	Yes	Yes	Yes	Yes
Yes	Yes	Yes	Yes	Yes	Yes	Yes	Yes
Yes	Yes	Yes	Yes	Yes	Yes	Yes	Yes
Yes	Yes	Yes	Yes	Yes	Yes	Yes	Yes
Yes	Yes	Yes	Yes	Yes	Yes	Yes	Yes
Yes	Yes	Yes	Yes	Yes	Yes	Yes	Yes
Yes	Yes	Yes	No	Yes	Yes	Yes	Yes
Yes	Yes	Yes	Yes	Yes	Yes	Yes	Yes
Yes	Yes	Yes	Yes	Yes	Yes	Yes	Yes
Yes	Yes	Yes	Yes	Yes	Yes	Yes	Yes
Yes	Yes	Yes	Yes	Yes	Yes	Yes	Yes
Yes	Yes	Yes	Yes	Yes	Yes	Yes	Yes
Yes	No	Yes	Yes	Yes	Yes	Yes	Yes
Yes	Yes	Yes	Yes	Yes	Yes	Yes	Yes
Yes	Yes	Yes	Yes	Yes	Yes	Yes	Yes
Yes	Yes	Yes	Yes	Yes	Yes	Yes	Yes
Yes	Yes	Yes	Yes	Yes	Yes	No	Yes
Yes	Yes	Yes	Yes	Yes	Yes	Yes	Yes
Yes	Yes	Yes	Yes	Yes	Yes	Yes	Yes
Yes	No	Yes	No	Yes	Yes	Yes	Yes

Table 11 Undergraduate courses available at Cambridge colleges (continued)

Course	Pembroke	Peterhouse	Queens'	Robinson	Selwyn
Anglo-Saxon, Norse and Celtic	Yes	Yes	Yes	Yes	Yes
Archaeology	Yes	Yes	No	Yes	Yes
Architecture	Yes	Yes	Yes	Yes	Yes
Asian and Middle Eastern Studies	Yes	Yes	Yes	Yes	Yes
Chemical Engineering	Yes	Yes	Yes	Yes	Yes
Classics	Yes	Yes	Yes	Yes	Yes
Computer Science	Yes	Yes	Yes	Yes	Yes
Economics	Yes	Yes	Yes	Yes	Yes
Education	Yes	No	Yes	Yes	Yes
Engineering	Yes	Yes	Yes	Yes	Yes
English	Yes	Yes	Yes	Yes	Yes
Geography	Yes	No	Yes	Yes	Yes
History	Yes	Yes	Yes	Yes	Yes
History and Modern Languages	Yes	Yes	Yes	Yes	Yes
History and Politics	Yes	Yes	Yes	Yes	Yes
History of Art	Yes	Yes	Yes	No	Yes
Human, Social and Political Sciences	Yes	Yes	Yes	Yes	Yes
Land Economy	Yes	No	Yes	Yes	Yes
Law	Yes	Yes	Yes	Yes	Yes
Linguistics	Yes	Yes	Yes	Yes	Yes
Management Studies (Part II course)	Yes	Yes	Yes	Yes	Yes
Manufacturing Engineering (Part II course)	Yes	Yes	Yes	Yes	Yes
Mathematics	Yes	Yes	Yes	Yes	Yes
Medicine	Yes	Yes	Yes	Yes	Yes
Modern and Medieval Languages	Yes	Yes	Yes	Yes	Yes
Music	Yes	Yes	Yes	Yes	Yes
Natural Sciences	Yes	Yes	Yes	Yes	Yes
Philosophy	Yes	Yes	No	Yes	Yes
Psychological and Behavioural Sciences	Yes	No	Yes	Yes	Yes
Theology, Religion and Philosophy of Religion	Yes	Yes	Yes	Yes	Yes
Veterinary Medicine	Yes	No	Yes	Yes	Yes

Sidney Sussex	St Catharine's	St Edmund's	St John's	Trinity	Trinity Hall	Wolfson
Yes	Yes	Yes	Yes	Yes	Yes	Yes
Yes	Yes	Yes	Yes	Yes	Yes	Yes
Yes	No	Yes	Yes	Yes	Yes	Yes
Yes	Yes	Yes	Yes	Yes	Yes	Yes
Yes	Yes	Yes	Yes	Yes	Yes	Yes
Yes	Yes	Yes	Yes	Yes	Yes	Yes
Yes	Yes	Yes	Yes	Yes	Yes	Yes
Yes	Yes	Yes	Yes	Yes	Yes	No
No	No	Yes	Yes	No	No	Yes
Yes	Yes	Yes	Yes	Yes	Yes	Yes
Yes	Yes	Yes	Yes	Yes	Yes	Yes
Yes	Yes	Yes	Yes	Yes	Yes	Yes
Yes	Yes	Yes	Yes	Yes	Yes	Yes
Yes	Yes	Yes	Yes	Yes	Yes	Yes
Yes	Yes	Yes	Yes	Yes	Yes	Yes
Yes	No	Yes	Yes	Yes	Yes	Yes
Yes	Yes	Yes	Yes	Yes	Yes	Yes
Yes	Yes	Yes	Yes	Yes	Yes	Yes
Yes	Yes	Yes	Yes	Yes	Yes	Yes
Yes	No	Yes	Yes	Yes	Yes	Yes
Yes	Yes	Yes	Yes	Yes	Yes	Yes
Yes	Yes	Yes	Yes	Yes	Yes	Yes
Yes	Yes	Yes	Yes	Yes	Yes	No
Yes	Yes	Yes	Yes	Yes	Yes	Yes
Yes	Yes	Yes	Yes	Yes	Yes	Yes
Yes	Yes	Yes	Yes	Yes	Yes	Yes
Yes	Yes	Yes	Yes	Yes	Yes	Yes
Yes	Yes	Yes	Yes	Yes	Yes	Yes
Yes	Yes	Yes	Yes	Yes	Yes	Yes
Yes	Yes	Yes	Yes	Yes	Yes	Yes
Yes	Yes	Yes	Yes	No	Yes	Yes

Appendix 1: Timetables

The academic year before you apply

Throughout the year, make sure that you have engaged with your subject by reading widely around it and by participating in activities such as attending lectures and entering competitions.

Spring term
- Go online and read the undergraduate prospectus and the alternative prospectus from the student unions of Cambridge or Oxford.
- Research other universities to which you are considering applying.
- Write the first draft of your personal statement.
- Find out when the summer open days are at Oxford and Cambridge. You will need to book a place for Cambridge. For Oxford, you only need to book a place for popular sessions.

June/July
- Sit any relevant end-of-year exams.
- Complete a first draft of your personal statement.
- Attend the open days at Oxford and Cambridge (check their websites for the exact days as they vary from one year to the next).

Summer holidays
- Gain relevant work experience, if you have not done so already.
- Participate in super-curricular activities.
- Continue to read widely around your subject.
- Revise your draft personal statement in the light of your summer activities. Get feedback on it from friends and family.

The academic year in which you apply

September
- Finalise your personal statement with your teachers.
- Visit the UCAS website (www.ucas.com) and register.
- Fill in the UCAS form.
- Register and book a place to sit the LNAT (if you want to study Law at Oxford) – www.lnat.ac.uk.
- Register for the BMAT if you are applying for Biomedical Sciences (at Oxford) or Medicine (at Oxford or Cambridge) – (www.admissions testing.org/for-test-takers/bmat/bmat-october/how-to-register).
- Register for other subject-related pre-interview tests for Oxford and Cambridge. See Chapter 9 for a complete list of Cambridge courses that require a pre-interview assessment.

October
- For Oxford applicants, register and book LNAT test by 5 October. The deadline for sitting the test is 15 October.
- The deadline for UCAS receiving your application, whether for Oxford or Cambridge, is 6pm on 15 October.
- The registration deadline for pre-interview subject-related tests is 15 October.
- Fill in the separate Cambridge SAQ. This will be emailed to you and must be completed by 6pm on 22 October.
- Receive the acknowledgement letter from your chosen college in mid to late October.

November
- Sit Oxford admissions tests and Cambridge pre-admissions tests. The date for 2022 is 2 November.
- Receive the letter inviting you to interview from Oxford or Cambridge and explaining if and when to submit written work. Alternatively, you may receive a letter rejecting you at this point.
- Submit written work with the special form – see faculty website for details. (Work should be sent directly to the college unless you have made an 'open application', in which case send it directly to the faculty. The work should be marked by your school.)

December
- If invited, attend interviews in the first three weeks of December (see precise interview dates for your subject in the prospectus).
- You may have to sit some tests at interview.

January
- Beginning of January: applicants who have been placed in the 'winter pool' are notified (Cambridge only). This may or may not entail going to Cambridge for another set of interviews.
- Around 11 January hear the outcome of your application from Oxford.
- End of January: hear the outcome of your application from Cambridge.

June
- Sit A levels (or equivalent exams).
- After A levels sit STEP (for students who have a conditional offer to read Mathematics, Mathematics with Physics and Computer Science at Cambridge only). Some colleges may also ask for the STEP for Chemical Engineering (via Engineering) and for Engineering.

July
- First week of July: IB results day.

August
- Mid-August: A level and Pre-U results day.
- If you get the grades your place will be confirmed by the university.
- If you don't get the grades, contact the college admissions tutor.
- You may be sent a letter of rejection at this point.

Appendix 2: Glossary

Adjustment
If you have met all of the conditions of your firm choice and exceeded at least one grade, you have the opportunity to enter UCAS Adjustment. Adjustment begins on A level results day and runs until 31 August. You can put your application on hold for a week to see if any institutions would be willing to offer you a place. If you register but do not find an alternative course, you will keep your place at your original firm-choice university. **NB Cambridge participates in Adjustment but only on results day; Oxford does not (see page 174 for more details).**

Admissions tutor
The tutor especially assigned the role of selecting candidates.

Alumni
People who once went to the college but who have now graduated.

ASNC
This is an abbreviation for the Anglo-Saxon, Norse and Celtic course at Cambridge.

Battels
The payments students and fellows at Oxford make to their college for accommodation, meals, etc.

Bedder
The person who cleans your room at Cambridge.

Clearing
When exam results come out in the summer, students who do not meet their offers can enter the competition for places at universities that have spare places. Clearing vacancies are listed in the UCAS search tool from early July to mid-September. **NB Neither Oxford nor Cambridge participates in the UCAS Clearing system.**

Collections
Exams sat at the beginning of each term at Oxford in the colleges. These are a good indication of your level of progress during the previous term, but do not count towards your final degree classification.

Collegiate system
This term describes the fact that both Oxford and Cambridge universities are divided into about 30 separate colleges, where students live and where their social lives are based.

Deferred entry
This means you would like to take a gap year (i.e. defer your entry for a year). You apply this year but will accept a place in two years' time.

Deselected
Some candidates will not make it to the interview; they are 'deselected' before the interview and will receive a letter of rejection.

Director of studies (DoS)
Your DoS at the University of Cambridge is an academic member of staff from your subject faculty who is also a fellow of your college. He or she is responsible for your academic development and will meet with you at the beginning and end of each term to check on your progress and will probably be your interviewer. The DoS at Cambridge is the equivalent to a tutor at Oxford.

Don
A teacher at a university; in particular a senior member of an Oxbridge college.

Exhibition
A scholarship you can win in recognition of outstanding work at Oxford.

Extenuating Circumstances Form (ECF)
Cambridge applicants who feel that their education has been severely disrupted and wish to have this considered can fill out a special online form to draw attention to their circumstances; this is to be submitted the week after the UCAS application submission.

Faculty
The department building dedicated to one particular subject, for example, the Faculty of Architecture.

Fellow
An academic member of a college. Each academic in every faculty is also assigned a college; this is where their office space is located. Some more senior fellows are given responsibility for the academic achievement of the students at their college and act as the DoS (at Cambridge) or tutor (at Oxford) of a number of undergraduates.

Fresher
First-year undergraduate student.

Go up
Traditionally, instead of simply saying 'go to university', for Oxford and Cambridge the term used is to 'go up' to university.

Hall
One of the places where you eat your meals in college. Usually you will be offered a three-course evening meal with wine. Formal Hall is a more elaborate affair and you may be required to wear your gown.

Head of House (Oxford)
This is a general term for the Head of a College, who is also known by different names at different colleges such as the Dean, the Master, the President, the Principal, the Provost, the Rector and the Warden. Many of these terms are also used at Cambridge.

Hilary Term
This is the second academic term of the year at Oxford from January to the middle of March. The equivalent term at Cambridge is called Lent.

HSPS
This is an abbreviation for the Human, Social and Political Sciences course at Cambridge.

Junior common room/junior combination room (JCR)
A common room for all undergraduate students of a given college. Each college has its own JCR.

Matriculation
Matriculation gives membership of the University to newly enrolled students who are embarking on degree-level programmes.

Michaelmas Term
The first term of the academic year which begins in October and ends in December.

Middle common room/middle combination room (MCR)
A common room for graduate students of a given college.

Norrington table
Oxford league table that measures each college's academic achievement at the final examinations.

Noughth Week
This refers to the week before full term begins in Oxford.

Open application
A way of applying to either Oxford or Cambridge without specifying a college.

Oxbridge
The collective term for Oxford and Cambridge.

Permanent private halls
These are like mini-colleges in Oxford. Two of them – St Benet's Hall and Regent's Park College – are for students studying most humanities subjects, but the remaining four are mainly for people who are training to be in the ministry.

Pigeon Post
This is an informal term for Oxford's internal postal service. At both universities, your pigeon-hole is referred to as your 'pidge'.

Pool

The pool is where applicants who may be rejected by their first-choice college are held. Another college may select them for an interview or make them an offer. The other college may do this for a variety of reasons, such as if it does not have enough good applicants and wants to find better ones, or if it wants to check that their weakest chosen student is better than another college's rejected student – a sort of moderation process.

Porters

The men and women who act as wardens of the lodge.

Porters' Lodge

Your first port of call at an Oxford or Cambridge college. This is where post gets delivered and where, if you get lost, they will be able to direct you – a bit like a reception desk.

PPE

This is an abbreviation for the Philosophy, Politics and Economics course at Oxford.

PPL

This is an abbreviation for the Psychology, Philosophy and Linguistics course at Oxford.

Prelims (Oxford)

This is short for Preliminaries, which are the exams at the end of the first year. There are only three results available: Pass, Fail and Distinction.

Proctors (Oxford)

A Senior and Junior Proctor are elected annually by colleges in rotation. Their role is to ensure that the rules and customs of the University are kept. Part of their role includes ceremonial duties (such as taking part in degree ceremonies), aspects of student discipline, ensuring exams are conducted properly and managing complaints.

Read

Instead of 'studying' a subject, the verb used is to 'read' a subject.

Scholar

Scholarships are usually awarded at the end of the first year for out-standing work. Oxford scholars get to wear a more elaborate gown and are given a small financial bursary (usually around £200 a year). Music scholars hold their award for the whole time they are at university.

Scout

The person who cleans your room at Oxford.

Subfusc

The black gown, black trousers/skirt, white shirt and black tie Oxford students must wear to take exams.

Summon
Another way to say 'to be called' for interview.

Supervision
A class held on a one-to-one basis or in a small group with your tutor (at Cambridge).

Supplementary Application Questionnaire (SAQ)
This is sent out by Cambridge once you have submitted your UCAS application. The SAQ gives Cambridge more information about you and your application and must be submitted within one week after you receive it. The SAQ is filled out online and costs nothing to send; if you do not have access to email you can contact the Cambridge admissions office for a paper version.

Tompkins table
Cambridge league table that measures each college's academic achievement at the final examinations.

Trinity Term
This is the summer term at Oxford. The equivalent term at Cambridge is Easter.

Tripos
Term used to describe Cambridge degree courses being divided into blocks of one or two years, called Part I and Part II. Some courses, such as Mathematics, also have a Part III.

Tutor
At Oxford, your tutor is an academic member of staff from your subject faculty, who is also a fellow of your college. He or she is responsible for your academic development and will meet with you on a regular basis to check on your progress, and will probably be your interviewer. The DoS at Cambridge is the equivalent to a tutor at Oxford.

Tutorial
A class held on a one-to-one basis or in a small group with your tutor (at Oxford).

Vacation
The period between university terms.

Viva voce
An oral exam given when you are being considered for a First Class degree and the examiners want to ask you further questions about your exam papers.

   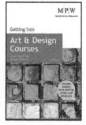